MW00396271

JOHN W. BARRIGER III

RAILROADS PAST AND PRESENT

George M. Smerk and H. Roger Grant, editors

John W. Barriger III

RAILROAD LEGEND

H. Roger Grant

INDIANA UNIVERSITY PRESS

This book is a publication of

INDIANA UNIVERSITY PRESS
Office of Scholarly Publishing
Herman B Wells Library 350
1320 East 10th Street
Bloomington, Indiana 47405 USA

iupress.indiana.edu

© 2018 by H. Roger Grant
All rights reserved

No part of this book may be reproduced
or utilized in any form or by any
means, electronic or mechanical,
including photocopying and recording,
or by any information storage and
retrieval system, without permission
in writing from the publisher.

The paper used in this publication
meets the minimum requirements of
the American National Standard for
Information Sciences – Permanence of
Paper for Printed Library Materials,
ANSI Z39.48–1992.

*Manufactured in the
United States of America*

*Library of Congress
Cataloging-in-Publication Data*

Names: Grant, H. Roger, [date]- author.
Title: John W. Barriger III : railroad
    legend / H. Roger Grant.
Description: Bloomington, Indiana :
    Indiana University Press, [2018] |
Series: Railroads past and present |
    Includes bibliographical references and
    index.
Identifiers: LCCN 2018004499 (print) |
    LCCN 2018003176 (ebook) | ISBN
    9780253032898 (e-book) | ISBN
    9780253032881 (cl : alk. paper)
Subjects: LCSH: Barriger, John W. (John
    Walker), 1899-1976. | Railroads—
    United States—Biography. | Railroads
    —United States—Employees—
    Biography. | Railroads—Management
    —United States—History—20th
    century. | Railroads and state—United
    States—History—20th century.
Classification: LCC HE2754.B37 (print) |
    LCC HE2754.B37 G73 2018 (ebook) |
    DDC 385.092 [B] —dc23
LC record available at https://lccn.loc.gov
    /2018004499

1 2 3 4 5   23 22 21 20 19 18

For

JOHN W. BARRIGER IV

Jack made this book possible

Contents

Preface

IN DECEMBER 1976 THE AMERICAN RAILROAD INDUSTRY mourned the death of John W. Barriger III, one of its best known, most talented, and most beloved figures. He was viewed by many as "selfless, scholarly, and dedicated." Said a coworker, "If you asked me to name the most giving (especially to newly minted railroaders), knowledgeable, bright, interesting guy, it would be very easy, JWB III." Hardly surprising – Barriger had received numerous awards during his nearly sixty-year professional career, including the prestigious "Railroad Man of the Year" in 1968 from the popular trade journal *Modern Railroads*.[1]

After graduating from the Massachusetts Institute of Technology (MIT) in 1921, this St. Louis, Missouri (technically Dallas, Texas), native wore many hats, and in the process he became an executive "boomer." Barriger had been a rising employee of the Pennsylvania Railroad; a Wall Street financial analyst; architect of the Prince Plan for railroad consolidation; head of the Railroad Division of the Reconstruction Finance Corporation; associate director of the Division of Railway Transport for the Office of Defense Transportation; manager of the Diesel Locomotive Division of Fairbanks-Morse Corporation; president of the Chicago, Indianapolis & Louisville (Monon), Pittsburgh & Lake Erie, Missouri-Kansas-Texas (Katy), and Boston & Maine railroads; vice president of the New York, New Haven & Hartford (New Haven) and Chicago, Rock Island & Pacific (Rock Island) railroads; and associated with the Federal Railroad Administration. Since the 1930s he had gained a national reputation as a public speaker on railroad and regulatory topics, and his 1956 book, *Super-Railroads for a Dynamic American Economy*, became

widely discussed among railroaders, government officials, business leaders, and others. Critics agreed that this study, which spelled out a course
of action for the industry's future focused on upgrading properties and
prompting traffic, presented a well-reasoned package of advice for the
railroad industry.

Writing a biography is a challenge. Subjects who are worthy of such
attention may take an author to places that the author might not wish to
go in research. No matter the vastness of primary and secondary materials, a biography is ultimately never definitive. Yet there is this positive
feature of examining an individual who has died: no life can be justly
judged until it has been completed. In this book-length account of railroad legend John W. Barriger III the task of exploring his event-filled life
is somewhat less difficult than with some subjects. First of all, Barriger
was an organized packrat, saving and organizing a multitude of professional papers, newspaper clippings, press releases, and diaries, and a
plethora of photographs, railroad-oriented books, reports, and even his
massive Christmas card lists. Toward the end of his life he began to write
his autobiography, although he failed to get beyond his teenage years. But
for the biographer, finding personal information from subjects' formative years can prove invaluable in learning what made them tick. Without question much of Barriger's worldview had been firmly established
before he matriculated at MIT in 1917.

Additional attractive aspects of this project are that the body of
primary materials is readily accessible in a single location, the John W.
Barriger III National Railroad Library, a unit of the St. Louis Mercantile
Library, located on the campus of the University of Missouri–St. Louis,
and that his sole surviving child, John (Jack) W. Barriger IV, possesses a
remarkable memory and has vivid recollections of his father, his family,
and the railroad industry for much of his father's life.

Every life has a pattern. Sometimes it is clear and sometimes hidden,
and for John W. Barriger III it is the former. His ongoing professional
desire was to modernize the railroad industry, making it more efficient
and profitable. This involved consolidating scores of competing companies, allowing them the financial means to upgrade their physical plants
and rolling stock in order to provide the best possible service for the
shipping and traveling public. He hoped that unfair and needless regula-

tory controls – what he called "super-regulation" – could be reduced or eliminated. As far back as his teenage years Barriger was consistently conservative in his personal outlook, living by a code of honor and loyalty that made for lasting and rewarding friendships. Politically, he was a staunch, pro-business Republican. Always there was Barriger's deep love of railroads – trains, stations, interlocking plants, yards, and the like – beginning with his earliest memories. His hobby became his life's work. "Barriger was an incredible railroader," opined Rush Loving Jr., a former associate editor of *Fortune* magazine. "Although warm of heart, he was an intense man, totally absorbed in the subject of railroads, and his dark eyes, peering steadily at you through rimless glasses, made him look all the more mirthless and venerable." Few, if any, people who knew him (or knew about him) would say that John W. Barriger III had not succeeded in becoming a twentieth-century American railroad legend.[2]

Acknowledgments

AN HISTORIAN IS ALWAYS FLATTERED AT BEING ASKED TO study a particular subject, in this case to write a biography of twentieth-century railroad executive John W. Barriger III. His son, John (Jack) W. Barriger IV, contacted me about such an undertaking. He had read my biography of his father's contemporary, Jervis Langdon Jr., published in 2008 by Indiana University Press, and he liked the book. Moreover, Jack is the last surviving child of John and Elizabeth Barriger, and only he can supply certain details about the family's life. Jack has a remarkable memory, and my numerous interviews with him and my frequent email requests generated information that often could not have been obtained elsewhere. Moreover, he gave the manuscript multiple readings, correcting errors and making suggestions. And Jack provided the financial support needed to conduct the required research. Fortunately, his father amassed an amazing library of railroad materials, and he retained an enormous number of his own personal papers, including childhood diaries and an unfinished autobiography.

The Barriger railroad collection has not been scattered to the winds. It is housed in the St. Louis Mercantile Library on the campus of the University of Missouri-St. Louis, and appropriately in the John W. Barriger III National Railroad Library. The head of the Barriger library, Nick Fry, not only possesses a thorough grasp of these research materials, but he kindly aided me in various ways, making my research much easier than for any previous railroad-oriented book. Nick, too, made thoughtful comments about an early draft of my completed manuscript.

Although John W. Barriger III died in 1976, there remain individuals who knew him. With one exception, they have all willingly provided me with their memories about this well-known and respected railroader. These include Ed Burkhardt, Dave DeBoer, Alan (Dusty) Dustin, Herb Harwood, Dick Hasselman, Bill Howes, the late Jim McClellan, and Bill McKnight.

Others also have contributed. They include Alden Dryer, Geoff Doughty, Ron Goldfeder, John Hoover, Jim Howarth, Scott Lothes, and Guus Veenendaal. Don Hofsommer kindly reviewed the Missouri-Kansas-Texas (Katy) chapter, enhancing coverage and analysis. As with previous book projects, I am indebted to the helpful staff of R. M. Cooper Library at Clemson University, and, as always, to my wife of more than fifty years, Martha Farrington Grant.

Well, Mr. Barriger, here it is, slightly more than forty years after your death. I hope I got your life's story right, or at least mostly right.

H. Roger Grant
Clemson University
Clemson, South Carolina

JOHN W. BARRIGER III

ONE

Early Life and Career

FAMILY AND LOVE OF RAILROADS

Throughout his adult life John W. Barriger III took great pride in his family lineage, and he developed a keen interest in its genealogy. His first paternal forefather in America was Josiah Barriger (perhaps Bergere), who arrived in the New World from Holland during the colonial period. One ancestor, Samuel Huntington, a Connecticut jurist and governor, gained lasting fame as a signer of the Declaration of Independence. In the course of western migration the Barriger clan crossed the Appalachians and settled in northern and then western Kentucky. His grandmother Barriger claimed to be a descendent of Davy Crockett, the legendary Tennessee frontiersman and hero of the Alamo. On the maternal side, Beck family members also reached back to the pre–Revolutionary War era. These English immigrants did not scatter until later in the nineteenth century, staying for several generations in Maryland, mostly along the Eastern Shore.[1]

Barriger admired greatly his grandfather, John W. Barriger Sr. (1832–1906). This native Kentuckian graduated from the United States Military Academy in 1856, ranking an impressive thirteenth in a class of forty-nine. Unlike so many West Pointers, the senior Barriger made the US Army his career. Although initially in the artillery, he became a commissary of subsistence officer, being a logistics and supplies specialist. During the Civil War Barriger served with both regular and volunteer forces, rising rapidly in the latter to breveted brigadier general "for faithful and meritorious services." Following the conflict he returned to the regular army but lost the temporary general rank and became a captain. Promotions, though, followed; he advanced from major to colonel in 1894. Like all military men, Barriger received numerous postings, including Jefferson Barracks near St. Louis, Missouri; New York City; and Washington, DC. During these post–Civil War years he displayed his talents as a researcher and writer, producing in 1876 a centennial history of the Subsistence Department. In 1896 Barriger retired from active service, although during the Spanish-American War the War Department recalled him temporarily to handle a desk job in Washington. Then in 1904 he became "Brigadier-General, US Army, Retired." Barriger continued to be active, however. From his retirement home in New York City, he joined the editorial staff of the *Army and Navy Journal*, a publication that helped to professionalize the US military.[2]

Shortly after General Barriger's death, a West Point classmate penned these insightful observations about his longtime friend: "His qualities of head and heart were such as soon to win the respect and esteem of his classmates, which the lapse of years never lessened. While always affable and courteous, he was as a cadet serious, thoughtful, studious and very conscientious in the performance of any duty." These were personal traits that John W. Barriger Jr. and John W. Barriger III would share.[3]

The marriage of the senior Barriger to Sarah Frances Wright, who came from a military family and "had a distinguished Revolutionary ancestry," took place at Carlisle Barracks, Pennsylvania, in 1863 and produced four children, three boys and a girl. John W. Barriger Jr. was the youngest of the couple's three sons, born in Washington, DC, on July 20, 1874. His precollegiate education included schools on several army posts, but when his father was stationed at Jefferson Barracks, he completed his school career at Central High School in St. Louis. Unlike the vast majority of contemporary male high school graduates, he pursued a collegiate education. John Jr. selected Washington University in St. Louis and entered its developing School of Engineering. While he was attending the university, his father was transferred to New York City, but John Jr. found lodging with family friends in St. Louis.[4]

John W. Barriger Jr., however, did not graduate from Washington University. This was not due to poor academic performance but rather

This photograph of the handsome John W. Barriger Jr. dates from 1898, a year before his marriage to Edith Forman Beck. (John W. Barriger III Collection, Barriger National Railroad Library at UMSL)

to a burning desire to launch a railroad career. In 1894, at age twenty, he joined the engineering department of the Terminal Railroad Association of St. Louis (TRRA) as an assistant to the resident engineer. It would be railroad entrepreneur Colonel Samuel W. Fordyce, a Civil War comrade of his father and family friend, who assisted in making this position possible. Although in the midst of the nation's worst depression, the TRRA was in the process of completing its St. Louis Union Station with its magnificent headhouse and massive train shed. This widely acclaimed facility opened officially on September 1, 1894. The initial assignment for John Jr. was to work on designing a complex series of tracks, crossings, and switches at the throat of the station. Next he turned his attention to the construction of a steel trestle that provided a connection between the station and the recently completed Merchants Bridge over the Mississippi River in north St. Louis.[5]

The relationship with Colonel Fordyce continued. When Fordyce became co-receiver of the Kansas City, Pittsburg & Gulf Railroad (KCP&G) in the late 1890s, John Jr. accepted his offer to join the company that somewhat earlier railroad visionary and promoter Arthur Stilwell had founded. Working in the engineering department, John Jr. participated in the survey of a projected line between Shreveport, Louisiana, and Beaumont and Port Arthur, Texas. His duties included those of rodman, compiler of statistics, and office manager. Following that undertaking, he joined the St. Louis Southwestern Railway (Cotton Belt), a carrier associated with Fordyce's railroad ventures. His base of operation was Tyler, Texas, and here he held the position of assistant engineer, maintenance of way.[6]

Not only was the younger Barriger developing his professional skills, but his personal life was about to change. On the evening of April 3, 1899, he married the bright, attractive, and vivacious Edith Forman Beck in the First Presbyterian Church in St. Louis. Born in the Gateway City on Washington's birthday 1877, his new wife was the daughter of Mary Forman Vickers, whose Baltimore family had been engaged in banking and shipping, and Clarence Benjamin Beck, a St. Louis fuel dealer who sold "bituminous and anthracite coal, coke and smithing coal." Edith, the oldest of four children, two of whom died in infancy, received a solid liberal arts education, having attended Monticello Ladies' Seminary, a

A radiant Edith Forman Beck poses in her bridal gown and veil. Her marriage to John W. Barriger Jr. took place on Monday, April 3, 1899, at First Presbyterian Church in St. Louis, Missouri. (John W. Barriger III Collection, Barriger National Railroad Library at UMSL)

Presbyterian female academy in Godfrey, Illinois, and the Mary Institute in St. Louis, a school affiliated with Washington University. Much later she would graduate from Washington University and eventually attend the law school of George Washington University in Washington, DC.[7]

The newlyweds made their home in Tyler, Texas, and quickly their first child was conceived. On December 3, 1899, John W. Barriger III was born to John W. Barriger Jr. and Edith Beck. "That 'blessed event' occurred, I am told, while my mother was en route to return to her parents' St. Louis home where better medical attention could be obtained than was available at that time in Tyler. But the stork would not wait a month, so my mother had to be taken off the train at Dallas and hurried to St. Paul's Sanitarium, where I first saw the light of day."[8]

Resembling so many railroaders, John Jr. led a nomadic life. In 1900 the family left Tyler for Kansas City, Missouri, and "lived in a little house on Vine Street [and] the scene of many happy memories for my mother." The new job of the young husband and father was in the office of the chief engineer for the Kansas City Southern Railway, the company recently created out of the bankrupt Kansas City, Pittsburg & Gulf property, and where Colonel Fordyce served as Kansas City Southern's first president. Edith Barriger recalled that her husband "was in charge of estimates for track, bridge and building work, together with masonry construction." Then in March 1902 the family relocated to St. Louis. At this time Fordyce had become involved with the recently organized St. Louis, Memphis & Southeastern Railway (StLM&SE). This company, which consisted of several predecessor roads, planned to open a direct connection between St. Louis and Memphis, Tennessee, largely along the west bank of the Mississippi River. The junior Barriger supervised building its bridges, trestles, and structures. It did not take long, however, before the St. Louis–San Francisco Railroad (Frisco) took control of the StLM&SE, and John Jr. "was given a position of increased responsibility in its Engineering Department as Engineer of Bridges and Structures."[9]

Unquestionably John W. Barriger Jr. possessed engineering talents. Yet he had others. Not only was he a skilled draftsman, but he made impressive pen and ink sketches of contemporary scenes "following [graphic artist] Charles Dana Gibson's style." Barriger was also a musician, playing such stringed instruments as the banjo, guitar, and mandolin. "He had a delight in music with a technical knowledge that marked him as an acceptable performer both for his own and other's enjoyment."[10]

On Friday, December 19, 1902, the promising life of John W. Barriger Jr. came to an abrupt end. That morning about ten o'clock a professional acquaintance, Thompson "Tom" McPheeters Morton, paid a call at his office on the fifth floor of the Granite Block at Fourth and Market streets in downtown St. Louis. The two men had previously worked together for the Kansas City Southern in Kansas City. But now an unemployed civil engineer, Morton hoped that Barriger could find him a job at the Frisco. For approximately ten minutes they talked, and Morton learned that there were no immediate openings. He also may have asked for a personal loan, something that Barriger had given him a few weeks earlier. At that point, workers in the adjoining drafting department noticed more than conversational voices. "Suddenly the men in the next room heard an oath blurted out in an angry tone, which was followed by a cry of terror," reported the *St. Louis Globe-Democrat*. "They rushed to the door, where they saw Barriger standing at bay, his face distorted with fright, trying to ward off his assailant." In his attempt to flee, Morton stabbed him twice with a common jack knife "of the barlow variety." One cut penetrated Barriger about an inch or so to the left of his heart, and the other entered in the right side of his back and pierced his kidneys. Almost immediately Barriger's coworkers wrestled Morton to the floor of the outside hall, and in the process he attempted suicide by digesting a compound of mercury pills. Morton, however, failed to end his own life. After he was subdued, these coworkers recognized that Morton had taken a suspicious substance. The assailant was rushed by the quickly summoned police to the St. Louis City Hospital, where his stomach was pumped. Nothing, though, could be done for the twenty-eight-year-old Barriger; he died in a pool of blood, victim of a tragic, brutal murder.[11]

A formal inquest followed. Testimony revealed that Tom Morton, who was thirty-one, single, a native of Shreveport, Louisiana, and "well educated," suffered from mental illness. "Morton would lie on his back and make incoherent replies to questions," observed Dr. H. L. Nietert, the St. Louis City Hospital superintendent, "and a few minutes afterward would revert to the same question again, and in a rambling way give another kind of a reply." Family members concurred. His cousin, Judge William Beckner of Winchester, Kentucky, and a brother, C. H. Morton, a Presbyterian minister from Sweet Springs, Missouri, indicated that he "had been unbalanced mentally for some time." Other witnesses reported that "Morton, once a talented civil engineer, had become a moral degenerate who expected others to provide him with an easy means of earning a living. Whisky and perhaps drugs have brought about the deterioration in his character." It was indicated, too, that he was slightly deaf and "had a horror of being in the society of other people." No member of the Barriger or Beck families attended the inquest; they believed that it would be too painful.[12]

The fate of Tom Morton surprised no one. In the ensuing trial the court issued its verdict. Rather than being sent to the Missouri penitentiary in Jefferson City where he might have faced execution for first-degree murder or more likely life imprisonment, Morton was committed to a mental hospital for the criminally insane. It had been a senseless crime, concluded the court, committed "in a seizure of insane rage."[13]

The events of December 19, 1902, and the aftermath left deep and lasting emotional scars. The murder sent Edith Barriger into an extended period of mourning. "She wore heavy mourning for nearly ten years, including for several years a heavy black veil over her face whenever she went out," recalled her son. "She occasionally mentioned to me what a terrible experience it was after kissing her husband goodbye when he left for his office in the morning to have his body brought home dead that afternoon." No amount of sympathy, even the sadness expressed by the Morton family, seemed to raise her spirits. "Paradoxically this man [Tom Morton] was a member of a distinguished family in another State. Neither she nor I have ever divulged their family name. The family of this man was greatly distressed and offered most sincere condolences." Her son also remembered that "she tried unsuccessfully to find solace in reading and writing." Edith Barriger never remarried, dying in 1974 after more than seven decades of widowhood. Yet later she would have several boyfriends and male companions, including a married US Supreme Court justice.[14]

The immediate sting of that cold-blooded murder of John W. Barriger Jr. came at what should have been the most joyous time of the year,

A young John W. Barriger III displays things nautical on a family outing to Asbury Park, New Jersey, in 1906. This photograph indicates that the future railroader had a childhood fascination with water transportation. (John W. Barriger III Collection, Barriger National Railroad Library at UMSL)

because it occurred only a few days before Christmas. At once, Edith and her three-year-old son left their home for a nearby family residence, and here they spent a most unhappy holiday. In a poignant commentary, John Barriger remembered that first Christmas after his father's death. "My father, as a railroad man, possibly intending to cultivate an interest in trains in his infant son, had bought a mechanical one among the gifts intended to go under my Christmas tree. This last gift from my father was kept for many years along with a young children's book entitled 'The A.B.C.s of Railroads,' which I still have, carefully bound."[15]

Since St. Louis held tragic memories, Edith early in 1903 took her son to stay for more than a year with relatives in Maryland. They spent much of this time in Baltimore with her uncle and aunt, the "moderately affluent" and childless Bastables. Alvin Bastable, who headed the Union Abattoir Company of Baltimore (stockyards), and his first wife, Geraldine

Vickers Bastable, were devout Presbyterians. Religion dominated their lives. "Mr. Bastable conducted family prayers and reading of the Bible every Sunday morning between breakfast and leaving for the nearby [Northminster Presbyterian] church. His wife spent several hours each morning reading the Bible and in prayer and meditation," and she loyally supported the Woman's Union Missionary Society of America. Not surprisingly, the young Barriger was taken to church on a regular basis. It would be in the Sunday School rooms at Northminster that he had his initial educational training.[16]

The relationship between the Bastables and John Barriger became close. Early on the couple indicated to his mother that they wanted to adopt him and to send him to the Country School for Boys (later the Gilman Country School for Boys, then the Gilman School), "Baltimore's best." But Edith Barriger did not want to lose her son, and so the two remained together, mostly in the St. Louis home of her parents, until he left for college in 1917. Still, when the Barrigers came to Baltimore, Bastable would take "little Jack" to his tailor to be fitted properly in clothing purchased from the "best boys' furnishings stores." There was more. "He also sent a monthly stipend of $25.00 to help support me in St. Louis and he paid for my college education." And Geraldine Bastable, who died in 1918, left him a small legacy, "which helped me get started in later life."[17]

Those repeated trips between Missouri and Maryland stimulated John Barriger's fascination for trains. "My first awareness of the delights of rail travel, which since then have been my lifelong principal source of pleasure, occurred in 1904, when my mother and I returned from Baltimore to St. Louis," he recalled. "The Bastables came with us. We traveled via a Baltimore & Ohio train and upon leaving Washington my uncle took me back to the observation platform to show me the unfolding scenery. I was thrilled by the passing railroad panorama. This trip was the first railroad ride to impress itself upon my consciousness." And Barriger retained vivid memories of a train ride two years later on the Pennsylvania's New York Limited from St. Louis to the east coast. "The observation platform held the greatest fascination for me and the next in order of importance was the dining car. It was the first time that I had ever seen on a train such special features as a ladies maid, barber, valet and stenographer." This experience had a special impact. "The maid gave me a set of post cards of the railroad and the train that are still in my collection of pictures; in fact they started it." At age six and a half that love of railroads had been firmly established.[18]

This infatuation with railroads did not mean that John Barriger lacked other interests. Based on diary entries from his teenage years, he apparently was a well-rounded lad. His Presbyterian church became a social center, as he made friends with boys and girls his age and participated in church-related programs and events. In spring 1911 Barriger joined the Boy Scouts of America, part of the recently launched international scouting movement. St. Louis had an early chapter; American scouting dated only from 1910. He rose rapidly from tenderfoot class to second class scout, and in April 1912 he achieved appointment as patrol leader, a hint of his future managerial skills. Barriger also enjoyed riding his bicycle, which he called his "wheel," and on occasions peddled for considerable distances. His diary entry from New Year's Day 1913 read: "Road [sic] on my wheel to Clayton and to Tower Grove Park," perhaps braving unpleasant winter weather. Some of his other activities were dancing school, music lessons, trips to the "motion picture show," and in summer repeated "bathing" outings. During his high school years he participated in various extracircular [sic] activities, including the editorship of the High School News, and "I was active in the school's literary, scientific and photographic clubs." That last activity had real appeal; he penned this diary entry for March 15, 1914: "Developed and Printed the pictures I took one day before."[19]

School emerged as a central part of Barriger's active youth. In fall 1904 he began his formal education. Because he was too young to attend public schools in St. Louis, his mother enrolled him in a small kindergarten conducted by the daughter of the rector of the Olive Street Episcopal Church. Attendance at another private school followed, one run in the home of Fanny Carr on Maryland Avenue. As he neared age seven, Barriger began classes at the Marquette Public School on McPherson Avenue. "I was put in room No. 18 instead of the beginners' room No. 22, because of my prior years in primary grades. I remained in the Marquette School until I graduated in June, 1913, and then went on to spend

In this mother and son portrait taken about 1910, John Barriger is dressed in his Sunday best suit, and Edith remains in a black mourning dress. (John W. Barriger III Collection, Barriger National Railroad Library at UMSL)

the next four school years in Central High School which was located on Grand Avenue near Finney." This was the same school where his father had graduated in 1892.[20]

Barriger excelled at his studies. His grammar school and high school academic records were consistently strong. In an age before rampant grade inflation, Barriger usually received all As and Bs. His final five weeks' report from Marquette School, posted in May 1913, for example, listed the following marks: "History A, Grammar A, Arithmetic A, Drawing B, Reading B." At Central High School Barriger took the rigorous "College Scientific Course." This curriculum required "four years of such technical studies as botany, physiology, physics and chemistry and four years of mathematics up to calculus." While at Central High he complemented these offerings with English literature, history and three foreign languages: Latin, French, and German. Athletics were much less important. "My school athletic interests were limited to the minimum requirements of two gymnasium sessions each week." He said, too, that "my school life in pre-college years followed the conventional pattern of boys of that period, except that I was more interested in books and current events than in sports in which I lacked the interest ever to become proficient." Yet on occasions, Barriger played football with friends, but more often tennis. Although he was a healthy young man, his rather modest stature of five feet eight inches and about 125 pounds may explain this lack of enthusiasm for things athletic.[21]

Barriger had positive feelings about his education in St. Louis, considering it a broadening experience. "My boy friends from well to do families were usually sent east to nationally prominent preparatory schools which were thought to provide a superior education, but I found that my Marquette (grammar) and Central High School years had equipped me for college and life thereafter quite as well as those better known secondary schools trained their students." He raved about his instructors. "These teachers were a dedicated group of men and women, devoting their entire efforts to educating their pupils in the subjects of their specialties and not in endeavoring to acquaint them with the social, political and economic problems of the times, and we were taught a healthy respect for the experience and guidance of our parents and our elders."

By the time he left St. Louis for the Massachusetts Institute of Technology (MIT), he held strong views of life and politics. As for the former, Barriger embraced "wholesome family values," and for the latter, "I was a staunch Republican and a hard-shelled conservative."[22]

During his precollegiate years matters of religion also shaped Barriger's worldview. In his diaries and other writings there are repeated comments about his ties to Second Presbyterian Church, located at Westminster Place and Taylor Avenue. This congregation of predominantly middle- and upper-class St. Louisians had become a family tradition. "My family have been identified with the 'Second Church' since my grandparents came to St. Louis in the 1870's, my material grandparents' two children and I were baptized in it, and I have been continuously a member of its congregation since formally joining the church through confession of faith in 1914 after attending its Sunday School classes since I was three years old." The longtime minister at Second Presbyterian, the nationally prominent Reverend Doctor Samuel J. Niccols, was held in high esteem. The commitment to the teachings of Dr. Niccols and core Calvinist tenets likely explains why members of the immediate family were Sabbatarians. "Religious observances occupied all Sunday mornings and during Sunday afternoons in St. Louis my grandmother [Beck] would read Bible stories to several of my friends and me and kept a box of candy conveniently available as a reward for our attention." Except for his grandfather Barriger, an Episcopalian, the family opposed the use of tobacco and liquor. "Possibly as a result of such upbringing," Barriger reflected, "I have never smoked and while not a complete abstainer my lifelong consumption of alcoholic beverages has been very small in total amount when spread over my long life."[23]

While occupied with church and home on Sundays, John Barriger had ample opportunities on Saturdays and during the summer months to pursue his growing love of railroads. Admitted Barriger, "My principal diversion between 1914 and 1917 was to cultivate my railroad interests through making the St. Louis Union Station and the principal freight yards located with this great terminal area my playground and club." On numerous occasions he and friends, who often included Norvelle Sharpe, son of a St. Louis physician, rode their bicycles, took streetcars, or walked to railroad sites. A diary entry for February 13, 1915, is representative: "Went on an all day walk with Sharpe. Spent most of time in the Union Station yards, walked the complete length of the trestle." A few days later he noted, "Another walk with Sharpe. Went through PRR [Pennsylvania Railroad] No. 30." He also spent late afternoons and Saturdays at both the St. Louis Mercantile Library and the St. Louis Public Library, where he devoured railroad books and periodicals.[24]

The diary reference to the Pennsylvania Railroad (PRR) reflects Barriger's growing fascination with this self-proclaimed "Standard Railroad of the World," the largest corporation in America. By 1916 his diary entries contained frequent quotations from PRR promotional materials. He began the new year of 1916 with this one: "The Broadway Limited (20 Hours en Route) is the Train for Busy People and is the Premier Train of the World." In July he wrote, "The Pennsylvania System – The crowning achievement of modern industry."[25]

Probably the laudatory statements about the Pennsylvania that Barriger recorded in his diary resulted from his personal contacts with Ivy Ledbetter Lee, who in the pre–World War I period served as assistant to the president of the PRR and later was hailed as the father of modern corporate publicity. On two occasions during Barriger's years at Central High, Lee, an alumnus, had been a guest speaker. "My interest in Ivy Lee led to meeting him and visiting with him. As a result of my meeting Mr. Lee under those congenial circumstances, he placed my name on the mailing list to receive all of the public relations and advertizing materials mailed out by his office."[26]

Not only did the railroad-minded John Barriger make contact with the famous Ivy Lee, but as a result of his frequent visits to Union Station he developed close ties with railroad employees, including Howard Trader of the Pennsylvania. "He encouraged my activities and occasionally introduced me to Pennsylvania officers arriving and departing on their trains in and out of St. Louis, usually occupying their business cars, which visits provided my first glimpse of their interiors." Over time he became friendly with Thomas Hamilton, a Princeton engineering graduate who served as general manager of the Pittsburgh, Cincinnati, Chicago & St. Louis (Vandalia) Railroad, a PRR subsidiary, and later general manager of the PRR's consolidated Northwestern Region. Hamilton further stimulated Barriger's fondness for the system. Said Barriger, "While all railroads interested me, my great favorite was The Pennsylvania."[27]

The Pennsylvania personnel with whom the young Barriger established personal relationships shaped his railroad career. The catalyst was "Achievement," an article about PRR passenger service that Barriger wrote during his senior year for his high school newspaper. Following its publication, he gave a copy to Howard Trader, who passed it along to local PRR officials. In time the piece found its way to Samuel Moody, passenger traffic manager for lines west in Pittsburgh. Moody subsequently sent it to William W. Atterbury, vice president–operations and future president. Barriger's writings apparently impressed everyone as the article made its way up the railroad's chain of command. Atterbury probably suggested to Moody that he inquire about the future plans of this St. Louis teenager. On February 13, 1917, Moody contacted Barriger and asked him about his ambitions. "Quickly responding to this opening, I mentioned that I would enter MIT in the fall and upon graduation hoped to secure appointment as a special apprentice in the Altoona Shops of the Pennsylvania Railroad or a similar trainee post in the Maintenance of Way Department." Moody responded. "[His] reply was more or less to the effect that 'eventually why not now,' and as a result I was offered summer employment with the Pennsylvania at Altoona, which I promptly accepted." Yet a self-effacing Barriger once told a financial writer that he considered the offer flattering, but indicated that initially he could hardly consider it before he had earned his college diploma.[28]

As a career path for John Barriger unfolded – railroad employment and college civil engineering – his mother came to realize that her son was no longer a child. Their relationship remained close and caring, yet tensions existed. The principal issue involved their diverse political perspectives. About 1906 Edith Barriger, who sought to occupy her free time, began to take courses at Washington University, and by spring 1922 she accumulated enough credits to earn a bachelor of arts degree. Her son, though, heartedly disliked the school's political environment. "Washington University then had a radical coterie of students and professors," he asserted. "My mother had very highly developed intellectual attainments, although unhappily she, like so many other persons who find radical doctrines attractive, was limited in her capacity to apply practical intelligence and experience to the problems under review." Edith became an admirer of Roger Nash Baldwin, a professor of sociology and a social activist who later founded the American Civil Liberties Union. This Harvard-educated Boston Brahman staunchly believed in democratic change and the concept of reform social Darwinism. "Roger Baldwin stood as a progressive who viewed matters from an elitist perspective," observed a biographer, "and believed that American institutions and American society required, at most, fine-tuning." He was no bomb-throwing radical. After moving to St. Louis in 1906, Baldwin attracted a number of upper-crust citizens to his various civic causes, including better treatment of juvenile delinquents and improved race relations.[29]

Energized by Roger Baldwin and other St. Louisians in a city that had become an exemplar of municipal reform, Edith focused on women's suffrage, a national movement that was rapidly gaining strength. She served as secretary for the Equal Suffrage League of St. Louis, an organization founded in 1910 that sought "Suffrage for Missouri in 1914." Edith was surely disappointed that this did not happen, although she may have agreed with Emily Newell Blair, a leader in this Show-Me State crusade, who wrote, "We did not win the 1914 suffrage amendment [to the Missouri Constitution]. We never expected to. But we changed the attitude of thousands." Edith likely participated in the well-publicized woman's rights protest at the Democratic National Convention held in the St. Louis Coliseum during June 1916. Known as "the Golden Lane," several thousand suffragists from the city and around the country stood quietly outside the convention hall in their white dresses and hats and held yellow parasols for protection from the blazing sun to support a suffrage plank to the party's platform. Their "walkless, talkless suffrage demonstration" succeeded in obtaining a modest pro-suffrage statement. About this time Edith participated in suffrage rallies in Idaho and Montana, and "in a couple of cases she was welcomed into bars by miners and cowboys, and was respectfully listened to and was well supported." Later as chair of the Missouri division of the National Woman's Party she picketed the White House to urge passage of the Nineteenth

Amendment to the US Constitution. The latter event made the national newspapers, complete with photographs – notoriety that embarrassed her conservative son, who was a student at MIT.[30]

During the 1910s Edith Barriger also became an active member of the Wednesday Club in St. Louis. This upper-class women's organization, founded in 1890, embraced more than social events, being also involved in civic activities. The club officially sought "to continue [members'] intellectual growth, stay abreast of the times, and contribute to the community." During the immediate postwar period, the Wednesday Club threw its support behind the humanitarian relief activities of the United States Food Administration. Edith and club members volunteered their services to assist director Herbert Hoover in his efforts to create "a common recognition of the obligation to help the stricken countries of the world until normal [food] conditions are once more restored."[31]

Edith's liberal acquaintances and reform activism long troubled her son. "I am confident that my father, her dead husband, would have disapproved of her radical friends as violently as I did," reflected Barriger, "but I am also sure that if he had lived she would not have suffered these aberrations. This is to me a painful subject, but I have always believed her turning to this outlet for distraction from her sadness was due to the extreme and unbalancing shock of my father's tragic death." He continued, "I have believed that my extreme conservatism, which is a source of personal satisfaction and mental comfort, is possibly due to my early keen dislike and complete distrust of my mother's radical friends. Happily she never married any one of the men among them, but I have always feared that her association with this group cost her the opportunity that she undoubtedly otherwise would have had as a handsome and well educated young widow in her late twenties and early thirties with only one child to make a second happy marriage." He closed with these thoughts: "If she had, it would have been her salvation and also beneficial to me."[32]

Edith, though, seemed satisfied with how her life was unfolding. She might have found employment outside the home, but she opted not to enter the job market. "She was a bit of a Victorian Elite in that she thought proper women did not work," recalled her grandson John W. (Jack) Barriger IV. Financially, Edith became dependent on her brother Clarence, a prosperous St. Louis coal merchant and mine owner, and then her son. When the Barrigers lived in Altoona, Pennsylvania, she joined their household. "Mom and Dad accepted, but probably resented the fact that she did nothing to support herself but showed up on their doorstep about the time I was born [1927]." That communal living arrangement, which involved several relocations, did not end until much later in Edith's life.[33]

RAILROADER AND COLLEGE MAN

The fortunate reaction by Pennsylvania Railroad officials to Barriger's newspaper article allowed him to begin his professional career. Following his graduation from Central High School, Barriger left St. Louis for Altoona, and on June 29, 1917, he started work as a laborer in Erecting Shop #2 in this sprawling railroad complex. Here Barriger could see firsthand a railroad that was "ever the experimentalist," an experience that became "perhaps my greatest thrill."[34]

An arrangement between the Pennsylvania and Barriger permitted him to matriculate at MIT in Cambridge, Massachusetts, on September 24, 1917. What the PRR called a "furlough" meant that Barriger would spend the academic months studying civil engineering and summers employed by the railroad. Because of World War I and a compulsory military science requirement at MIT, the only interruption in this four-year routine involved a stint in the US Army as part of its Student Army Corps program. Barriger did reasonably well academically, taking a variety of challenging courses. Although the school used a pass-fail grading system but with explanatory gradations, his official transcript indicates that he excelled in descriptive geometry and industrial relations yet struggled somewhat in physics and advanced mathematics. Barriger thrived in the college setting, being socially active and relishing his off-campus field trips, including one to explore an interlocking plant outside Boston, and enjoying a summer surveying camp required for civil engineering majors in East Machias, Maine. Barriger also found his hands-on experiences with the PRR to be educational and an agreeable change from his formal studies.[35]

Not long after joining the Pennsylvania Railroad, John Barriger made an important decision. He became less interested in mechanical

In 1917 a young and excited John Barriger began his railroad career with the
Pennsylvania Railroad at Altoona, Pennsylvania. His talent as a budding photographer
is readily seen in this photo from July 1917, where he captured on film a portion of the
massive Altoona shops complex that extended for 3 miles and where 16,000 people
and their families gained their livelihood. (John W. Barriger III Collection, Barriger
National Railroad Library at UMSL)

repair and more intrigued with operations. So he obtained a transfer
to the Maintenance of Way Department and received an assignment
on the busy New York Division. Here he worked as an assistant to the
civil engineer in charge of track construction between the Pennsylvania
communities of Bristol and Morrisville. This involved surveying, making engineering computations, and checking material supplies. Next
Barriger was placed with the engineering corps to prepare valuation and
track maps, and later he took charge of a surveying party that rechecked
bridge plans and their specifications.[36]

As Barriger learned more about the nuts and bolts of the PRR physical plant, he completed his college education. In June 1921 he graduated
from MIT with a bachelor of science degree in civil engineering and
engineering administration. Since the program required a senior thesis, Barriger predictably selected a subject that pertained to the PRR,
and he undertook an ambitious one: "The Corporate History of the

Pennsylvania Railroad, 1846–1890." The research and writing consumed much of his final months in Cambridge. In a diary entry for May 13, 1921, he described a wager that he made with a fellow student. It called "for me paying a forfeit of a certain sum for every page under 20 of thesis turned out per day until completion, while I receive a similar amount as bonus for all over 20." And he had one exceptionally productive day. "By working until 1:20 AM on Saturday morning, made 54." But that impressive spurt tired him out, and in the following entry he recorded a page shortfall: "lose 45c." Two weeks later he had finished about 200 pages that he then submitted to his adviser, Professor F. E. Armstrong. Finally, Barriger completed the project on the thirtieth, and it subsequently won approval. His PRR thesis turned out to be more historical than engineering, an indication of his love of railroad history that lasted until his death.[37]

Anticipating graduation from "Boston Tech" in June, Barriger scurried to find a permanent job with the Pennsylvania. The developing post–World War economic downswing – the nation's "forgotten depression" – forced the railroad industry, including the mighty PRR, to reduce its workforce. Luckily he landed an entry-level position as a rodman with the engineering corps on the New York Division. But within months he learned that because of impending force reductions he would be furloughed. Barriger scrambled again, and success followed. On September 26, 1921, he reported to the division engineer of the Toledo Division. Unlike his previous assignments, his job was less physical: "Principal duties consisted of preparing a Traffic Census of the Detroit Metropolitan area and miscellaneous work in connection with the Pennsylvania-Detroit Railroad." In reality this was a market survey. Corporate headquarters wanted this study because it planned to resume construction of a Toledo to Detroit extension, which wartime federalization had stopped. By 1923 the PRR, through its Pennsylvania-Detroit Railroad subsidiary, had gained access to the "Motor City" from Toledo through a combination of leases and construction of a 20-mile cutoff line.[38]

Always ambitious and "being very anxious to enter the Transportation Department as an 'apprentice,' but there being no such course," Barriger took action. Through contacts that led him to R. C. Morse, superintendent freight transportation, Eastern Region, he audaciously proposed such a training program. There was good news: Morse was receptive. As a test of sorts, Barriger in January 1922 reported to the general manager in Chicago, where he studied operations of the Polk Street Freight Station. "This was my first contact with the Transportation Department and the purpose of the assignment was evidently to determine my suitability for the work I desired to take up." After nearly a month in the Windy City, he returned to Toledo for "special duty" with the division's transportation inspector. Soon Barriger received a much different assignment. On May 1, 1922, he began work on a temporary basis with the assistant to adviser in publicity, aiding him in the launching of a Northwestern Region edition of the *Pennsylvania News,* the company news organ. Barriger, who had been his high school newspaper editor and had completed a substantial collegiate thesis, was hardly a fish out of water. When volume 1, number 1, appeared, he jumped at the chance to deliver a copy personally to General Atterbury in Philadelphia, but once at company headquarters he regretted that "I can't get to see him." This association with the *Pennsylvania News* foreshadowed his future interest in public and employee relations and also his "natural flair for promotion."[39]

By the fall of 1922 the pace of Barriger's rapidly changing career with the PRR slowed somewhat. For the next two years he participated in the company's pilot transportation apprentice program, something that he relished, and he worked out of his earlier stomping grounds, the New York Division. His initial assignments were varied, including yard service, clerical duties, and a longer stint as an assistant yardmaster. His latter job was made more nerve-wracking because of the bitter national Shopmen's Strike that began on the PRR in mid-1922 and lasted for nearly a year, a stoppage that led to the humiliating defeat of the shopcraft unions. In the course of his apprentice placement, Barriger passed the book of rules and air brakes examinations, and he qualified as a freight conductor. He also had contact with the office of freight trainmaster. Eager to expand his knowledge of railroading, he recalled another learning experience. "During this period I spent all available spare time studying train dispatching through 'listening in' on the circuit while seated alongside of the dispatcher." Subsequently Barriger was assigned to the office of the superintendent, where he worked on divisional and interdivisional freight and passenger runs. At this time Barriger took advantage of specialized training for engine service "to learn the proper handling of locomotives."[40]

Barriger was never a wallflower when it came to his employment experiences. In consultation with fellow trainees, he explained to his superiors in 1924 how the pilot transportation program could be strengthened. His multipage letter made fourteen recommendations, including "Reduction of Yard Service from 12 months to 9 months," "Require the Apprentice to pass examination as Trains Dispatcher," "Specify road service to include braking and firing," and "A course of outside reading to be prescribed and we [trainees] be required to submit abstracts of the subjects covered." Barriger closed with these tactful remarks: "We trust that the seeming boldness of our requests will not be taken amiss but received in the spirit in which we send it. We believe that the quality, as well as the quantity, of our work suffers because of certain limitations of the course which we believe can be best changed before any apprentice has completed the course and thus established a <u>precedent</u> [underlining in original]."[41]

The year 1925 brought about more exposure to the workings of the Pennsylvania. No longer wet behind the ears, and preferring analytical work, Barriger became an "inspector for manager of mail and express traffic." He spent months studying through mail and express trains and also terminal operations in Chicago, New York, and St. Louis. His charge was to see if milk, parcel post, Railway Express, and other nonpassenger operations could be consolidated, along with less-than-carload (LCL) freight, into a third service that would be distinct from the freight and passenger sectors. Barriger reveled in this assignment and his system-wide travels.[42]

Being single and with some free time, Barriger often explored various divisions of the PRR and other steam and electric interurban roads. He had an insatiable desire to see and understand the total railroad network. Barriger took a dim view of those railroaders who were not interested in experiencing the industry beyond their work assignments. "I remember one superintendent bawling the daylights out of me because I spent my time that way. He boasted of the fact that he had never been west of Pittsburgh and he was nearly ready to retire, so you can see what kind of parochial attitude he would take towards me who believed in having a national viewpoint."[43]

The following year Barriger received a placement on the Middle Division of the Pennsylvania. In early January he became an assistant yardmaster in Holidaysburg, Pennsylvania. This was an arduous job, and consistent with such a post it always created workplace stress and sleep deprivation. But his stay at Holidaysburg was of short duration. Several months later he took a "special duty" stint with the company's Committee of Association of Transportation Officers to study comparative operating methods of the PRR, Baltimore & Ohio, New York Central, and Reading railroads. After that five-week assignment ended, he once more became an assistant yardmaster, this time on the Middle Division in Altoona. This job lasted until April 1927.[44]

FAMILY MAN

Railroading was constantly on John Barriger's mind until love blossomed. During the summer of 1925 the latter occurred while he was visiting friends at Wequetonsing, Michigan, located on the north shore of Little Traverse Bay near Petoskey. This upscale resort community, established by Indiana Presbyterians in the late 1870s, consisted of a hotel, assembly hall, and about one hundred cottages and was a popular summertime retreat for well-to-do St. Louisans who wanted to escape their home city's oppressive heat and humidity. Here Barriger met and fell in love with the attractive and sociable Elizabeth Chambers Thatcher, who lived at her ancestral estate, Glen Owen, on Chambers Road in Ferguson, Missouri. She had been born on September 17, 1902, in Parral, Chihuahua, Mexico, where she also spent her childhood. Elizabeth's father, Thomas Hudson Thatcher, a graduate of the Missouri School of Mines (today's Missouri University of Science and Technology) and a "kind and gentle man," worked for fourteen years in Mexico, managing silver mines for Consolidated Kansas City Smelting & Refining Company in Parral and then operated his own commission business in that community. The rapidly developing Mexican Revolution of 1910 forced the family, which consisted of her parents, Elizabeth, and four younger

Thomas H. Thatcher holds his baby daughter, Elizabeth Chambers Thatcher, a portrait likely taken in early 1903 in Parral, Chihuahua, Mexico. (John W. Barriger IV Collection)

This family portrait shows Thomas and Odille Thatcher and their six children. It was made in the 1920s, probably in St. Louis or in nearby Ferguson, Missouri, location of the Thatcher ancestral estate, Glen Owen. *Back row from left to right:* George, Hudson, Fusz, Chas, and Elizabeth. Joe, the youngest family member, is to the right of his father and mother. (John W. Barriger IV Collection)

brothers (a fifth son would be born in Missouri in 1913) to return to the United States. Because of illness Thatcher needed to delay his own exit to safety until May 1910, but once back in the Show-Me State the family did not suffer financially. Although Thatcher had "much money invested in Mexico, where he retains extensive mining interests," his father-in-law, Eugene Fusz, a prominent St. Louis businessman associated with the Chateau & Harrison Valley Iron Works, came to Thatcher's aid, having excellent business connections. Thatcher, though, subsequently went into business for himself, becoming a dealer in mining supplies. Much later, in 1934, this sixty-five-year old businessman won election on the Democratic ticket as presiding judge of St. Louis County, a quasi-judicial and legislative post.[45]

Elizabeth did not come from old Protestant stock. The Thatchers were Roman Catholics, and she became one who "adores the Catholic Church." Her education included the four-year liberal arts course at the small, all-female College of the Sacred Heart (later Manhattanville College) in Manhattanville, New York, where she graduated in 1923.

A red-letter day in the life of John Barriger was his marriage to Elizabeth Chambers Thatcher on Saturday, September 25, 1926. This elaborate affair took place at the Thatcher family home, Glen Owen, located on Chambers Road in the St. Louis suburb of Ferguson, Missouri. (John W. Barriger III Collection, Barriger National Railroad Library at UMSL)

Then during the 1923 holiday social season Elizabeth was presented to St. Louis society in a fancy ball held at Glen Owen.[46]

Not only was Elizabeth Thatcher well-schooled and socially prominent, but she was also bilingual; she learned Spanish before she mastered English. In the Mexican Thatcher household when her parents wished to speak confidentially, not wanting her or her siblings to listen in, they spoke English. Throughout her adult life Elizabeth remained fluent in Spanish, and this became an useful skill when she later lived with her husband in Washington, DC.[47]

Romance led to the engagement of John and Elizabeth on Christmas Eve 1925, and then to their marriage. That anticipated event occurred on September 25, 1926, at Glen Owen. In a letter a few days before the wedding, Barriger wrote his mother, "Elizabeth's and my life together will certainly be born amid splendor and most happy surroundings." And his mother, a staunch Presbyterian, did not object to her son marrying outside of Protestantism, perhaps attributable to her liberal values. Since the Thatchers were a prominent family, this elaborate ceremony made the front page of the Society and Women's Section of the *Sunday St. Louis Globe-Democrat*, featuring a photograph of the radiant Elizabeth and her eighteen-member wedding party. The following year a gossip writer for the *St. Louis Censor* made this observation: "John W. Barriger is said to be an exemplary type of young man and making Elizabeth the best of husbands."[48]

This would be a happy marriage. John often referred to Elizabeth as "Sweetie Pie" (occasionally "My Tweetum Pie" and "Lovest Lamb-pie"), and according to their son Jack, "She was enthusiastic about him." During their early years of marriage John occasionally sent Elizabeth a letter, note, or telegram that revealed his funny side. Take this telegram sent to her from Montreal, Canada: "Have you heard of the Montreal baby who was just born with a broken arm because he had to hold on until the marriage license was issued?" Fortunately, these newlyweds had an understanding about their mixed-religion marriage. John became a "nominal" Presbyterian, but "really ecumenical, and he became close to at least one priest." The four Barriger children, John Walker Barriger IV (August 3, 1927), Elizabeth Thatcher Barriger (August 28, 1928), Ann Biddle Barriger (September 5, 1930), and Stanley Huntington Barriger (August 13, 1933), would be raised Roman Catholics, and they remained strongly committed to the faith.[49]

With a wife and an expanding family, John Barriger sought employment opportunities with better pay. At the time of his marriage, he worked as an assistant yardmaster in Altoona, where he supervised about one hundred employees, but in April 1927 he left that nerve-wracking job to take special duty assignments for the chief of passenger transportation. The couple, though, remained in Altoona. By the time he left the PRR later in 1927, he earned $275 monthly ($3,800 in current dollars) or $3,300 annually ($45,000 in current dollars), a decent living wage.[50]

Although John Barriger considered his decade of employment with the Pennsylvania worthwhile, he had mixed feelings about his fellow railroaders. In a March 1969 interview with *New York Times* reporter

The marriage of John Barriger and Elizabeth Thatcher was a most happy union. Throughout his life he repeatedly referred to her as "Sweetie Pie" and used other terms of endearment. When this picture was taken, the young Barriger was a proud Pennsylvania Railroad man. (John W. Barriger III Collection, Barriger National Railroad Library at UMSL)

Robert Bedingfield, he reminisced about these years. "On the PRR there were always some men, officers and employes alike, who believed in me implicitly, even when I had no experience, but most people thought I was nuts." He continued, "I remember in those days I used to talk at length about PRR finishing the great plans of [President Alexander J.] Cassatt [1899–1906], putting a long tunnel under the Allegheny Mountains, reducing grades and curves, modernizing major yards, and dozens of things like that. Some of the officers of the Pennsylvania Railroad whom I worked for thought I was probably the most promising young man on the railroad and nothing would stop me from being president some day." Others were not so pleased and wanted him off the property. Barriger elaborated:

> Those were the days when there was a considerable gulf between officers and employees. I always believed that when I went into a new place, tell the men, '*I am completely at your mercy. Do a good job for me so I can get along as I want to and if you don't, you can give me a royal frigging and I will fail* [italics in original].' I've tried to work with the men under me all my life. Some of the officers I worked for

> thought my ideas would undermine all discipline on the railroad, others thought
> it was a great thing to do, but as I say, I was a controversial figure.

He added, "Everything I did or said a few thought was progressive and that I should be encouraged and pushed along. Some other people thought the quicker they cut my throat, the better."[51]

In reflection Barriger realized that his time with the Pennsylvania Railroad set him on the proper career path. He felt that those opportunities to become more than a minor operating official produced great benefits. "I think that those special assignments which led to my being taken off routine jobs and getting a wider view, somewhat unfitted me to return to those routine assignments," he reflected years later. "In other words, being singled out for them made me stand out in ways that led to my becoming what might be called a very controversial figure."[52]

All in all John Barriger developed an amazing understanding of the American railroad industry. One indication involved his extensive traveling, having covered by the time that he left the PRR a substantial portion of the 250,000 miles of the nation's rail system. This boundless traveling did not end; it continued through the remainder of his life. "My father has the almost uncanny faculty of being able to identify locations continuously in his travels over most of America's principal rail routes," said his younger son Stanley years later. "On many of them he can tell where he is at night without looking out the window, and has even been aware, upon waking, that he was on a detour route that began after he had gone to sleep! Dad has the basic physical characteristics and track patterns of many thousands of rail line in his memory."[53]

FINANCIAL ANALYST

Barriger's detractors probably smiled when they learned that he had accepted a position in New York City with Kuhn, Loeb & Company, a firm heavily involved in financing the railroad industry and responsible since the 1890s for handling most of the Pennsylvania's securities. This was a good move for Barriger. The job paid a starting annual salary of $4,000 ($55,300 in current dollars), and within two years his compensation reached $6,000 annually ($83,000 in current dollars). This was the advancement that he sought, providing him with a strong income but also the professional exposure that produced other opportunities.[54]

Why Kuhn Loeb? Barriger explained to Robert Bedingford his decision to join this prestigious investment banking house. "Having a great interest in railroads generally and knowing that Kuhn, Loeb & Co. was the banking firm identified with PRR financing, I became interested in making a change of base to it." Although Barriger did not have frequent contacts with General Atterbury, who became PRR vice president in 1924 and president the following year, they did have informal talks. "In some of my conversations with General Atterbury, I took up with him the possibility of solving my personal problems by in effect transferring from PRR to Kuhn, Loeb & Co. He gave me an introduction to Kuhn, Loeb & Company, and at any rate I got a job in its then newly formed statistical department."[55]

Now that John had a Wall Street job, was recently married, and was father of an infant son, the Barrigers, including Edith Barriger, relocated to the suburban community of Upper Montclair, New Jersey. For the new financial analyst this was a practical location for commuting to work by public transportation. As with the years on the PRR, Barriger was eager to learn more about the business of railroading, and working in the Manhattan financial district made that possible.

At Kuhn, Loeb & Company Barriger had varied duties. The position provided him with a chance to work on the final details for the reorganization of the bankrupt Chicago, Milwaukee & St. Paul Railroad (Milwaukee Road) and to examine the financial situation of various carriers and holding companies. He also got exposure to matters of railroad consolidation. Explained Barriger, "Since leaving the Pennsylvania, my work has centered exclusively on railway securities." And he saw his job this way: "I have believed that it was of paramount importance to be thoroughly familiar with the facilities and problems; have direct knowledge of the economic and physical geography of its territory, its sources of traffic and competitive position, and above all the caliber of its official family, and keep abreast of actual or potential technical and economic developments affecting the future of the carriers." Barriger noted, too, "Not less than one-third of my time has been spent in field

As an employee of the Wall Street financial powerhouse firm Kuhn, Loeb & Company, John Barriger dressed appropriately. For the remainder of his life he preferred a three-piece suit, white shirt, and tie. (John W. Barriger III Collection, Barriger National Railroad Library at UMSL)

investigations, in all parts of this country, in carrying out these objectives." In February 1929, for example, he traveled to Montreal, Quebec, to assess the Canadian Pacific Railway, including both its railroad and non-transportation operations.[56]

Barriger, however, developed qualms about Kuhn, Loeb & Co., and after two years he resigned. "I expect the most important reason I left was that I had always heard before I went in financial work that bankers took a very direct interest in advising railroads about their policies and affairs." He discovered otherwise. "The wholesale underwriters of securities were essentially sales agencies and not counselors. In my work as an analyst I wasn't looking only for the good points in a railroad necessary to sell its securities, but for its weak points, too. I considered that an analyst was a professional man like a doctor or lawyer to tell a railroad about its deficiencies, too." As he opined, "I soon concluded a truly critical approach to railroad analysis wasn't one that would lead to fame and fortune within investment banking organizations whose business it was to sell securities of their railroad clients. I realized that I didn't fit into the scheme of things of a banking firm selling railroad bonds any more than I had fitted into the Pennsy scheme of things at the divisional level, because I wanted to look at railroads from the point of view of a constructive critic, as the great railroad builders did."[57]

Still, the Kuhn, Loeb experience had benefits. He particularly liked his frequent contacts with economist Paul Gourrich, who later became the statistics director for the Securities and Exchange Commission. In the process of his travels he met hundreds of railroad leaders and others associated with the industry, helping him to develop a "big picture" sense of what railroads needed and didn't need. "I learned a great deal while with Kuhn, Loeb," reflected Barriger. "I shall always be deeply grateful for the privilege of having worked for this firm."[58]

Before submitting his letter of resignation to Kuhn, Loeb, Barriger had lined up another position on Wall Street, making on September 1, 1929, a seamless transition to Calvin Bullock & Company. This job paid considerably more; his starting pay was $8,500 annually ($119,000 in current dollars). When he left on June 1, 1933, his annual earnings had nearly doubled, amounting to $15,000 ($227,000 in current dollars), an

In the fall of 1929, a railroad investment company was organized. In the fall of 1929 came a new face to Room 2860 to keep this company organized.

In the summer of 1929, we had no railroad department. In the summer of 1930, one of the most complete departments of the organization was the railroad department.

A year ago we went out and sought information on the rails. Now people come to us for that information.

Those who have trod on the well worn rug to the second "door on the right" in Room 2860 know why. That's"the General's office." The General himself is the reason for our rise in esteem as a "railroad house" as well as a "utility house."

John Barriger has earned his name as a rail authority. He has lived with the railroads all his life and he has studied them most carefully. Indeed, John himself typifies his beloved "Twentieth Century, Limited" --- he always runs full steam ahead.

Many of us have been impressed by his ability as an after dinner speaker. Whether he dines with Generals (recent buddies were Atterbury, McRoberts and Pershing) or with the rest of us, John is liable to punctuate, if not dominate the gathering, with items of current comment, quite loquacious and quite to the point.

"The Penn, my friends, is mightier than etc., etc., etc."

Attaboy, John.

Shortly before the stock market crash of October 1929 John Barriger joined the International Carriers unit of New York–based Calvin Bullock & Company. He showed a passion for its railroad department and became known to his associates as "the General," as this scrapbook copy attests. A colleague took this photograph of Barriger in his everyday workplace attire. (John W. Barriger III Collection, Barriger National Railroad Library at UMSL)

impressive amount during difficult economic times. This salary boost was much appreciated. "That was big money for me and urgently needed, with two young children and probably more in the future." By the time of his departure his work responsibilities had also increased, including supervision of five employees.[59]

Barriger had more focused duties at Calvin Bullock, work that better suited his railroad interests. Specifically he joined International Carriers Ltd., the investment trust managed by Calvin Bullock that claimed a $20 million portfolio of rail securities. In this capacity Barriger served as a vice president, and in April 1932 he became a company director. The International Carriers trust included several historically strong railroads, notably Norfolk & Western, Pennsylvania, and Union Pacific. He also was associated in various capacities with other trusts managed by Calvin Bullock. Said Barriger about his duties, "I felt the place where a critic should be was in an investment management institution and not in a security selling institution. I think I was probably the very first analyst to make a practice of going out on railroad inspection trips." This he did, claiming "not less than one-third of my time has been spent in field investigations." In 1933 one assignment involved "a trip of observation" that covered over 20,000 miles in the West and Pacific Northwest, where he studied the efforts of railroads to regain traffic lost to trucks. Such journeys made good business sense, and it was what this peripatetic lover of railroads so enjoyed.[60]

While at Calvin Bullock, Barriger also remained in his office to analyze companies, including the Pennsylvania. In mid-September 1930 he produced a positive overview of this company, designed to encourage investors to acquire Pennsylvania securities. The result was a slick eighty-eight-page publication, *The Pennsylvania Railroad*, profusely illustrated and featuring numerous tables about financial and operating matters. Barriger remained that avid admirer of his first employer. He wrote in his concluding statement: "Emerson has said that an institution is but the lengthened shadow of a man. The Pennsylvania Railroad today is the embodiment of the vision and personality of its master builder, J. Edgar Thomson, who laid its foundation of greatness, and A. J. Cassatt, who developed the inherent strength of the System to its present position of power and prestige." Not to be overlooked was his idol, President Atterbury. "The third of its great leaders, General W. W. Atterbury, is now guiding the destinies of this organization, which is crossing the threshold of a new era." But little did Barriger realize that the nation was on the verge of its worst economic crisis since the mid-1890s.[61]

Employment at Calvin Bullock broadened John Barriger's knowledge of the railroad enterprise. Such insights became imperative following the onset of the Great Depression, triggered by the stock market crash of October 1929 and the sharply worsening economic conditions by the early 1930s. This inquisitive man-on-the-make made contact with numerous railroaders, trade association personnel, shippers, and government officials, and he continued to increase his understanding of the industry. When Barriger felt deficient in matters of rate making, for example, he took a correspondence course from the La Salle Extension University of Chicago. His remarkable memory enhanced these experiences. It would be during the Calvin Bullock years that Barriger also launched his public speaking career, initially lecturing on railroad and business topics at the University of Pittsburgh, a commitment that for an academic semester necessitated monthly trips between New York and Pittsburgh.[62]

In the opening weeks of 1933 John Barriger received an offer that catapulted him into the national limelight. This involved preparation of a voluntary plan for railroad unification, what came to be known as the Prince Plan of Railroad Consolidation. Between February and May 1933 Calvin Bullock gave him a paid leave of absence to participate in this historic undertaking. Barriger enthusiastically plunged into this heavily complex and controversial project.

TWO

Government Man

THE PRINCE PLAN

By 1933 a growing number of prominent railroaders considered John W. Barriger III a rising star in the industry, a man who possessed a flare for facts and figures and a remarkable knowledge of the layout and workings of the nation's railroad system. It would be Walker D. Hines, former Atchison, Topeka & Santa Fe Railway (Santa Fe) board chair and second director general of the US Railroad Administration, and Leonor F. Loree, president of the Delaware & Hudson Company and executive committee member of the Kansas City Southern Railway, both staunch advocates of railroad consolidations, who suggested to Frederick Prince that the thirty-three-year-old Barriger play a leading role in preparing a plan for voluntary railroad unification. Prince was a wealthy Boston financier who served as president of the Association of Railroad Securities Owners and had been an active railroad investor. In January 1933 president-elect Franklin D. Roosevelt asked him at a conference on the "railroad problem" to direct such a study.[1]

Why a desire to bring about railroad consolidation? Such discussions had long been ongoing. Since the industry had developed largely from a patchwork of short lines, a growing movement developed in the mid-nineteenth century to merge and lease properties or to have some form of traffic relationships. In the 1870s and 1880s, beginning with the Iowa Pool, there had been efforts to prevent ruthless rate cutting through various nonbinding "gentlemen's agreements." It was investment banker

J. Pierpont Morgan Sr. who made this revealing observation: "I like competition, but I like combination better." And that is what he did during the Gilded Age and after. For years Morgan strove to make railroads larger and more efficient, as with his work in assembling the Southern Railway in 1894 from various smaller and mostly weak lines. Morgan and other men of money, including Jay Gould and E. H. Harriman, promoted "system building" and established "communities of interest" between competing properties. These captains of industry were strongly devoted to laissez-faire principles.[2]

Not all Americans endorsed railroad consolidations. Antimonopolists blasted these actions, believing that the emerging giants had an unfavorable impact on rates and services and threatened democratic institutions. Such views were shared by Grangers, Alliancemen, and Populists and, after the turn of the twentieth century, by a rapidly increasing number of socialists and progressives. Reformers spearheaded passage of the Interstate Commerce Act in 1887, which created the Interstate Commerce Commission (ICC), and such landmark legislation as the Elkins Act (1903), Hepburn Act (1906), and Mann-Elkins Act (1910), collectively bringing about rate controls and expanded jurisdiction of the ICC. It would be President Theodore Roosevelt, "Square Deal" advocate and "trust buster," who led the attack on the Northern Securities Company, a holding company that controlled the Great Northern (GN), Northern Pacific (NP), and Chicago, Burlington & Quincy (Burlington) railroads. These so-called Hill Lines were named for James J. Hill, who built the GN and later controlled the NP. (The GN and NP jointly owned the Burlington.) In 1904 the US Supreme Court in a landmark 5–4 decision gave Roosevelt and his supporters a victory, ruling that Northern Securities must disband, being in restraint of trade and thus violating the Sherman Antitrust Act of 1890.

Although political reformers expanded the regulatory codes at the federal and state levels, railroads continued to buy and lease other carriers, usually feeder lines. Scores of railroads also absorbed their subsidiaries. The public generally did not fuss much about most corporate expansions, believing that Progressive Era reforms protected its interests. Such stringent regulation prompted Henry Cabot Lodge, the "stand pat"

Republican US senator from Massachusetts, to astutely observe: "The ICC has undertaken as its mission not the protection of the public, but the destruction and prosecution of the railroads." There is little doubt that federal regulations damped the spirit of entrepreneurship within the industry.[3]

In 1917 a new take on the railroad enterprise occurred. The outbreak of the Great War in 1914 had placed strains on American transportation. Even before the United States declared war on the Central Powers in April 1917, the Woodrow Wilson administration backed war-related aid for Great Britain and France. With entry into the conflict, wartime traffic soared, and chaos reigned in Atlantic and Gulf terminals. Loaded freight cars clogged port sidings while shippers craved empties. The Railroads' War Board (RWB), a voluntary industry organization, sought to untangle the mess and alleviate equipment shortages. Yet it failed to forge an efficient railway network. The industry had been growing financially weaker and was in no position to acquire additional motive power and rolling stock, largely because of stiff regulations, forced concessions to railroad unions, and increased motor vehicle competition. In fact, by 1915, about one-sixth of the nation's railroad mileage was in the hands of receivers, and fewer miles of lines had been built than at any time since the Civil War era. Furthermore, the RWB lacked legal authority to require carriers to cooperate, relying instead on moral suasion. Old rivalries, jealousies, and suspicions among the trunk roads, most notably between the New York Central (NYC) and Pennsylvania (PRR), and the complexities of the task forced federal intervention. Washington could not turn a blind eye; railroads were the nation's number-two war industry. The rail crisis led to formation of the US Railroad Administration (USRA), and by early 1918 it began to increase network efficiencies.[4]

What had lawmakers created with the USRA? This powerful government agency "federalized" most of the nation's steam railroads and strategic electric interurbans. Regulation by the ICC temporarily lapsed when Washington leased the essential properties. Then in March 1918 legislators passed the Railroad Control Act, which guaranteed to companies compensation based on net operating income averages for the three years ending on June 30, 1917. A revolving fund of $500 million

($9.35 billion in current dollars) was established for the costs of federal control, and the government promised to return lines to their owners no later than twenty-one months after the conflict had ended.

The USRA largely fulfilled its mission, helping to ensure a victory for the Allies in November 1918. It realized its goal for the improved movement of military personnel and especially military cargo and agricultural goods, assisted by a combination of industry operating experts and a push for standardization of locomotives and freight cars. There were negatives with this "emergency" measure. Some carriers, for example, suffered from USRA policies, mostly from the rerouting of traffic away from their lines that resulted in a prolonged or permanent loss of business, and consumers felt the sting of major increases in freight rates.[5]

With federalization due to expire on March 1, 1920, debates erupted over extending Washington's involvement. Should the USRA continue? Industry and financial people mostly sought the immediate end to federalization. Yet there were government officials and some others who urged continuation of control for another five years, allowing time to formulate a reasoned regulatory policy. Labor, which had gained strength during the war years, wanted Washington to play an even greater role.

It would be railroad labor that sparked a public discourse about the ultimate relationship between government and industry. In 1919 Glenn Plumb, general counsel for the operating unions, sought government ownership, resembling what had occurred in several European countries and in Canada, first with its Canadian Government Railways and then with the Canadian National Railway System, a 23,000 mile publicly owned sea-to-sea network. Railroaders sought good wages, worker-management harmony, industry efficiency, and protection of the public interest – or at least those were their stated intentions.

Debate on what became the Plumb Plan followed. This labor scheme called for Washington to raise funds for public ownership of the carriers through the sale of about $18 billion ($249 billion in current dollars) of long-term government bonds. The money generated would provide a fair price to compensate the thousands of investors. Once the railroads were nationalized, Washington would lease its rail holdings to a federally chartered corporation that fifteen presidentially appointed public and labor representatives would control. Yet there would not be a monolithic labor bloc; workers would be divided into two classes, "A" for salaried employees and "B" for wage earners. It was assumed that these separate white- and blue-collar groups would act as countervailing powers, making it difficult for either one to dominate. Under the plan the ICC would remain, retaining rate-making authority, and railroad-generated profits would be divided equally between government and labor. As with other proposals for industry unification during the 1920s and 1930s, strong objections developed. "This is lunatic thinking," exclaimed a railroad official, a not uncommon reaction. Labor found little support among industry executives or for that matter from other parties; the Plumb Plan was considered extreme. For many Americans nationalization smacked of "Bolshevism"; after all, the "Red Scare" hysteria gripped the country in 1919 and lasted for several more years. Furthermore, a majority of citizens wanted to return to "normalcy," and that meant less government intrusion in their lives. There was the worry, too, that government ownership might lead to increased passenger and freight rates and reduced service.[6]

Although the Plumb Plan was dead on arrival with policymakers, a railroad consolidation plan nevertheless emerged. The logic demonstrated by the USRA and to a lesser degree by Glenn Plumb influenced passage the Transportation Act of 1920 or the Esch-Cummins Act. Its lead sponsors, Representative John Esch, a progressive Republican from Wisconsin, and Senator Albert B. Cummins, a progressive Republican from Iowa, headed their respective congressional bodies' committees on interstate commerce. The legislation, which took effect February 28, 1920, on the eve of the official termination of the USRA, was a product of extensive debate, yet it won bipartisan support. Not surprisingly this measure had great complexities.

A key section of the Transportation Act of 1920 responded to the inadequacies of railroad earnings. The immediate postwar period revealed the negative impact of highway and water competition and the damaging aspects of progressive regulations. Although the ICC could continue to establish maximum and minimum rates, its rate-making actions were to be set at a level that would guarantee an equitable rate of return on investments. However, one-half of any excess income beyond 6 percent would be taken by the government, the "recapture of excess earnings clause," and shared with the financially weakest carriers through low-interest loans. (At this time the nation had more than 1,000 railroad companies, including 186 Class 1 carriers, those earning more than $1 million annually or about $14 million in current dollars.) The measure contained a provision that for the first six months of operations after federalization companies would be guaranteed a net railway operating income equal to the annual rental received during the control period. This proved expensive for taxpayers, costing the national treasury about $530 million ($6.35 billion in current dollars). The law further allowed carriers during a two-year period following resumption of private control to tap a revolving loan fund of $300 million ($3.6 billion in current dollars).[7]

The 1920 legislation did not overlook labor. There would be a nine-member US Railroad Labor Board, consisting of three representatives each from the railroads, labor, and the public. This body exercised considerable power over wages and worker grievances. Generally, the Labor Board, which in the mid-1920s morphed into a more labor-friendly Railroad Board of Mediation, took a pro-management stance. It sparked widespread hostility from union rank-and-file members when because of tough economic times it recommended substantial wage reductions in 1921 and 1922. The latter cuts triggered a bitter national shopmen's strike.[8]

While the recapturing and labor provisions had strident backers and detractors, a highly controversial aspect of the 1920 law involved company groupings. Consolidations, in the minds of supporters, became the panacea that competition had once been. While the Interstate Commerce and Sherman acts, together with the Northern Securities decision, emphasized competition, the new statute embraced the consolidation approach, yet still attempting to preserve a degree of hallowed competitiveness.

The Transportation Act of 1920 mandated that the ICC produce a comprehensive plan for amalgamation of most steam roads. The more-or-less unified system of railroads during USRA control had made a substantial number of congressional lawmakers, railroad officials, and labor leaders see the value of a more rationalized rail network. There also existed the belief, repeatedly articulated by Senator Cummins, that in the postwar era weak roads could not survive. Even if reorganized through bankruptcy proceedings, these struggling carriers could never expect to become profitable. Therefore the weak should be combined with the strong, creating a limited number of systems with approximately equal financial strength. The act also gave the ICC certain powers to bring about these consolidations: it had authority to approve any proposed merger and had control over the issuing of railroad securities. Still, the law had a glaring flaw: any grouping would be *voluntary*.[9]

ICC commissioners and others were not certain about the practicability of the congressional mandate to endorse what amounted to a private cartelization of America's railroads. Consolidations of the 1,000 or so companies into regional systems to reduce or end redundancies and to forge an efficient and solvent network had merit. The consensus among regulators, though, was that the devil was in the details.

The grouping task went forward. The ICC hired a transportation expert to formulate the consolidation framework: William Z. Ripley, a professor of political economics at Harvard University, was charged with developing this tentative plan. He was well-known and respected within industry and government circles, having produced several academic books, including *Railway Problems: An Early History of Competition, Rates and Regulation* and *Trusts, Pools and Corporations*.[10]

Ripley plunged into preparing a unification plan. Data was checked, including statistical materials generated by government agencies, especially the ICC and USRA, and he interviewed business, financial, and railroad executives. At the close of January 1921 Ripley submitted his 196-page proposal to the Commission.

Ripley adhered to the act's mandate that existing routes and channels of commerce be maintained. He avoided coast-to-coast systems that would create actual transcontinental railroads as well as configurations of carriers that failed to fit into geographic and rate-making divisions.

Ripley suggested six principal groups and named them as follows:

1. Trunk Line Territory (Atlantic seaboard
   to Chicago and St. Louis)
2. New England
3. Chesapeake Region
4. Southeast
5. Western Transcontinental Region
6. Southwestern-Gulf Region

In these six major groupings (or what Ripley called "Divisions") there were twenty-one systems. Specifically there would be five eastern trunk lines, five western combinations, four southeastern systems, two Great Lakes to tidewater coal roads, and two southwest combinations. Lastly, three regional systems would also be formed: Florida, Michigan, and New England.[11]

Ripley believed that the chief seaports – New York, New Orleans, Galveston, San Francisco, and Seattle – had been provided with good, competitive service, and he took care to make certain that Chicago and St. Louis remained leading railroad centers. He contended, perhaps correctly, that a more radical reduction in the number of systems – something that the Prince Plan later suggested – would injure rail options for smaller communities. He also argued that the rate of earnings for the multiple systems would be high enough to ensure their financial well-being. Ripley did not include the plethora of short lines and terminal companies, deciding to leave them independent.

After studying the document for six months and discussions with Ripley, the ICC released its own tentative report on consolidation. In reality it was a modified Ripley proposal, and on August 21, 1921, the public learned of its recommended groupings. Most significantly the ICC plan cut the number of systems from twenty-one to nineteen. On several issues there was a significant departure from Ripley. The greatest variations occurred in the West. The ICC endorsed a Chicago & North Western–Union Pacific merger, but objected to bringing that system into San Francisco over the old Central Pacific as Ripley proposed. Ripley had placed the Denver & Rio Grande Western and Western Pacific with the Burlington–Northern Pacific, while the ICC had those two roads going to the Santa Fe. Under the ICC plan, the Santa Fe also picked up Burlington affiliates Colorado & Southern and Fort Worth & Denver City rather than having them assigned to the Missouri Pacific as Ripley did.[12]

Predictably, controversy erupted over the proposed units. At ICC hearings held between April and December 1923, with Professor Ripley as a participant, numerous railroad officials attacked the groupings. Pennsylvania Railroad president Samuel Rea, for one, blasted the severance of the coal-hauling and prosperous Norfolk & Western from PRR's control to form a separate system of roads in the Pocahontas coal-producing region. During these deliberations, which produced approximately 12,000 pages of testimony and more than 700 exhibits, two camps developed. Major carriers generally objected to the anti-Darwinian notion of the strong aiding the weak, and the less-prosperous carriers expressed their desire to align with moneymakers.[13]

What the extensive hearings in 1923 revealed was that the tentative plan for railroad consolidations was a hot potato, being seemingly an almost impossible task. Even with additional study, ICC commissioners became ever more frustrated. In February 1925 the Commission told the Senate Interstate Commerce Committee that a majority of its members wanted only mergers that developed "in a more normal way." Congress, however, demanded a master plan, even though for the next three years the ICC repeatedly asked to be relieved of the mandate. When lawmakers refused, the Commission reluctantly pushed ahead with what it called its "Final Plan."

On December 9, 1929, the ICC announced the "Complete Plan of Consolidation." Again there would be nineteen systems, and they would be clustered around one or two major roads. There would also be two additional systems involving the monster Canadian railroads, Canadian National and Canadian Pacific. Both carriers controlled US properties, and so System 20, "Canadian National," incorporated the Central Vermont, Grand Trunk Western, and several short lines and terminal roads, and System 21, "Canadian Pacific," absorbed the Duluth, South Shore & Atlantic, Soo Line, and Spokane International railroads.[14]

There were other notable changes, including a rather peculiar one, namely System 7, "Wabash-Seaboard." John Will Chapman, a financial analysist, went so far as to say that "System 7 startled the world." Earlier the Wabash, which operated between Buffalo, Detroit, Kansas City, and Omaha, had been divided at the Mississippi River between System 4, "Erie," and System 13, "Union Pacific–Chicago & North Western." Wabash management heartedly disapproved of dismemberment, so now the company remained intact, becoming a key component in System 7. (Under the earlier plan, System 12, the Seaboard Air Line – the Wabash

partner – had been more logically grouped with the Illinois Central.) Included with the Wabash and Seaboard were the Lehigh Valley, Norfolk &
Western, Pittsburgh & West Virginia, and a gaggle of anemic short lines
in the South. System 7 also gained trackage rights over portions of the
Grand Trunk Western, PRR, and Reading. "It would run from Omaha to
Miami via Buffalo," observed historian Richard Saunders, "and did not
appear to have much geographic cohesion except that, in an odd way, it
resembled the later CSX and Norfolk Southern systems."[15]

The onslaught of hard economic times, triggered by the stock market
crash in October 1929, diminished discussions about implementing the
ICC's Final Plan; in fact, it essentially died and surely to the delight of
Commission members. Yet in 1930 several Eastern trunk roads – Baltimore & Ohio, Chesapeake & Ohio–Nickel Plate, New York Central, and
Pennsylvania – substantially agreed among themselves to pursue their
own scheme of regional mergers. But internal and regulatory disagreements failed to produce any unions. Then with the rapidly deepening
national depression, interest again developed for consolidations.[16]

The Great Depression was just that for American railroads. Rail
traffic contracted severely, cutting gross revenues in half. In 1930, for
example, weekly freight car loadings ranged from about 800,000 to 1
million, but two years later these numbers were only about 550,000.
The passenger business hardly fared better. In 1926 railroads carried 874
million riders; in 1932 it was about half that volume. Also in 1932 approximately three-quarters of the national railroad mileage failed to earn
enough to cover interest charges or other fixed obligations. In September
Democratic Party presidential candidate New York governor Franklin
Roosevelt said it well: "Now there is no reason to disguise the fact that
the railroads as a whole in this Nation are in serious difficulty. They are
not making both ends meet."[17]

Lawmakers were hardly oblivious to the growing railroad crisis. In
January 1932 the Herbert Hoover administration, with congressional
backing, grudgingly launched the Reconstruction Finance Corporation
(RFC). Soon this pump-priming agency began to provide emergency
loans mostly to beleaguered banks and railroads, having $500 million
($8.76 billion in current dollars) in capitalization and authorization to

borrow up to $1.5 billion (26.3 billion in current dollars). For years to come the Railroad Division of the RFC would be a godsend to scores of beleaguered carriers. As early as November 1934 loans totaling $512.5 million ($9.2 billion in current dollars) had been awarded to eighty-one cash-strapped railroads.[18]

During the waning years of the Hoover administration Congress provided an additional way to assist the troubled industry. Lawmakers added Section 77 to the Bankruptcy Act of 1898. This measure streamlined railroad bankruptcy proceedings and gave the ICC enhanced powers to protect investors and the public interest. Significantly, the Commission became involved at a much earlier stage in a bankruptcy case then what had occurred under the existing statute.[19]

In November 1932 a political earthquake shook the nation. The White House and Congress would soon see the arrival of activist Democrats who stressed the necessity for immediate relief, recovery, and reform. These "New Dealers," led by President-elect Roosevelt, did not ignore the plight of the railroad industry.

Even before his landslide election victory, Franklin Roosevelt focused on the railroad crisis. In a nationally broadcast radio speech that he delivered on September 17, 1932, from Salt Lake City, Utah, he recommended rectifying unfair competitive advantages enjoyed by commercial buses and motor carriers. He also sought regulation of railroad holding companies and the reduction of what he called an "overbuilt railroad plant." As for the latter, Roosevelt said, "The public generally does not realize that thirty percent of railroad mileage in this Nation carries only two percent of the freight and passenger traffic. That is worth thinking about!" Washington needed to act, suggesting that problems stemmed from "the entire absence of any national planning for the continuance and operation of this absolutely vital national utility."[20]

Action followed. Roosevelt and his advisors, famed "brain trusters" A. A. Berle Jr. and Raymond Moley, wasted no time in requesting public and private groups to explore ways to improve the economic health of the railroad enterprise. In January 1933 Berle and others held such meetings and reported back to the president-elect. "Mr. Roosevelt leaned strongly toward consolidation, but he wasn't taking sides on the issue." There was agreement, though, that "the case for mergers was handicapped because there was no up to date consolidation plan." It would be Frederick Prince, friend of Roosevelt, generous contributor to his 1932 political campaigns, and participant in the January planning sessions, who spearheaded recommendations about consolidation that the administration had requested from the financial community. Prince would personally contribute the $33,000 that covered the costs of this undertaking.[21]

Frederick Henry Prince was a man of talent and drive. Born in Winchester, Massachusetts, in 1859, one of the six children of Harvard College–educated lawyer and prominent Democratic politician Frederick Octavius Prince, Prince attended private schools before entering Harvard. But in his sophomore year he left the campus to get an early start in the business world. This was a good decision. Prince joined the New York Stock Exchange, and over time his F. H. Prince and Company became active in various business ventures, including railroads. One carrier was the Pere Marquette Railroad, and early in the twentieth century he led a syndicate that allegedly milked the company. A happier story involved his heavy financial involvements in the sprawling (and highly profitable) Union Stock Yard & Transit Company and the Central Manufacturing District in Chicago. As an indication of his business insights, Prince anticipated the stock market crash of 1929, surviving with a fortune estimated at $250 million ($3.5 billion in current dollars). His enormous wealth allowed him in 1932 to buy the famed Marble House "cottage" in Newport, Rhode Island, built in the late nineteenth century by Alva and William Kissam Vanderbilt. Prince's worldviews were consistent: "rugged individualism" and the Anglo-Protestant work ethic.[22]

When asked by Frederick Prince to join the consolidation study, John Barriger jumped at the chance to become involved with the "Prince Plan: A Plan for Coordinating the Operations of Railroads in the United States," or simplified to the "Prince Plan" and occasionally the "7-System Plan," "Prince-Barriger Plan," or even the "Barriger Plan." Recalled Barriger, "Happily I found my ideas on the subject and those of Mr. Prince ran very closely parallel." It was in February 1933 that he began this work in Washington, DC. Family members, however, remained in Upper Montclair, New Jersey, although on October 1, 1932, they had moved from their earlier rental house at 8 Garfield Place to another rental property located at 446 Park Street. Since much of the work on unification took place in the ballroom of the swanky, albeit financially strapped, Metropolitan Club at H Street NW, near the White House, Barriger stayed in a nearby hotel during the week and commuted home by train on weekends.[23]

Barriger did not start cold with his unification labors. An ardent believer in fewer, more efficient railroads, he was knowledgeable about the Plumb Plan and the consolidation proposals that emanated from the Transportation Act of 1920. Barriger had already prepared his own thoughts on "Consolidations of Railways." In a well-crafted document, which he prepared for his employer Calvin Bullock in January 1931, he outlined the advantages of reducing the number of carriers by focusing on the region north of the Ohio and Potomac Rivers and east of the Mississippi River. At the heart of his arguments were these points: "Reduction of all 'overhead' expenses are the most obvious to the general public, but far more important are those which accrue from reorganization of traffic routing and movement, equipment utilization and concentration of car and locomotive repairs." He further addressed a controversial aspect of unification, an especially hot-button issue during hard times, namely the fear of reducing the railroad workforce. Barriger was not too worried. "Indeed, it is within the range of possibility that the economies and service improvements from consolidation will achieve a sufficient growth in the demand for railroad transportation to lead to future employment of a far greater number of men than they could use if they must continue to lose traffic because of arbitrary hindrances in the way of producing the highest grade transportation at the lowest possible cost."[24]

As February 1933 began, the Metropolitan Club ballroom became a beehive of activity. "It was a strange arrangement with people, desks, typewriters and adding machines scattered around under crystal chandeliers." The work area foreshadowed what would be taking place in Washington after Roosevelt's inauguration on March 4; the First Hundred Days of the New Deal meant that thousands of government employees and advisors burned the midnight oils. At the Metropolitan Club a group of railroad experts, including at times Frederick Prince, became part of that workforce. Barriger, though, played the principal role, the work "following the ideas of an intensive railroad student, J. W. Barriger, 3d."[25]

The plan rapidly emerged, culminating in a first draft that was readied by March 15, with a revised version released in September. While production was lightening fast, the Prince Plan achieved what its backers desired. "It was only a theoretical plan proposed from outside the industry to illustrate a more or less ideal grouping of the railroads from the standpoint of maximizing their service potential and minimizing the costs of operations," as Barriger later remarked.[26]

What did the Prince Plan propose? The initial eight regional systems as set forth in the first draft became one fewer in the final version, and they were dramatically fewer than what had been proposed under consolidation schemes generated by the Transportation Act of 1920. Specially, the Eastern Region contained a North System (System No. 1) and a South System (System No. 2). The former was built around the New York Central and had such additional components as the Boston & Maine; Delaware, Lackawanna & Western; Erie, and New York, Chicago & St. Louis (Nickel Plate). The latter used the Pennsylvania as its core and included major carriers Baltimore & Ohio, Norfolk & Western, and Wabash (except lines west of Decatur, Illinois, and St. Louis). The Southern Region likewise had two parts: Southeast System (System No. 3) and Mississippi River System (System No. 4). Number 3 contained trunk roads Atlantic Coast Line, Louisville & Nashville, and Seaboard Air Line, and Number 4 had Illinois Central, St. Louis–San Francisco (Frisco) (lines east of Memphis), and Southern. The Northwestern Region (System No. 5) stood alone, and was appropriately labeled the Northwest System. It included these majors: Burlington, Milwaukee Road (except its east-of-Chicago subsidiary Chicago, Terre Haute & Southeastern), Great Northern, and Northern Pacific. Then there was the Central Western Region (System No. 6), the Central System. It contained the Chicago & North Western (North Western); Chicago, Rock Island & Pacific (Rock Island); Southern Pacific, and Union Pacific. Finally, the plan called for the Southwestern Region (System No. 7), the Southwest System. Its principal carriers consisted of the Santa Fe, Missouri-Kansas-Texas (Katy), Missouri Pacific, and the Frisco (lines west of Memphis). The US affiliates of the Canadian National and the trackage owned by the Canadian Pacific in Maine and Vermont were unassigned. The plan also suggested jointly owned properties, mostly switching and terminal companies, and some trackage rights arrangements. Six Class 1 switching and terminal roads went unassigned, being industrial plant operations.[27]

Barriger spent extended workdays crafting the various systems. He considered a multitude of factors before he began to have typed drafts – ones he repeatedly revised – prior to the first and final plans being released. A good illustration of his thought process is found in this commentary about System No. 5, the Northwest System:

> The System #5 has lines in the Southwest, but it is being extended into the Southwest for the single major purpose of being given a Gulf outlet. Its lines to the gulf must have access to adequate traffic to sustain them at a profitable basis, but it would defeat the purpose of the grouping to endeavor to create around these System 5 Southwestern extensions a System which is the equal of #7, a purely Southwestern Region development, or System #6 which, while termed the Central System, of necessity includes lines in all Western states, although in two, viz – Montana and North Dakota – its mileage is unimportant. The System 5 mileage in the Southwest should be strengthened by giving it access to New Orleans and the lower Rio Grande Valley. This can be done perfectly by giving it a half interest in the New Orleans–Texas & New Mexico, and the San Antonio–Uvalde & Gulf. In this way, the System #5 will have a direct line from New Orleans to Denver and Seattle with a reasonably direct route to San Francisco, and the present route of the Katy will be strengthened by having its own direct access to the perishable freight producing districts around Brownsville, and also access to the Brownsville Gateway into Mexico, which in future years will probably be the main point of entry into that country, taking the place of Laredo today.[28]

Once these voluntary seven systems came into being, each would become a new corporation. These units would acquire their constituent companies through a fifteen-year lease and make rental payments to their owners. Ultimately these leases could turn into purchases. And the RFC would become involved. It would buy the companies' debenture bonds at par, and the money generated could be used for physical betterments, replacement of rolling stock, and the like. Railroad workers would not be forgotten. Those displaced by these systems would receive a protection allowance of one-half to two-thirds of their salaries. However, if railroads did not embrace the plan within a reasonable time, Barriger and his associates believed that Congress should make it compulsory.[29]

Barriger attached to the final version a well-reasoned rationale for the groupings. His principal consideration: "The proposed systems must be possible of formation with a minimum disturbance of present corporate control, conserving in all cases for the consolidated operating unit, the benefit of the historical developments of the constituent companies." Dismemberment of existing carriers was to be avoided, yet allowing for exceptions. The second major objective: "No system shall penetrate any new area through inclusion of a weak or attenuated line that will be at a traffic and an operating disadvantage. It is essential to establish only strong groups which can provide superior service at a profit throughout their entire extent." There was this consideration: "The plan strengthens competition in those respects where it now serves a useful public purpose and eliminates rivalry where it is only productive of waste and hence is actually a detriment to service." The pairings therefore were designed to preserve the value of two competing lines between the most important traffic centers, and "local competition serves no beneficial purposes but causes heavy unnecessary expenses notwithstanding the fact that the opportunity for such a type of traffic rivalry has probably never been as extensive in scope as is imagined."[30]

Then there were the anticipated financial benefits. Barriger and his associates believed that the savings generated by these proposed consolidations would be considerable. Based on 1932 traffic data, the amount computed to an impressive $743,489,000 ($13 billion in current dollars) or about 30 percent of total railroad operating expenses that year. The largest dollar savings would come from System No. 1 and System No. 2, with $173,192 ($3 million in current dollars) for the former and $185,192 ($3.2 million in current dollars) for the latter. Over time benefits for all systems were expected to increase. Commented *Railway Age* early on, "Savings which are in many cases, if reports are true, little short of amazing."[31]

Paralleling reactions to the consolidation plans proposed by Professor Ripley and the ICC, there were similar responses to the Prince Plan. There came both praise and criticism. "The Plan simply threw overboard all the old concepts of mergers," explained an industry observer. "It was ruthless, shrewd, radical, and as compellingly plausible to some people as it was preposterous to others."[32]

On the positive side, Roosevelt apparently approved of Barriger's handiwork. Raymond Moley believed that the president liked its creativity, being "interested in anything novel." After all, this proposal was more sweeping than anything since that Plumb Plan for a nationalized railroad system. Frederick Prince also seemed satisfied. As he told the Boston News Bureau, "[This plan] is the most revolutionary and the most completely worked out of any railroad-unification scheme so far presented." A number of railroad leaders applauded it. Since the seven groupings centered around such major trunk roads as the New York Central, PRR, Santa Fe, Southern Pacific, and Union Pacific, their executives believed that their corporate cultures would dominate these new systems and that their jobs would likely continue. General Atterbury of the PRR, for one, "openly espouses it."[33]

The industry's leading trade journal, Railway Age, expressed caution. "Attempts to deal with major economic problems in emergencies by important but hastily conceived measures are always fraught with the danger that the results will be widely different from those anticipated." It raised this provocative question: "Cannot railway systems, regional or otherwise, be made so large that no single organization can manage them efficiently and satisfactorily?" This publication, though, strongly believed that healthy railroads were absolutely necessary to the nation's economic recovery.[34]

But there were howlers, and most of them came from the ranks of labor. Said a spokesman for the Railway Labor Executives' Association, "Of all the dreams of huge profits from railroad consolidation, the so-called Prince Plan, the largest share of which will be realized by adding more than 300,000 to the already intolerable number of unemployed rail workers, will be utilized to strengthen the railroad securities and bring about a higher rate of return from such securities." Allegedly George Harrison, president of the Brotherhood of Railway and Steamship Clerks, Freight Handlers, Express and Station Employees, believed that Barriger had convinced Prince that if these unification proposals became reality, he "could make a [financial] killing." Much later Jesse Clark, president of the Brotherhood of Railroad Signalmen, charged that the plan was based on "the false notion that the railroads had an excess capacity."[35]

Others, too, complained. Joseph B. Eastman, who served as federal coordinator of transportation under the recently enacted Emergency Railroad Transportation Act and was a well-regarded former ICC commissioner, expressed his reservations, "seeing few advantages in it." Most of all, he questioned the envisioned savings. Eastman had appointed a committee, headed by William B. Poland, "who has much railroad experience, both as an engineer and as an administrator," to study the potential economies, and it calculated savings of $218 million ($3.8 billion in current dollars), or $525 million ($9.1 billion in current dollars) less than what had been estimated based on 1932 operations or $321 million ($5.6 billion in current dollars) when 1929 data was used. "The economics of such a plan would not be nearly so large as claimed, and that in other respects it would not be in the public interest," said Eastman. Understandably there were industry executives who objected to having their railroads downgraded or dominated by other, especially rival, ones. The Baltimore & Ohio was one such road, saying the plan "[is] unsound in principle, is not required by the existing conditions, and disregards the national welfare, the public interest, and the destructive economic effect on localities." The company's general counsel labeled it as "the most radical suggestion in connection with the railroads of which I have any knowledge," characterizing it as "destructive in its very phase except as to the interests of the seven big railroads in the country to which it would hand, without mercy, all the others." Communities and state railroad commissions worried about the loss or reduction of rail service; the plan estimated the abandonment of approximately 11,000 route miles. There also was concern that freight rates would increase. And fiscal conservatives shuddered at the potential cost to taxpayers, perhaps reaching $2 billion ($35 billion in current dollars).[36]

John Barriger expected criticisms of the Prince Plan, knowing that it would be a tough sell. The negative reaction apparently did not bother him. He remained convinced that carrier consolidations were in the interests of the railroad industry and the nation. Barriger appeared eager to defend the plan's merits before any federal committee or agency, and he wanted to be able to make the best possible impression. Although Barriger continued to be employed officially by Calvin Bullock & Company, he rejected an offer of $15,000 ($262,781 in current dollars) by Frederick Prince for doing the plan. "I declined it because I said I might be asked to defend it before a congressional committee and I would be in a better position to do so if I were unpaid."[37]

The Prince Plan fared better than either the Plumb or ICC proposals. Even though no railroad consolidations resulted, Congress, with Barriger's preliminary proposal in mind, passed in mid-June 1933 the Emergency Railroad Transportation Act. This measure, which President Roosevelt hurriedly signed, created the Office of Federal Coordinator of Transportation (OFCT). Lawmakers sought as its principal purpose to encourage railroads to eliminate duplication of services, promote joint use of terminals and tracks, and rationalize equipment fleets. Needless waste would ideally end or at least be reduced, and major economies achieved. As with the National Industrial Recovery Act, the Emergency Railroad Transportation statute also promoted cartelization and allowed exemptions from antitrust laws. But since the OFCT, under the guidance of Joseph Eastman, did not force compliance with its proposals, its accomplishments were modest. Yet indirectly the Prince Plan and the OFCT led in 1934 to creation of the nonprofit Association of American Railroads (AAR), successor to the Association of Railway Executives, designed in part to assist member carriers to coordinate their operations. Presumably the AAR would speak for the industry. Later Barriger could take satisfaction that his ideas about railroad consolidation had been about thirty years or so ahead of his time.[38]

RECONSTRUCTION FINANCE CORPORATION

While the Prince Plan never became a New Deal achievement, it advanced the professional career of John Barriger. His stature rose considerably; he was no longer an obscure New York financial analyst, but a person whom more people in the railroad industry, business community, and federal government knew about or recognized. Connections that Barriger made with members of the Roosevelt administration led to an offer to join the Reconstruction Finance Corporation as chief examiner of its newly launched Railroad Division, a position that he enthusiastically assumed on June 1, 1933. Although his compensation was less than what he had earned on Wall Street, starting at $8,500 ($157,250 in current dollars) and increased to $15,000 ($244,000 in current dollars), it was an "acceptable" amount during this time of national depression. It would be A. A. Berle Jr., Roosevelt's point person on railroad matters, who recommended to RFC chair Jesse Jones that Barriger be hired to take this federal post. And this recommendation pleased Jones. "[Barriger] well understood both the operating and the financing end of railroading and had an excellent comprehension of the whole nation-wide transportation problem." Although Barriger did not care for Jones's Democratic Party politics or the New Deal generally, the two men harmoniously worked together.[39]

A Washington job meant another family move. So in June 1933 the Barrigers relocated from Upper Montclair, New Jersey, to a large, relatively new six-bedroom rental house at 3611 Fulton Street NW, near the Washington National Cathedral; this would be their home until May 1944. The household included John, Elizabeth, Edith Barriger, and the three children, Jack, Betty, and Ann. Not long after establishing their new residence, Elizabeth gave birth to a fourth child, Stanley. There was also a live-in maid who had a third-floor bedroom, a cook who arrived daily, a laundress who came once or twice a week, and a yardman who seasonally worked one day a week. All of these servants were African Americans, and they used public transportation to and from Fulton Street. In Barriger's mind this was just fine; people of color should remain in subservient positions.[40]

For years to come Barriger remained close to Frederick Prince, and between 1933 and World War II the Barriger family enjoyed summer vacations at Prince's Padlock Ranch, a large working cattle spread located in the Wind River Range about 20 miles west of Thermopolis, Wyoming. Although rejecting that earlier $15,000 ($280,000 in current dollars) check from the always generous Prince, Barriger accepted one for $500 ($8,760 in current dollars). This money paid moving expenses to Washington, DC, and sustained the family until the RFC pay began.

As a result of the close relationship between John Barriger and the wealthy Boston financier Frederick H. Prince, which developed with their work in 1933 on a plan for national railroad consolidation, the Barriger family prior to World War II enjoyed summer vacations at Prince's sprawling Padlock cattle ranch west of Thermopolis, Wyoming. Barriger took this photograph en route to Thermopolis during the summer of 1934. *Left to right:* Betty, age 6, Ann, age 4, Elizabeth, baby Stanley in the arms of the family nurse, and Jack, age 7. (John W. Barriger IV Collection)

At this time Barriger was not invested in the stock market, including railroad securities, a somewhat surprising occurrence considering his Wall Street contracts and background. That had been a fortunate turn of events, since railroad securities, even those of the leading companies, lost much of their value or became worthless.[41]

Because of the desperate financial plight of the railroad industry, the Railroad Division of the RFC was confronted with applications for millions of dollars of loans from both large and not-so-large carriers. For railroad officials, even those who may have been reluctant to seek federal assistance, the Barriger office was commonly viewed as their last best hope for preventing bankruptcy. And for those fifty-eight roads already under court protection, the RFC meant a chance to rehabilitate and modernize their physical plants and perhaps avoid an unwanted sale or dismemberment.[42]

Barriger faced a heavy workload at the Railroad Division. It was his duty to analyze each railroad loan application and then to place the essential statistical, corporate, operational, traffic, and historical information before Jesse Jones and members of the RFC board of directors, allowing them the essential background information when they reviewed a request. Barriger had additional responsibilities. He needed to inform Jones and directors about all of the RFC's outstanding railroad loans, especially those in default or in danger of default.

At the Railroad Division offices, located on Connecticut Avenue across from the Mayflower Hotel, Barriger did not work alone. Although tiny when compared to other New Deal relief and recovery agencies, the division by 1936 employed forty staff members. They included seven examiners, including himself, six draftsmen, five statisticians, nine stenographers, and two file clerks. And members of a legal section consisted of four attorneys, six stenographers, and a file clerk.[43]

In order to perform his responsibilities Barriger not only spent considerable time in his Washington office – perhaps at many as seventy-five or more hours a week – but he needed to travel. This he did. Nearly always with briefcase, "grip," and camera in hand, Barriger covered tens of thousands of miles of the American railroad network, riding often in office cars but also in regular freight and passenger movements and in other flanged-wheeled conveniences. Being bright and gregarious he knew what questions to ask railroad people, the important and the not-so-important. His eagle eyes also discerned strengths and weaknesses.

In the course of his eight years as chief examiner, Barriger oversaw the granting of more than $1.3 billion in railroad financing. These dollar injections strengthened, even saved, scores of roads, ranging from the Baltimore & Ohio ($87.5 million) to the Missouri Southern ($99,200). In some cases loans were approved but subsequently were not needed. Yet not all applicants received the good news that the RFC would honor their loan requests, or perhaps they won only partial or limited financial support.[44]

After John Barriger joined the Railroad Division of the Reconstruction Financial
Corporation (RFC) in 1933, he traveled extensively, including a trip to Dotsero,
Colorado, east of Glenwood Springs. On June 16, 1934, Barriger joined the celebration
of the grand opening by the Denver & Rio Grande Western Railroad of its 38-mile
Dotsero Cutoff between Orestod (Bond) and Dotsero. This construction, financed by
a $3,850,000 RFC loan, shortened the distance between Denver and Salt Lake by 173
miles, making through service via the Moffat Tunnel to the Pacific Coast possible
for the first time. The new line strengthened Denver as a convenient "gateway" for
transcontinental freight and passenger traffic. (John W. Barriger III Collection, Barriger
National Railroad Library at UMSL)

With his RFC duties, Barriger continually increased his exposure
and positive image, especially among individuals associated with the
railroad industry. While Jesse Jones became the public face of the RFC,
Barriger gained a similar stature among railroaders, bankers, and investors. In November 1934 newspapers nationwide ran a brief story, often
including his photograph, claiming that he was a likely candidate to
succeed General Atterbury, who would retire from the Pennsylvania
presidency in spring 1935. Following publication of this bogus story Barriger received positive comments, including this one from a southern

During his years as chief examiner for RFC's Railroad Division, John Barriger nearly always had camera at hand, taking thousands of photographs. Showing that he had interest in all things railroad, he captured the expansive Chicago, Burlington & Quincy Railroad bridge over the Mississippi River at West Quincy, Missouri. This is a visual masterpiece, revealing a strong use of horizontal/vertical lines and vanishing point. (John W. Barriger III Photo, John W. Barriger III Collection, Barriger National Railroad Library at UMSL)

railroad official: "If you wish the position sincerely hope you will land it." While the piece was mere speculation, this rumor must have been an ego booster for the young RFC official. A few years later his ego was surely enhanced when a Washington, DC, newspaper described his career "rising with the rapidity of a Horatio Alger hero," and reported another false rumor made by newspaper and radio gossip commentator Walter Winchell that "Mr. Barriger has been spoken of in Wall Street as the next president of the Pennsylvania Railroad."[45]

While there was no job forthcoming with the mighty PRR, Barriger continued his busy work schedule. In 1935 he and an assistant, Hilton Moore, visited one of the nation's most beleaguered carriers, the Georgia & Florida Railroad. This small Class I road with approximately 500 route

During the awful snow events of winter 1935–36, Barriger photographed in February 1936 this dramatic scene of a steam-powered snowplow train at work on the Chicago, St. Paul, Minneapolis & Omaha (Omaha Road), part of the Chicago & North Western Railway System, near Fairmont, Minnesota. (John W. Barriger III Photo, John W. Barriger III Collection, Barriger National Railroad Library at UMSL)

miles, based in Augusta, Georgia, stretched between Greenwood, South Carolina, and Madison, Florida, via Douglas and Valdosta, Georgia. Founded in 1906 by Richmond, Virginia, banker John Skelton Williams, the company failed in 1915, and this bankruptcy lasted until 1926. Three years later the G&F faltered again, remaining under the protection of a federal court until its sale in the early 1960s to the Southern Railway. The G&F gained the dubious distinction of being the longest Class 1 bankrupt railroad in American history.[46]

Almost as soon as the Reconstruction Finance Corporation opened its doors, the G&F applied for financial assistance. In March 1932 it asked for $1 million to pay various obligations, mostly outstanding receivers' certifications and local property taxes, and also to purchase track materials and other supplies. A loan came, but not what the railroad had requested. The RFC agreed to extend only $271,221, designed for redeeming receivers' certificates held by struggling Georgia banks and to pay down taxes owed to county and municipal governments. The rationale was sensible. Officials believed that the railroad was at best shaky and doubted if it could survive. Undaunted, the company appealed. In the modest victory that followed, the G&F got an additional loan of $83,000, one earmarked to pay interest on specific receivers' certificates and to retire maturing equipment trust certificates.[47]

The G&F badly needed more federal aid. For several days in spring 1935 Barriger studied the property, specifically its main line between Augusta and Valdosta and its shops in Douglas. He seemed impressed (perhaps surprised) by its overall physical condition, including bridges, track, and motive power. Although the railroad was no transportation slum, he agreed with colleague Moore that additional loans should not be forthcoming. "We pointed out to them [RFC board of directors]," wrote Moore, "that the Georgia & Florida was so completely devoid of earning power that it would be quite impossible for the Examining Division to recommend to the Board a further loan of any kind, and it would not be possible to find that this Corporation [RFC] would be adequately secured." Always that advocate of unification, Barriger thought that the G&F should be taken over by a competitor, most likely the Atlantic Coast Line. A corporate obituary for the "God Forgotten" was in order.[48]

While the railroad industry paid little or no attention to RFC loans granted or not granted to the Georgia & Florida, it did pay attention to the battle over the fate of the much larger and also bankrupt Minneapolis & St. Louis Railroad (M&StL). This 1,647-mile granger road, which extended between Peoria, Illinois, and Aberdeen, South Dakota, via the Twin Cities, and with additional lines that penetrated sections of Minnesota and Iowa, had been in receivership since 1923. Efforts at reorganization had sputtered, and by the time of the Great Depression the M&StL was in dire straits. Its not-so-kind monikers of "*Maimed & Still Limping*," "*Misery & Short Life*," and "*Midnight & Still Later*" seemed appropriate.

Because the M&StL sought loans from the RFC, Barriger began a study of the property not long after he became chief examiner. At first he believed that the railroad could be reorganized and made profitable as a stand-alone entity. The M&StL, however, would need a new and talented management team and a sizable cash infusion. As the months passed, the railroad continued to hemorrhage red ink, and the feeling grew among employees, shippers, regulators, and others that it might have to cease operations. Initially Barriger had recommended a substantial loan, but this request got derailed by the RFC board. Yet wanting to save as much service and employment as possible, he decided that another carrier could possibly take over the troubled property, and so he contacted a half-dozen presidents of neighboring railroads. Recalled Barriger, "Nobody wanted the road as it was, but each agreed to take a part; happily, no two roads wanted the same part." Therefore, he concluded that the best hope in protecting the public interest would be multiple carrier ownership. Such a fate for the M&StL would in a modest way help to fulfill his treasured goal of greater rail consolidation.[49]

By 1935 Barriger, joined by Jones, advocated dismemberment of the M&StL. What evolved during late 1934 and into 1935 was a response that called for eight connecting railroads to take the desirable pieces, scrap the unwanted trackage, close the two principal shops, and eliminate about two-thirds of the employees. A new firm, Associated Railways Company, would implement this proposal. "The plan seems an equitable solution of an unhealthy railroad situation in a particular territory," opined Jones, and Barriger agreed. RFC would help finance the restructuring process, committing $7.2 million ($126 million in current dollars).[50]

Then the unexpected happened. Receiver Lucian Sprague and his associates orchestrated a successful campaign to save their railroad. Joined by investors, employees, shippers, politicians, and online communities, some of which would be devoid of rail service if the Associated Railways Company succeeded, the crusade drummed up much-needed business. Barriger admitted that Sprague had been the right person to take command, calling him a leader with "lots of charisma, a good salesman." Not only did carloadings increase, but management made some essential improvements to the physical plant, motive power, and rolling stock. It also won approval to abandon about 100 miles of money-draining branchlines. By 1938 the plan for the Associated Railways quietly died; commented an observer: "The corpse got up and drove them off."[51]

The M&StL miracle convinced Barriger and Jones that the RFC should provide assistance. In late 1938 Barriger returned to the railroad. During an inspection trip and consultations with officials and others he found the physical property to be markedly improved. Moreover, traffic pointed to future profitability. A year later the RFC agreed to a $5 million ($86.3 million in current dollars) loan, but a regulatory complication prompted the ICC to reject this cash infusion. Fortunately, the M&StL steadily grew its revenues, and in 1943 it ended two decades of court protection.[52]

John Barriger correctly judged the financial health and likely fate of the Georgia & Florida, but he underestimated the ability of the Minneapolis & St. Louis to save itself. While the concept of the Associated Railways had merit and fit his desire for a more consolidated industry, he revised his assessment of the "Misery & Short Life." In time Barriger would see striking parallels with the Sprague renaissance on the M&StL and the one that he brought about to the struggling Chicago, Indianapolis & Louisville Railway (Monon).

Those long hours in the Washington office and inspection trips to view such railroads as the Georgia & Florida and Minneapolis & St. Louis did not leave much time for Barriger to enjoy family life. Less than year after he joined the Reconstruction Finance Corporation a feature writer for the *St. Louis Daily Globe-Democrat* visited Elizabeth in her Washington home. The story, which appeared in late January 1934, noted that "Mr. Barriger was called to Washington and has been so engrossed with his duties that he works day and night, managing dinner at home only a few nights a week." Apparently, Elizabeth functioned just fine. "Mrs. Barriger's obvious pleasure is in her family, the City of Washington, and life generally, makes meeting her a refreshing experience." When possible the Barrigers had their big family meal on Sundays – "roast beef, turkey, something substantial." In some ways, this made up for Barriger's repeated absences. "Usually the family didn't see him for meals during the week or when he was on an extensive trip," recalled son Jack. "He might come home at 7 or so in the evening, past the time that the family had eaten. We always looked forward to Sundays when Dad was home." Since government employees worked five and a half days a week, Barriger usually did not return from the office on Saturdays until early afternoon.[53]

The family celebrated Sundays and times when Barriger could be at home. Yet having Edith Barriger, "Didi" to the children, living in

While seemingly working day and night for the Reconstruction Financial Corporation, John Barriger had limited opportunities for family activities. Yet he squeezed out time to join Elizabeth in New York City to send off her father, Judge Thomas Thatcher, and her mother, Odille Thatcher, on an extensive ocean voyage and overseas holiday. (John W. Barriger III Collection, Barriger National Railroad Library at UMSL)

Always the doting father, John Barriger poses with his two younger children, Stanley and Ann. The location is Washington Union Station and the date is about 1940. A love of railroads early on developed for both Barriger sons, Jack and Stan. (John W. Barriger IV Collection)

their midst caused some strain. Barriger remained a fiercely political and social conservative and never a New Dealer, and he did not care for his mother's progressive friends. Didi understood. "Didi had a group of 'liberal' friends whom she would entertain in our home, usually when

Mother and Dad were away," noted her grandson. "Sometimes it was for tea and occasionally for lunch or dinner." He added, "I don't think her ideas changed as she aged, but probably she was less outspoken." The grandchildren adored her. Didi read and listened to the radio with them, attended their school functions, and did other activities. When in 1943 she began her first wage-earning job, taking a wartime clerk's position at the nearby US Naval Observatory, she had a regular schedule away from the Fulton Street house. That was also true for Elizabeth; she was not always a stay-at-home mother. During the war she served as a block warden in the District, making certain that windows were covered at night. She also put her Spanish language skills to work as a translator of documents for various groups, including the Pan American Railroad Association. And Elizabeth accompanied her husband on some of his business trips, entertained his associates, and participated in other social activities.[54]

Although the health of American railroads improved as the decade of the 1930s waned, Barriger and the Railroad Division remained active. Revenues generally had not returned to pre–October 1929 levels, and numerous carriers remained under court protection. A variety of roads continued to seek financial assistance.

One assignment that occupied Barriger involved the bankrupt Chicago & Eastern Illinois Railway (C&EI), a 1,271-mile road that linked Chicago with Evansville, Indiana, and St. Louis, Missouri. In April 1933 the collapse of the regional soft-coal industry catapulted this property into receivership. "The Chicago & Eastern Illinois Railway is an exceptionally good example of how a 'one commodity road' may be much more adversely affected by changes within the particular industry producing that commodity than a road whose traffic is well diversified," explained *Moody's Manual of Investments*. Because of substantial RFC loans, Jesse Jones recommended to Federal Judge John Barnes, who oversaw the C&EI bankruptcy, that Barriger be named one of three reorganization managers. During 1940 he functioned in that capacity. Then from January 1, 1941, until the road's annual meeting in May 1942, Barriger held a seat on the board of directors and served on its executive committee. During that time the company, reorganized as the Chicago & Eastern Illinois Railroad, saw its bottom line strengthen by soaring wartime traffic and increased coal tonnage.[55]

Barriger had been no stranger to the Chicago & Eastern Illinois. When he worked for Kuhn, Loeb & Company, he became acquainted with the road since his employer served as its banker. Once he joined the RFC, Barriger became familiar with its financial problems. For years he had mixed feelings about the future of this Chicago-based carrier, believing that the C&EI should be merged with another carrier. While working on the Prince Plan he thought that it should join the New York Central, and he recalled that when president of the Monon, "I was a constant and continuous advocate of a C&EI-Monon merger." Alas, it would not be until the "merger madness" of the 1960s that the C&EI disappeared, its lines going to the Louisville & Nashville and Missouri Pacific.[56]

Coinciding with his involvement with the C&EI, John Barriger resigned from the Railroad Division of the Reconstruction Finance Corporation. His last day on the job was July 31, 1941, and it was a busy one for him, organizing paperwork, packing books and personal items, and saying good-byes. His departure came with sadness, not so much for Barriger, but for his workplace associates. "He sure left a sad office force as there was not one there who was not all choked up when the goodbyes came," wrote staffer Helen Boland to Elizabeth Barriger. "As I remarked to one of the girls it reminded me of the after effects of a funeral when everything seems so quiet and empty. Our place has been like a morgue, everyone looks so downhearted and they have talked of nothing else but Mr. Barriger's leaving." The formal exit resolution, signed by Jesse Jones and other RDC officials, read in part: "RESOLVED: That the Board of Directors of this Corporation accept Mr. Barriger's resignation, effective, as he requests, and that they take this action with very sincere regret. BE IT RESOLVED FURTHER, That the Members of this Board express to Mr. Barriger their deep appreciation of the able and valuable service he has rendered the Corporation. He has handled the important tasks committed to his care with high degree of skill and efficiency, and has won the respect and admiration of his associates."[57]

Such positive performance comments pleased Barriger. He had no regrets about what he had done in a job that saw $1.5 billion of railroad financing passing through his department. Only $165,000 in loans eventually were not repaid. Barriger seemed especially proud that "this organization operated at substantial profit to the government and not at any loss." For any Washington agency and at any time this was a remarkable accomplishment.[58]

OFFICE OF DEFENSE TRANSPORTATION

So why did Barriger end his eight-year tenure with the Reconstruction Finance Corporation and with colleagues who treasured his presence? In a 1973 security clearance form, he explained tersely: "To improve earning power." Yet it was not in his personality to stay with a position for a long period. His next job? On August 15, 1941, Barriger joined the staff of the Chicago-based Carriers' Conference Committee as a consultant to assist with a national labor wage case, a project chaired by Fred G. Gurley, vice president (later president) of the Santa Fe and an admired acquaintance. His pay was $100 per day ($1,625 in current dollars), and he worked seven days a week. This employment lasted until the end of 1941, when the work of the Committee officially ended.[59]

Once again Barriger used his knowledge of the railroad industry, especially its requirements for capital, to prepare a counterproposal to the wage demands made by 1.26 million unionized workers. If demands were not met, these railroaders threatened a national strike at a time when war clouds were rapidly gathering. It was the charge of the Gurley group to present its study to a presidential fact-finding board. This it did, announcing tentative results in October. The core concept was to have wage payments adjusted by averaging changes in the cost of living at full value, with half the value of changes in the gross revenues of the roads. Gurley and his associates defended this formula on the grounds that payrolls absorbed more than half of the roads' gross revenues, while rises in the cost of materials and lags in freight and passenger rate adjustments by the ICC deprived companies of net income, even though their gross revenues were improving. These would be points that Barriger made that autumn before the fact-finding board. As with the Prince Plan, the operating and craft brotherhoods were not favorably inclined toward this proposal.[60]

Before the Gurley group concluded its work, Barriger reentered federal service. On January 30, 1942, less than two months after the United States entered World War II, he began a year's tenure as associate director,

Division of Railway Transport for the US Office of Defense Transportation (ODT) at an annual salary of $8,500 ($138,250 in current dollars). Not only was his income good, but the Barriger family could remain in Washington. Always the diplomat, Barriger before he joined the ODT sought and received blessings from Jesse Jones and Frederick Prince.[61]

John Barriger was prepared to take on his new duties. He knew and respected the agency's head, Joseph Eastman, and he grasped the mandate of this hastily established government unit, namely to regulate the transportation of goods and people considered vital to winning the war in Europe and the Pacific. Although Barriger understood why the government federalized most steam railroads during World War I, he preferred the ODT approach. "The railroads in private hands needed a Federal organization such as the O.D.T. to 'run interference' for them in solving certain of their problems in order to permit them to produce all of the transportation service of which their plants are potentially capable." Barriger also knew his immediate supervisor, Victor (Vic) V. Boatner, a former president of the Peoria & Pekin Union and Chicago Great Western railroads who had assisted Eastman when he served as federal coordinator of transportation. Housed on the fifth floor of the ICC building, located at 12th and Constitution NW, the Railway Transport Division of the ODT became an immediate beehive of activity, and that meant long hours for Barriger both in his office and on the road.[62]

John Barriger received various assignments. Immediately he became involved in preparing reports on commodity movements (citrus fruit for one), freight and passenger equipment requirements, and terminal operations in St. Louis. He also began work on a lengthy analysis of what the ODT called "Lake Superior Ore Transportation Capacity." During these early weeks Barriger received a request to become the receiver for the American Railroad Company of Puerto Rico, a struggling 310-mile sugar hauler. He knew this road; the previous year he had been on the island to work on a labor-wage dispute. Barriger declined this flattering offer, although for several years he continued to be involved with the company's labor matters.[63]

No two days' busy routine at ODT were the same. February 24, 1942, was typical, and Barriger made these diary notations:

V.V.B. [Boatner] and I have breakfast with George Carr [chair of the board of Dearborn Chemical Company], Dan Ellis of C&O and Mr. Riddle, Engineer, Maintenance of Way, P&WVa R.R. Meeting with Messrs. Buford and Kendall of AAR in Turney's office to review "Morning Report." This takes all of morning and have lunch with Bochtaller and Mahaney. McMullen stopped in office. H.C. Oliver called from Pittsburgh and Fred Prince from Aiken, S.C. Afternoon spent working on memoranda on railroad property and protection, 1942 car requirements, etc.[64]

When possible Barriger, both before and after his tenure at the ODT, always preferred breakfast meetings. When he later served as president of the Monon, some people referred to him as John "Before-Breakfast" Barriger, "because of his habit of transacting business before 8 a.m." Barriger felt that business could be accomplished in a "sober" and "timely" fashion. He also enjoyed the food and drink options, often ordering a poached egg on a toasted English muffin with an extra muffin. He would then place the egg on a fresh English muffin since the first one had become soggy. There also would be a side of bacon or sausage. Barriger usually had juice and always plenty of hot coffee. This, too, would be the fare for his guests. And Barriger could host, this being the least expensive meal of the day, and one where no alcoholic drinks would be expected.[65]

Although Barriger used the telephone, telegrams, and letters to conduct long-distance business, he also needed to leave Washington. In mid-March, for example, he flew to Los Angeles, having that rare wartime priority status for air travel. In California Barriger discussed with Santa Fe officials an array of ODT matters and spoke in San Francisco on the government's wartime involvement with railroads. But because of poor weather conditions, he missed his return flights, and consequently was unable to attend a C&EI board of directors meeting in Chicago. Not long after he arrived home, Barriger learned that he would be on the road again.[66]

On Saturday, March 21, 1942, while attending a business luncheon with several others at the Washington Press Club, Boatner and Barriger were summoned to go at once to the office of Joseph Eastman. There they learned that President Roosevelt, using his power under the Federal Possession and Control Act of 1916, had signed Executive Order No. 9180 for the immediate government takeover of the strike-ravaged and strategically important Toledo, Peoria & Western Railroad (TP&W). "This means I am to go out there as Federal Manager," wrote Barriger in his diary. "A busy afternoon arranging, through Commissioners Mahaffie, Atchison and Director Lewis for members of the ICC's Bureau of Accounts and Valuation to accompany me there. Leave on 'Capital Limited' [B&O] at 5:45 P.M. [for Chicago] with Otto Beyer, Hallan Huffman, Assistant General Counsel and four members of the ICC staff. Before I leave, call George Voelkner [railroad official] at Chicago and notify him to join the TP&W organization as Assistant Federal Manager." He later noted, "I left so quickly that my formal written authorities and instructions had to follow me."[67]

Once at the TP&W general offices, located in Peoria Union Station, Barriger, whose official title was federal manager of the properties of the Toledo, Peoria & Western Railroad, and his associates faced a challenging situation. The road's president, the feisty George Plummer ("G. P.") McNear Jr., was furious about the Roosevelt order and was not anxious to cooperate with Barriger or anyone else. Since 1926 McNear, a University of California and Cornell University–educated investor-turned-railroader, had been involved with the this 239-mile bridge, or "outer belt," line. The TP&W offered a time-saving freight bypass around the congested Chicago and St. Louis gateways by connecting Effner, Illinois, with Keokuk, Iowa, via Peoria and interchanging cars with nineteen railroads. At the foreclosure sale in 1926 McNear orchestrated the purchase of this property for $1.3 million, becoming its largest investor and its "boss." Under his reign the railroad greatly improved, making such derogatory nicknames as "Two Ponies & a Wagon" and "Totally Pathetic & Weary" largely inappropriate. In 1927 McNear took pride in cutting operational expenses by winning regulatory authority to exit the money-losing passenger business. While a master of rehabilitation and economy, McNear had sparred repeatedly with the railroad brotherhoods, including taking a strike by train service, shop, and maintenance-of-way forces between November 1929 and June 1930, a job action that was marked by considerable violence. Then in 1941 McNear refused to go along with an industry-wide pay raise, offering instead hourly wages, and also demanding elimination of what he considered to be inefficient labor practices or make-work "featherbedding." On December 28, 1941, a bitter and seemingly intractable strike by engineers, firemen, and trainmen began. Nonstrikers were stoned and threatened, and an attempt was made to dynamite a bridge in Peoria. The antilabor McNear refused an arbitration order made by the National War Labor Board. Because of the need to expedite wartime freight, the government could not allow the TP&W to become a streak of rust.[68]

Barriger sought a rapid and equitable solution to the TP&W labor crisis. As soon as he established his temporary offices in Peoria Union Station and in the downtown Pere Marquette Hotel where he stayed, he consulted a range of company employees, both labor and management, in what he called a "kaleidoscopic series of meetings." He quickly restored a previous set of schedules for pay and work rules, voiding those McNear had imposed in late December that had led to a virtual operational shutdown. The hundred or so strikers returned to their jobs, and trains once more began to roll. Barriger also spent time, often in the wee hours of the morning, observing switching operations in the East Peoria yards and riding with crews on both the Eastern Division (Effner–East Peoria) and the Western Division (East Peoria–Keokuk). Although federal officials promised substantial military backup from Fort Sheridan outside Chicago, Barriger did not need soldiers to restore service. For a short period, however, three armed military guards provided protection, and their presence reminded McNear and his associates of the federal involvement.[69]

As days and weeks passed, Barriger seemed pleased with what he had been able to do on the TP&W. "Reach Peoria and find our railroad is at last enjoying a traffic boom," he noted in his diary for May 1, 1942. "Some record-breaking days. The morale is high, everybody is in good spirits." And he continued to be involvement as federal manager. "I address the Rotary Club's luncheon. Call on some shippers, visit the yards."[70]

Following extensive inquiries and ongoing consultations with associates, Barriger on July 1, 1942, placed into effect a set of schedules that contained features that aided labor but also allowed some work-rule flexibility that management sought. As for the latter, at any time extra yard engines in East Peoria could be started to handle traffic conditions. His policies were fair and effective, and they pleased Washington. McNear, however, continued to fume.

When not in Peoria or traveling on behalf of the TP&W, Barriger returned to Washington. When at the office he worked on ODT business, mostly on how to increase passenger train efficiencies. In late 1942 he also accepted a not-so-time-consuming role as a director of the 960-mile Alton Railroad, nee Chicago & Alton Railroad, that had just entered bankruptcy. Barriger remained in that position until 1946, assisting that road with its successful efforts to merge with the Mobile & Ohio Railroad.[71]

During this period Barriger had those cherished times at home. Elizabeth understood that her husband must be gone for extended periods, but when in July 1942 Barriger received a offer from the Office of Economic Warfare to head a railroad mission to India, she emphatically said no. "If I go to India," commented Barriger, "she will go to Reno or its equivalent!"[72]

When Barriger left ODT at the end of 1942 and terminated his ties with the TP&W, his associate George Voelkner took charge of this fully functioning railroad. During federal control McNear had no choice but to remain on the sidelines, but with the coming of peace, Washington returned the property to his control, a transfer that officially took place on October 1, 1945. Thus ended three and one-half years of continuous government operation. McNear, though, stuck to his tough, anti-union ways, and a general strike soon erupted. As with earlier management-labor confrontations, this walkout turned violent, highlighted when railroad guards in February 1946 killed two union pickets at Gridley, Illinois, east of Peoria. After extended negotiations, the strike ended in October, but unresolved issues and bitter feelings remained. Then on the evening of March 10, 1947, while walking near his Peoria home, McNear fell mortally wounded from a shotgun blast fired from a speeding car. There were no credible witnesses, and law enforcement never solved this heavily publicized assassination. Professional hit men from Chicago, hired by disgruntled union members, may have been the perpetrators.[73]

After the holiday season of 1942 John Barriger returned to the private sector, although toward the end of his professional career he would again become a government man. So why did he leave Washington? Barriger felt that he had done his job well for Eastman's ODT, including getting dependable service restored on the TP&W and maintaining "its proper share of the commercial traffic." As in the past he relished challenges and opportunities to advance his stature and income in the industry that he loved.

THREE

Monon

BACK TO THE PRIVATE SECTOR

When 1943 began, John W. Barriger III no longer claimed a government check; instead he received a substantial pay hike from his friend Frederick H. Prince. His annual salary now amounted to $12,000 ($166,000 in current dollars). Barriger became a vice president of the Union Stock Yard & Transit Company, succinctly describing his job this way: "Special assignments for the Chairman [Prince]." Simultaneously, he rejoined the Carriers' Conference Committee on an "as needed" basis to conduct statistical work for a national labor wage case that involved a vacation-with-pay controversy with train crews. Barriger was based in Chicago, although the family, except for son Jack, remained in Washington until late August 1944, when they moved to a rented house on the Archibald MacLeish Estate, located on Sheridan Road in the North Shore bedroom community of Glencoe, Illinois. Before relocating to the Chicago area, Barriger stayed at the downtown (and exclusive) Chicago Club, enjoying a membership paid for by Prince and being within convenient walking distance of his office in the First National Bank Building. Jack joined his father at the Chicago Club since he decided not to finish his secondary education at Landon School in Bethesda, Maryland, but rather to complete his studies at New Trier High School in suburban Winnetka before entering the Massachusetts Institute of Technology.[1]

During a seventeen-month tenure working for Frederick Prince, Barriger took on varied assignments. Since the late nineteenth century Prince had invested heavily in Chicago's South Side Union Stock Yard

The connection between John Barriger and Frederick Prince continued into the 1940s. In 1943 Barriger joined Prince's profitable and sprawling Union Stock Yard and Central Manufacturing District located on the south side of Chicago. As a vice president he became connected with the Chicago Union Stock Yard & Transit Company. (John W. Barriger III Collection, Barriger National Railroad Library at UMSL)

and its Chicago Junction Railway Company, a switching road that connected with area trunk carriers. In 1905 he spearheaded creation of a "community of industries" north of the stockyards, resulting in the 265-acre Central Manufacturing District, bordered roughly by 35th Street on the north, Morgan Street on the east, Pershing Road on the south, and Ashland Avenue on the west. "Mr. Prince was one of the first men to visualize the future of industrial real estate," observed a chronicler of his Windy City business operations. A variety of enterprises, including meat-related ones, became part of this sprawling complex, and even during the Great Depression it was a good and steady moneymaker for Prince.[2]

Barriger spent time dealing with the Chicago Junction Railway, where he assisted with traffic and regulatory matters. This was a 20-mile double-track road together with numerous sidings and industrial trackage that a New York Central Railroad subsidiary leased. Barriger also promoted the Central Manufacturing District. Yet his involvement with these Prince enterprises was neither time consuming nor pressure filled. "I don't think Dad did more than add his name to the list of vice presidents of the Chicago Union Stockyards & Transit," remembered his son Jack, "plus entertain some of his business friends including VP Transportation of Armour, Swift, Cudahy and more." These affairs frequently took place at the Saddle and Cycle Club next to the Stockyards Inn, where the "best steaks in Chicago" were served.[3]

Still another career change took place. On May 1, 1944, Barriger turned his attention to a full-time position, becoming manager, Diesel Locomotive Division of Fairbanks-Morse & Company (F-M). This well-established and diversified business enterprise, which dated back to the 1830s and was headquartered in Chicago, had evolved from making commercial scales to producing pumps, stationary steam engines, and other machinery. In the 1890s F-M expanded into the railroad supply field, and early in the twentieth century it began manufacturing motors and generators. Between the world wars the firm produced for marine use, especially to propel US Navy submarines, heavy-duty diesel engines that featured a distinct design, specifically opposed pistons. Cylinders contained two pistons, each driving a crankshaft and providing nearly twice the power per unit of engine volume. These diesel units, which were mechanically simple with few working parts, pleased customers and were financially attractive.[4]

Fairbanks-Morse executives decided to apply their diesel engine technology to railroad locomotives. Initially the opposed piston concept did not work well, but later refinements proved encouraging. On the eve of the Pearl Harbor attack, F-M engineers had designed both a 1,000-horsepower switch engine and a 2,000-horsepower dual-purpose cab locomotive. But because of the critical need for submarine and other marine engines, the US Supply and Production Allocation Board and its successor, the US War Production Board, stopped the company from producing any railroad power. Then during the summer of 1943 the government gave F-M the green light for production. The first diesel locomotive, scheduled to be ready in August 1944, was a 1,000-horsepower yard switcher, and Chicago, Milwaukee, St. Paul & Pacific (Milwaukee Road) wanted this unit.[5]

Enter Barriger. While working for Frederick Prince in Chicago he made contacts with Fairbanks-Morse personnel. At a March 1944 luncheon at the Chicago Club with Colonel Robert H. Morse, company

By the 1940s public speaking had become "old hat" for John Barriger. Toward the close of World War II he spoke in Chicago to a group associated with his recently obtained position as manager, Diesel Locomotive Division of Fairbanks-Morse & Company. (John W. Barriger III Collection, Barriger National Railroad Library at UMSL)

president and general manager, the two likely discussed employment possibilities. Morse embraced locomotive production, seeing the need to fill the void that declining war orders would soon create. An agreement was reached; Barriger joined the company on May 1, 1944, at the substantial annual salary of $25,000 ($340,000 in current dollars). "I was designated manager [of the diesel division] and supervised all phases of the work involved in doing so and remained for two years until I left for the presidency of the Monon." The likelihood for strong potential sales encouraged Barriger; after all, many of the nation's steam locomotives were undergoing heavy usage handling wartime traffic, and most needed replacement. This sense of optimism (and wishing to succeed) prompted him to engage famed industrial designer Raymond Loewy, whose earlier major corporate patron had been the Pennsylvania Railroad, where his assignments including the design of the stunning, futuristic T1 4-4-4-4 duplex-drive steam locomotive. Lowey would create the distinctive body style for these emerging F-M locomotives.[6]

Employment at Fairbanks-Morse required a hectic schedule, reminiscent of when Barriger was a government man. Not only did he supervise about 200 employees, but he made frequent trips, exploiting his vast number of industry contacts. To promote locomotive sales, Barriger personally called on railroad officials who ranged from representing large Class Is to short lines and terminal roads. "I talk Diesels to all of these men." There also were visits to parts manufacturers and other locomotive builders and frequent meetings in Chicago and at the production facility in Beloit, Wisconsin. Tuesday, August 15, 1944, was no slow workday:

> Breakfast at Chicago Club with R. C. White, J. G. Lyne, and Arthur C. Knies.
> Several out-of-town r.r. executives here for C. H. Buford's meeting at Stevens Hotel call on me during the morning, among them Russell Coulter. Mr. Buford and Mr. White are my guests for lunch at the Chicago Club. Although I go to Continental Bank to keep previous engagement with Mr. Cummings and two of his Vice Presidents. 2:00, meeting in J. T. Gillick's office with him and O. N. Harstad, E. B. Finnegan, J. W. Severs, and D. C. Curtis. Presented Mr. Gillick with the souvenir bottle with which Mrs. Gillick christened the 1802 [first F-M locomotive] on August 8th in Beloit. We discussed various phases of the FM OP Diesel engines and locomotives and the possible purchase of five of the 1,000 h.p. switchers by CMSTP&P. 3:00 Call on J. M. Nicholson, Warren Kelly, and G. H. Minchin of the Santa Fe to discuss locomotives. Dinner at Blackstone with R. C. White and J. G. Lyne. Overnight at Chicago Club, having finished some work at the office about midnight in preparation for a trip to Beloit next day.[7]

Elizabeth Barriger helped with her husband's business activities. "She was a wonderful hostess," recalled son Jack. "She had a wonderful facility to remember names. She'd meet a group of people in a room and when they left, she would call them each by name." Not long after arriving in Illinois, Elizabeth attended a luncheon at the Glenview Country Club, hosted by the wife of Fred Gurley of the Santa Fe, and there she spent time with the wives of officials from the Milwaukee Road, a company that contemplated additional locomotive purchases and one that became a good F-M customer. There would also be family-initiated gatherings, and perhaps Elizabeth would show off her prowess as a talented bridge player.[8]

Although Barriger worked diligently in his efforts to make Fairbanks-Morse a major player in the diesel locomotive field, production at the Beloit factory never rivaled that of the leading manufacturer, Electro-Motive Division of General Motors (EMD). By the early 1950s F-M claimed just 4 percent of the national market, building only a modest number of smaller and medium-size units; EMD had more than a 60 percent market share. Admittedly, opposed piston engines were compact, efficient, and powerful, yet when placed in railroad locomotives, they developed troubling maintenance problems. Buyers discovered excessive piston and crankshaft failures in both their switchers and road units. In the case of the Santa Fe, which purchased a number of F-M locomotives, road diesels especially performed poorly. "They failed miserably in over the road freight and passenger service because the lubricating and cooling systems could not take the rugged conditions and long times under full throttle of railroad service." Moreover, these engines were much more complicated to work on than those used by EMD and other builders. "Mechanical department personnel hated them." Barriger, in fact, told Colonel Morse that F-M needed to redesign these diesel engines for railroad use. But the colonel did not want to make the necessary financial commitment, and his decision angered Barriger. Then ten years after he left, F-M sold its final unit to a domestic railroad, and by that time EMD totally dominated the field. "A combination of poor management, insufficient resources, an inadequate finished product, and ineffectual marketing programs defeated the company's bid in the diesel locomotive market," concluded historian Albert Churella. "Fairbanks-Morse entered the market too late to be effective." Still, the company built or supervised construction of 1,256 locomotives, with peak production between 1944 and 1954.[9]

A WOEBEGONE RAILROAD

John Barriger could not resist becoming a railroad president; he relished having a railroad to call his own. "There is a lot more fun in a railroad than on a golf course, or at a football game," as he said to a group of railroad financial officers, reflecting his love for the industry. In a similar vein he told the *Indianapolis Times*, "[The Monon is] small enough to be fun, big enough to be interesting." Barriger accepted the presidential offer made by Arthur T. Leonard, senior vice president of the City National Bank of Chicago and chair of the board of directors of the broken-down Chicago, Indianapolis & Louisville Railway, universally known as the Monon.

(In 1956 the Monon moniker became the official name.) Representatives of the three largest investors in the railroad – New York Life Insurance Company, Chase National Bank, and Robert R. Young interests – knew of Barriger and his multiple talents, and they made known their feelings. They sought an executive who would be capable of "building up the Monon, giving the people of Indiana up-to-date, modern railroad service." In February 1946 Barriger became one of three court-appointed reorganization managers, and on May 1, 1946, he officially took the throttle of this now-out-of-bankruptcy road at a starting salary of $25,000 ($310,000 in current dollars) and later increased to $36,000 ($368,000 in current dollars). Barriger made these cogent comments about his selection to *Business Week*: "Practically the only place you can join a railroad is at the bottom or the top, and there's a lot of competition for the top job on the big roads." So it would be the Monon. "The Monon will make me famous as either a top-notch railroader or a terrible flop," as he opined.[10]

What was this railroad that John Barriger would oversee? The Monon, a 552-mile freight and passenger road with more than 2,000 employees, connected the three cities of its corporate name, although not directly. The railroad made an elongated "X" in the northern Indiana town of Monon. The main stem linked Chicago, Monon, Lafayette, Crawfordsville, Bloomington, and Bedford with Louisville, Kentucky. A secondary main line continued southeastward from Monon to Indianapolis. Less-traveled trackage extended north from Monon to Michigan City, Indiana. The company also operated several branches, including an 18-mile one that served the popular twin resort communities of French Lick and West Baden in southern Indiana, where "genteel gambling," invigorating baths, and Pluto mineral water had long been part of their attraction. Fortunately, the Monon was more stem and less branch and twig.[11]

The Monon had a long history, dating back to the late 1840s with the formation of the New Albany & Salem Rail Road. By the time of the Panic of 1857, this Hoosier State line extended from the Ohio River to Lake Michigan at Michigan City. Resembling other pioneer roads, this railroad experienced several reorganizations, becoming in 1873 the Louisville, New Albany & Chicago Railway (LNA&C). Another Monon component was the Indianapolis, Delphi & Chicago Railway, a company

that emerged during the post–Civil War period, and for financial reasons
it also had its own need to reorganize. In 1881 what had become the Chicago & Indianapolis Air Line Railway entered the orbit of the LNA&C.
There would be modest additions, and after a bankruptcy reorganization
in 1897, the property emerged as the Chicago, Indianapolis & Louisville
Railway. Five years later the Louisville & Nashville (L&N) and Southern railroads gained joint stock control, providing them with a friendly,
direct access to Chicago. This involvement by the L&N and Southern in
the Monon, however, was not ideal. "The record indicates that in view of
the keen rivalry between the owners and the competitive situation north
of the Ohio River," explained Barriger, "they treated the Monon more as
a stepchild than as a family member."12

During the early years of the twentieth century the Monon did reasonably well, but the company faltered following World War I. There
were fewer and fewer online-generated carloadings, being mostly bituminous coal and building stone, and modest interchange traffic, including
somewhat erratic northbound coal movements to U.S. Steel Corporation
plants in greater Chicago. With the coming of the Great Depression,
the railroad experienced a grave money shortfall, but owners L&N and
Southern would not come to its aid. The Monon struggled. In 1933 the
company made a desperate loan request to the Railroad Division of the
Reconstruction Finance Corporation, but it was rejected. Barriger, who
studied the property, realized that its earnings potential was poor and
its finances needed reorganization; he was not supportive of a railroad
whose plight "seemed so hopeless." On December 30, 1933, this negative
decision forced the Monon into bankruptcy. Trustees cut freight and
passenger service and won authority to reduce its branchline mileage.
They went so far as to consider total abandonment, but the company
remained intact and managed to cope through those busy war years.13

By the mid-1940s the future of the bankrupt Chicago, Indianapolis
& Louisville Railway looked problematic. Although the bankruptcy allowed the company to restructure its debt at reasonable rates of interest,
little was done to rehabilitate the property. Moreover, employee morale
had plummeted; shipper after shipper had turned to trucks; the public,
who preferred automobiles and buses to Monon trains, had developed
a dim view of the railroad. Hoosiers, though, enjoyed poking fun at it.

Went the lyrics to one local song: "Ireland must be heaven / 'Cause the Monon don't go there." Take this joke that involved the parent of a newborn baby: "Asked if the infant had been named, 'not yet.' Well, why don't you name her Monon? If she's like the rest of them, she has a yowl like a locomotive whistle; she keeps the person living nearby awake; and she was late in arriving!" Journalist Douglass Welch offered this assessment. "Among Class A railroads the Monon was a seedy tramp, black with coal dust and arrayed in a hundred-year old suit of clothes." A Santa Fe official, who toured the property, concluded scornfully that the Monon was really nothing more than "a right-of-way and a franchise."[14]

There were good reasons to avoid and to mock the Monon. Passenger operations were modest, and remaining trains were powered by outdated (some said "antique") steam locomotives and consists featured turn-of-the-century equipment. "Its passenger service," noted one source, "degenerated into a reasonable facsimile of the traditional slow train in Arkansas." Moreover, the company hardly offered fast, on-time freight deliveries. Its seventy-four "coal-burning teakettles" were mostly worn out; its newest steam power dated back to the late 1920s. The Monon owned only four diesel locomotives, all EMD switchers, which it had purchased in 1942. Resembling the passenger equipment, the freight car fleet was old, much of it either obsolete or in need of heavy repairs. "Its yard tracks were so clogged with bad order cars of its ownership that yard switching was seriously impeded." There also were problems with old lightweight rail, having limited 112- or 115-pound steel, and there were miles of rotten ties and thin ballast. Numerous depots, bridges, and other structures needed replacement, major repairs, or at least a coat of fresh paint. For years deferred maintenance had been ongoing, and it showed. Adding to Monon woes the line south of Bainbridge – midpoint between Chicago and Louisville – suffered from numerous and steep grades, often greater than 2 percent, and excessive track curvature. This section featured a classic sawtooth profile.[15]

"THE GUINEA PIG LINE"

If John Barriger was to make the Chicago, Indianapolis & Louisville Railway a profitable small Class I carrier, he would need to work some magic. This he did to the best of his ability, employing a plan that he called "super-railroads." In the mid-1950s Barriger would spell out details of this concept in a book-length publication, *Super-Railroads for a Dynamic American Economy*, but for years he had been formulating his core ideas. While at the Pennsylvania Railroad in the 1920s, he became convinced that railroads must raise their main-line standards of freight and passenger service by running heavy tonnage trains that were adequately powered without intermediate restrictions on their speed. Barriger became that vocal proponent of "low grades and easy curves." By 1940 this message frequently became part of his public speeches to railroad and other groups. He summarized his progressive thinking this way: "To me, the term 'super-railroad' means integrating the best engineering methods and standards of operation into a railway's entire property. Too small a part of the total mileage of any company now embodies these characteristics." Added Barriger, "Railroads do not presently need to attain trainloads and train speeds and service qualities above present maxima, but they must narrow the spread between their average performance and their best."[16]

The Monon for John Barriger became his "super-railroad guinea pig," or what he jokingly called the "Guinea Pig Line." But before he could implement ideas that had been percolating in his mind, he discovered upon arrival that he needed to be more than company president. "I not only had my own specific assignment to fill, but found that the heads of the Operating and Traffic Departments had either resigned or retired, so at least temporarily, I had these two other jobs to fill." It didn't take him long to hire replacements. Fortunately, Barriger found two outstanding railroaders who were willing to join him at corporate headquarters in the Transportation Building on Dearborn Street in Chicago. Colonel Frank Cheshire, a former officer in the military Transportation Corps who had worked in the mechanical department of the Baltimore & Ohio and later served as master mechanic on the Missouri Pacific for its lines west of Kansas City, became the chief mechanical officer and subsequently vice president–operations, and Warren Brown, previously the general freight agent for the Nickel Plate Road in St. Louis, assumed duties as head of traffic. Barriger found additional talent to fill top-ranking posts, exploiting again his contacts throughout the industry. These men shared

A professional photographer took this formal portrait of John Barriger as the new Monon Railroad president. He posed in his regular three-piece business suit and his signature wire glasses. (John W. Barriger IV Collection)

Barriger's overall philosophy of railroading, and they gave support to the notion that less-affluent companies seem to attract more venturesome people. Cheshire, Brown, and other officers also accepted the Barriger dictum: "If you don't want to work 70 hours a week, we can't use you." As team captain Barriger set the workplace example of long hours.[17]

Almost immediately after he took over as president, Barriger concluded that his traffic personnel must know the present condition of the railroad and what he planned to do to bring about substantial upgrades in freight service. So he summoned the fourteen offline traffic agents and those online for a thorough inspection of the property. Amazingly for some of these traffic representatives, it was the first in a decade (or longer) that they had seen what they were being paid to sell shippers.[18]

Before Barriger tackled a basic component of his super-railroad concept, namely the challenges of grades and curvatures, he focused on ending the Age of Steam. Already Barriger realized that diesels were superior to steam locomotives. They were in his words, "super-power." The Monon not only owned those obsolete iron horses, but it lacked a single one of adequate capacity to serve its requirements for faster, less expensive freight operations.

Immediately Barriger and his staff went to work to dieselize the property. An existing order to EMD was modified and increased in size. Small orders were also made to American Locomotive–General Electric and Fairbanks-Morse. Barriger, however, did not enthusiastically embrace Beloit products that he had earlier so vigorously promoted, likely because of limited production and maintenance problems. He also rejected an earlier Baldwin Locomotive Works dieselization proposal; no units from its Eddystone, Pennsylvania, plant would appear on the property. The Monon dieselization strategy, nevertheless, was typical of the period, namely, acquisition of locomotives from a variety of builders and diversification in types. A red-letter day took place in early November 1946 when a F-M switcher arrived at the railroad's shops complex in Lafayette. Chief mechanical officer Cheshire called it "the first material evidence of the beginning of Monon's modernization program." By the close of 1947 the railroad had only eighteen steamers remaining on its roster.[19]

Significantly, the process of dieselization did not result in a single employee losing his Monon job. For example, boilermakers, who worked in the Lafayette shops, received training as diesel mechanics. It was, according to one observer, "business humanized."[20]

Progress continued. As 1948 ended, the Monon had nearly completed dieselization of its main-line operations. Finally, on June 28, 1949, the last steamer, an 0-6-0 switcher that worked the New Albany yards, was retired from active service, and the Barriger goal of all-diesel motive power had been achieved, with considerable cost savings realized. Immediately, the company boasted that it was "America's First Completely Dieselized Class 1 Railroad." That was a not-so-true statement. In July 1948 the New York, Ontario & Western had dieselized, and somewhat earlier so had such smaller roads as the Texas-Mexican, Atlanta & St. Andrews Bay, and New York, Susquehanna & Western. The rapid dieselization program pleased Barriger, and arguably the Monon could not have avoided financial disaster without the diesel. Yet he was not certain that the triumph of this type of locomotive would continue. "I believe the coal-fired gas turbine will take over within 10 years," he predicted in 1947. Later, though, he decided otherwise, especially after the Pennsylvania and several other carriers had little success with this experimental power. Barriger, nevertheless, remained a strong advocate of electrification. Innovative power would fulfill the mission of any carrier that sought to become a super-railroad.[21]

Hand-in-hand with the success of dieselization came improvements to the physical plant. If the Monon were to emerge as a super-railroad, such betterments were essential. Deferred maintenance long had been a problem. Barriger and his supportive board of directors launched a quest to replace lighter rail with heavier steel. On the main line from Hammond, where the Monon's own line began, to New Albany, where it connected with the Kentucky & Indiana Terminal for entrance into Louisville, by 1950 299 miles sported rail of 100 pounds or heavier, except for 1.6 miles of 90-pound rail through the Lafayette yards. Crews installed better steel on the Indianapolis line, but more was needed, and all of the Michigan City trackage got relay rail, increasing average weight from 75 pounds to 90 pounds. Along with rail betterments came a massive installation of treated ties together with the spreading of thousands of cubic yards of crushed stone ballast to strengthen the roadbed. Yard facilities and communications also saw modest rehabilitation. Bridges, too, were not overlooked. Although limited financial resources precluded all that Barriger sought with better stream crossings, the company in 1949 spent $300,000 to upgrade the substantial structure over the Wabash River at North Delphi on the Indianapolis line with seven new piers and fifteen modern heavy-deck plate-girder spans. Maintenance on other bridges was accelerated.[22]

The signature line betterment involved relocation of track away from the shores of Cedar Lake south of Hammond. This Cedar Lake Cutoff reduced maximum grades to 0.24 percent and curvature to one degree. It also eliminated the nearly 1,000-foot-long Paisley Trestle that crossed what was considered to be a bottomless quicksand bog. Its 60-foot piles did not touch bottom; friction alone held up trains. Barriger (and the insurance carrier) considered an accident on this trestle to be a disaster waiting to happen.

The Monon could ill afford to lose any of its expensive diesel locomotives or the overall financial blow a derailment would cause. Barriger and everyone associated with the railroad had vivid memories of the worst freight accident in modern company history, a head-on collision in June 1947 near Lafayette that resulted in the death of three trainmen and loss of three costly F-3 diesel units. With the opening of the Cedar Lake Cutoff on November 30, 1948, train speeds were increased considerably, no longer needing that maximum 25-mph restriction over the former Paisley Trestle.[23]

Barriger wanted more grade and curvature reductions and additional line relocations. These betterments would do much to achieve that super-railroad objective. He repeatedly argued, perhaps to the surprise of some, that "the greatest single railway problem is not truck or water competition or even wages or taxes or freight rates, but grades and curves." In his mind, "grades and curves are the principal handicaps to the operation of trains on a speed and cost basis which would make the railroads immune to competitive transportation."[24]

There was real need to upgrade the southern part of the main line and portions of the Indianapolis secondary by reducing grades and curvature and eliminating interurban-style street running in Bedford, Lafayette, Monticello, and New Albany. The Barriger team formulated a number of specific plans, but for financial, political, or other reasons, such improvements – so critical to the super-railroad philosophy – remained only paper dreams. Barriger realistically concluded, as company historian George Hilton observed, that the "railroad south of the Tree of Hope was so bad that no small number of betterments would have

A champion of fast, streamlined passenger trains, John Barriger did not miss the opportunity to arrange for the Train of Tomorrow, a four-car demonstration train created by General Motors Corporation and the Pullman-Standard Company, to travel on Monon rails during its pre-exhibition national tour. He and a fashionably dressed Elizabeth are about to board this state-of-the-art postwar train. (John W. Barriger III Collection, Barriger National Railroad Library at UMSL)

much improved it, and thus small improvements north of Bainbridge would be marginally more beneficial." Even though the Monon had relatively little in the way of fixed charges when Barriger took charge, had more than $13 million in cash, and was operating in the black by 1948, it required extremely deep pockets and great political clout to upgrade its route structure to preferred levels. The Monon was hardly a Santa Fe or Union Pacific.[25]

Although the major plans for upgrading the route structure of the Monon, with exception of the Cedar Lake Cutoff, came to naught, Barriger and his staff realized that improving freight rolling stock and passenger equipment together with upgraded service were possible, and hardly "pie-in-the sky," objectives. As with nearly every American railroad, freight trains were a company's bread and butter; the Monon was no exception. In order to meet customer needs, Barriger speedily sought to revamp the freight car fleet. Hundreds of obsolete pieces became junk. Scores more, which could be repaired, went to the Lafayette shops, and in the process they received modern AB brakes "where the prospective service life justifies this improvement." Within a year of Barriger's arrival, the company ordered from Pullman-Standard 500 all-steel, 50-ton, 40-foot boxcars and 100 70-ton covered hoppers. The following year an order was placed for 550 additional cars, specifically 100 50-ton boxcars, 100 70-ton coal hoppers, 300 50-ton gondolas, and 50 70-ton composite gondolas. The latter were designed to carry quarried limestone; steel framing and wood lining were more durable than all-steel cars.[26]

Even before the arrival of husky diesels and better rolling stock that offered round-the-clock operation and relative freedom from on-line maintenance facilities, Monon freights began to operate on regular schedules. The company no longer dispatched trains until they had the desired maximum tonnage and car numbers. (The railroad had avoided running a freight with more than sixty-nine cars; Indiana's full-crew law meant an additional brakeman if there were seventy or more cars in a train.) Under the Barriger regime a freight would run even if it wasn't pulling anything but a caboose. "The new timetable was a bold stroke, setting up train service far in excess of what traffic would support," observed journalist J. E. O'Brien in September 1946, "but already carloadings have increased so rapidly that several extras have been needed."

As a 1947 advertising message proclaimed: "The MONON is writing a new chapter in freight service with new equipment, new plans of railway development, new schedules and higher speeds. Overnight deliveries between all points on its lines are already assured." Previously it might take from one to three days for cars to move from downstate Indiana to Chicago. A clear trend had been established; customers no longer shipped on the Monon because they had no other choice.[27]

The passenger picture dramatically changed with Barriger at the throttle. Although World War II saw troop-train extras, the trustees by 1945 had slashed service to the bone. The Monon was on the verge of becoming a freight-only carrier. The main line had only a single train each way between Dearborn Station in Chicago and Union Station in Louisville, with a connecting bus between Mitchell and French Lick. The Indianapolis line also had one round-trip train between Dearborn Station and Union Station in Indianapolis.[28]

Part of the Barriger super-railroad concept involved the belief that fast, attractive, and conveniently carded passenger trains would please the public and bolster the balance sheet. Although increasing automobile ownership and airplane usage pointed toward still more competition with postwar passenger train service, Barriger was not about to give up on intercity passenger operations; he was an unabashed passenger train optimist. "As long as we must maintain the road anyway for freight, let's run any passenger service which more than pays operating expenses. If it contributes anything at all to fixed expenses, we are still ahead." He accepted the argument of the marquee value of good passenger trains. If shippers liked the equipment and service, they would likely become freight patrons. Barriger noted that roads like the Baltimore & Ohio, Chicago & Eastern Illinois, Chicago, Burlington & Quincy, Santa Fe, Seaboard Air Line, and others made their passenger operations attractive and achieved a reasonable level of profitability; there was no wholesale retreat from the passenger business. In an honest expression of optimism, he believed that the Monon could, too. The strategy involved creating new business and regaining traffic lost to the highways.

No wonder Barriger jumped at the chance to score a public relations coup by inviting to Monon tracks the renowned Train of Tomorrow on its pre-exhibition national tour. In May 1947 this General Motors and Pullman-Standard four-car demonstration train, which claimed to be the ultimate in the post–World War II era rail travel, even featuring the excitement of a dome car, made a round trip run between Chicago, French Lick, and New Albany. Thousands watched from trackside a train that Barriger so admired.[29]

After the Barriger regime began, any observant person along the Monon sensed that "tracks are back," meaning increased, convenient, and comfortable passenger trains. The August 1947 public timetable noted that the main stem sported in- and outbound trains the Night Express and the Day Express between Chicago and Louisville, including a restored Pullman connection to French Lick. Bus service between Mitchell, Orleans, and French Link was also increased. Indianapolis line patrons could select either the Tippecanoe, which left the Capital City at 7:00 a.m. or the Hoosier, which departed at the once-popular time of 5:15 p.m. The former returned from Chicago at 1:05 p.m. and the latter at 9:00 p.m. On both routes, these trains operated on faster schedules, even before dieselization could occur. Barriger also reopened Boulevard Station in Indianapolis, a suburban facility that resembled Wabash's famous Delmar Avenue station in St. Louis. The Michigan City trackage remained freight-only, although Barriger considered reviving passenger service with a Budd-built rail-diesel car.[30]

There were also significant equipment upgrades. When Barriger arrived, most of the passenger rolling stock possessed museum qualities. The typical heavyweight car, which dated from the early twentieth century, was potentially dangerous, being constructed of wood with metal sheathing for that "modern" look. Furthermore, these dowdy cars were uncomfortable and poorly suited for high-speed service. So what to do? Barriger realized that streamlined passenger cars were in high demand, and potential buyers faced a sizable waiting period before delivery. This equipment was also expensive. But better be lucky than good. Through his network of contacts, Barriger learned that the US Army planned to divest itself of a fleet of carbon-steel hospital cars that American Car & Foundry Company had recently built. The basic dimensions of these air-conditioned cars, together with floor plans and window placements, resembled twenty-eight streamlined cars delivered in 1946 to the L&N at

John Barriger revitalized passenger service on the Monon's main lines between Chicago and Louisville and Chicago and Indianapolis. He took advantage of the opportunity to acquire a fleet of recently built and surplus US government hospital cars and had them reconditioned at the company shops in Lafayette, Indiana. A public relations photographer captured this snappy Monon passenger train as four boys look on from their summer swimming hole. (John W. Barriger III Collection, Barriger National Railroad Library at UMSL)

Hoping to capture passenger traffic to and from the resort community of French Lick, Indiana, the Monon provided streamliner service to this off-the-main-line location. (John W. Barriger III Collection, Barriger National Railroad Library at UMSL)

a cost of $2.5 million ($30.7 million in current dollars). An ample number were available, and they came at a bargain-basement price, $16,500 each ($203,000 in current dollars).[31]

It did not take long before streamliners came to the Monon. With board approval Barriger ordered twenty-eight of these US government surplus hospital cars. During 1947 workers at the Lafayette car shops fashioned from this former military rolling stock thirteen coaches, five grill coaches, two dining-parlor cars, two parlor cars, three dining-bar-lounge cars, and two mail-baggage cars. Another car was to be a full-length diner, but with declining passenger demand for food service it was converted into an office car. Raymond Loewy, with whom Barriger had worked on body designs for Fairbanks-Morse locomotives and who was then shaping postwar Studebaker automobiles, was hired to create an exterior color scheme and replacement corporate herald. The result were units painted in a gray, white, and bright "Monon Royal Red" – a livery honoring the "cream and crimson" colors of Indiana University. As for the new herald, the Monon got a circle containing a sanserif letter

M with an Indian arrowhead that pointed upward. Not one to overlook details Barriger had the public timetables redesigned. The previous one of the reorganization period was a dull black-and-white, resembling the austere timetables issued by the US Railroad Administration during World War I. New timetables were a striking yellow, red, and black, and then red and gray, and screamed "look-at-me." They contained more than schedules, general information, and system map; they also provided equipment descriptions, promotional materials, and a message from the publicity-conscious Barriger.[32]

The public liked how the Monon passenger sector had changed, and ridership initially spiked. The parlor cars were particularly sumptuous, thanks to the additional handiwork of Raymond Loewy. Yet, Barriger's foray into the modern passenger train business failed to replicate the success that dieselization had been. The investment of approximately $1 million ($10.7 million in current dollars) had not been a good decision. Monon historians Gary and Stephen Dolzall minced no words: "The Monon's great passenger train experiment was a failure." More automobiles and better roads constantly drew people away from Monon trains as they did on other passenger-carrying roads. Although in 1948 passenger revenues looked promising, with a passenger count of more than 300,000, up from 259,751 for 1947, that figure would decrease. By mid-1949 the Monon was losing about $85,000 ($898,000 in current dollars) per month. Commented Barriger, "Monon passenger service is favorably known and much appreciated by the communities served, but poses a continuing problem, due to the persistent loses which it incurs." Retrenchment began. In September 1949, the company dropped, without public protest, the overnight trains between Chicago and Louisville and forever ended service to French Lick. Freight would have to be the railroad's salvation. Still, the Monon maintained its remaining service. The Chicago–Indianapolis Hoosier, for example, operated daily with six cars, including a coach, observation-lounge-parlor, and dining consist. And this train took an acceptable three hours, fifty minutes, to travel the 184 miles southbound, and five minutes longer northbound.[33]

Notwithstanding passenger-revenue disappointments, John Barriger orchestrated the launching of the Varsity in January 1950. He realized that his relatively modest railroad served an amazing number

of colleges and universities: St. Joseph (Rensselaer), Purdue (West Lafayette), Wabash (Crawfordsville), DePaul (Greencastle), and Indiana
(Bloomington). To exploit the weekend student market the Varsity left
Bloomington for Chicago on Friday evening and returned on Sunday
evening. Yet this train lasted for only six months. However, in early 1953
it was revived, but finally discontinued that May.[34]

Going back to his teenage year contacts with Ivy Lee and knowing
the extensive promotional work carried on by the Pennsylvania Railroad, Barriger understood how to be a good cheerleader. And he excelled
at this calling. His unusual business card as Monon president read: "John
W. Barriger, President and *Traveling Freight Agent* [italics added]." He
looked upon himself as Monon's number-one traffic man, and energetic
sales were his passion. Throughout his Monon tenure Barriger hustled
for every carload, although some may not have been profitable. Barriger
called on active and former shippers and potential new ones. And he
entertained and always paid attention to details. Take his first big shipper dinner held at French Lick. What exactly happened may have been
somewhat distorted, but it characterizes his entertainment philosophy:
"Mr. Barriger had ordered 'nothing but the best' (including roast beef)
for his shippers. He went behind the bar to see that his orders had been
complied with and found that the hotel manager was serving well drinks
rather than what had been ordered." Barriger was not pleased. "He invited the hotel manager to come to the bar whereupon he began breaking
bottles of the inferior drinks. 'Sir, I intend to pay for these, however, you
will comply with my wishes to serve them only the best.'" Barriger also
began an almost frantic series of speeches to civic leaders, service organizations, business groups, school assemblies, and practically anyone
who would listen. It was not unknown for Barriger to make a half-dozen
contacts or speeches in a day. "Barriger was full of energy," remarked
an acquaintance. "He couldn't relax." And throughout his life, Barriger
enjoyed being around people. "As far as I know," according to his son
Jack, "he never ate alone but would skip eating rather than dine alone."[35]

Just as Barriger relished meeting people, he met them with confidence and with respect. Resembling practically every railroad president
of his generation, he wore "proper attire." This generally meant a three-
piece suit with his gold watch and chain in the vest pocket, tie and hat,

but on infrequent occasions, especially in hot, humid weather, he took off the jacket and rolled up his shirtsleeves. Elizabeth bought him sport coats and slacks, but they were rarely taken out of the closet. Barriger, too, wore his signature rimless bifocal glasses. When in conversation or discussion with workers and others, Barriger never admonished anyone with profanity. And there would be virtually no instances of an off-color joke or story. That behavior was often not the norm among railroad officials.[36]

When Barriger headed the Monon, the family, accustomed to his long work days and out-of-office travels, often did not see much of him, except usually on those cherished Sundays. In January 1947 a move from Glencoe to another rented house, located on Scott Avenue in the North Shore town of Winnetka, made for about the same commute between home and office. Later that year John and Elizabeth purchased their first house, a property at 622 Oak Street, also in Winnetka. As Jack remembers, "It was beautifully situated in Winnetka opposite the SE corner of the Winnetka Village Green, three blocks from the CNW [Chicago & North Western] Commuter Station and four blocks from downtown." The family would stay there for the next nine years, and the four children benefited from local public and private schools. Edith "Didi" Beck was also part of the Chicagoland household. Beginning in 1944 she found work at the nearby Great Lakes Naval Training Center and was assigned to the Naval Separation Office.[37]

Barriger, the aggressive booster of the Monon, changed the image of the railroad, kept old customers, and attracted new ones. "Down here in southern Indiana we refer to the stages of the Monon as BB and AB, Before Barriger and After Barriger," wrote Steward Riley, publisher of the *Bedford Daily Times-Mail*. "In the BB days the Monon was commonly known as the god-damn Monon. In the AB days, the name has been shortened to simply Monon, and there is a definite ring of respect, almost of obeisance, in the very name." Riley continued, "The Monon has worked with our Chamber of Commerce to establish new industries in this community. Men like Barriger win friends for the railroads." E. R. Kiefner, vice president of Gunnison Homes in New Albany, gave this testimonial: "Since January 1947, the date of completion and occupancy of our present facilities, we have been served exclusively and efficiently

Having a good time was part of the July 1947 Monon centennial celebrations. Joining in the fun were three Barriger children, Jack, Betty, and Ann. Jack has been repeatedly kissed by a bevy of "Belles of the Monon" and is unmistakably enjoying this once-in-a-lifetime experience. Sister Betty is to his immediate right, and younger sister Ann is in front of Betty. Most of the online beauty queens are wearing the white Monon painter-style caps distributed by the company at this and other public events. (John W. Barriger III Collection, Barriger National Railroad Library at UMSL)

by the Monon. Dependable overnight schedules applying between all points served by this carrier, plus the close cooperation afforded by their interested departments, have been of valuable assistance in solving numerous rail transportation problems."[38]

The public persona of John Barriger and the Monon became well known in Indiana. He did not miss a beat when it came to good will and promotion. Just as he did not ignore those individuals and groups outside the railroad, he paid close attention to employees. Not long after Barriger arrived, he made an effort to instill a new spirit among white- and blue-collar workers. In September 1946 the *Indianapolis Times* reported that "of the Monon's estimated 2,000 employees, Mr. Barriger judges he knows about half by name. He hopes to know all in a few months."

During that elaborate celebration of the Monon Railroad centennial, the "Belles of the Monon," these online young beauty queens happily gather on the special train for their group picture. (John W. Barriger IV Collection)

Employees appreciated his honest frankness, his "down-to-earthness," and his accessibility. "All I ever saw of our railroad president was closed curtains on his car until Barriger came," commented a station agent in 1946. "Now he's stopped his train twice just to come and see me." Remembering his stint with an in-house publication at the Pennsylvania, Barriger in 1947 launched an employee magazine, *The Rail and Tie: Monon the Hoosier Line*. This 24-page illustrated publication featured news stories and personal happenings about members of the extended Monon family. As a lover of railroad photography, Barriger took advantage of the photo artistry of F. J. Bennett, telegrapher at the McDoel Yard in Bloomington, to adorn the cover of the company's 1949 annual report. Editorialized *Railway Age*, "Perhaps there's a hint there for those roads that would like to make their reports even more attractive by utilizing the talents of some of their camera-using employees." It did not take long before that abysmal employee morale had become a condition of the past.[39]

The greatest publicity triumph at the "New Monon" came when Barriger orchestrated an elaborate centennial celebration in 1947. A student of railroad history and knowledgeable about his company's past, Barriger was not about to miss a serendipitous opportunity. The year was 1847 when the New Albany & Salem Rail Road, initial component of the Monon, had its ceremonial groundbreaking, although it did not begin freight and passenger service for another two years. The birth of the Monon would be properly observed.[40]

The idea of a railroad-sponsored centennial celebration predated the Barriger spectacular. Well-remembered by industry personal and the general public was the gala that the Baltimore & Ohio held to commemorate its claim as "the pioneer railroad of the country," a year-long birthday party that took place in 1927. Its centenary exhibition and pageant, called "The Fair of the Iron Horse," turned out to be a smashing success, attracting more than 1.3 million visitors. In the immediate post–World War II most railroads had discretionary funds to "do something extra." Since a number of companies traced their origins to the late 1840s and early 1850s, when the rail network began its first major wave of expansion, a centennial was there to recall. Such railroads as the Chicago & North Western, Erie, Illinois Central, Louisville & Nashville, and Milwaukee Road did not forget.[41]

Barriger, that publicity hound, planned to spare no effort and expense in taking this golden opportunity to promote the Monon. The railroad took out newspaper advertisements that described "A Century of Service at the Crossroads of America." Wrote Barriger, "So it is that 'the Hoosier Line' – one hundred years *young* – is today celebrating not only a full century of service to Hoosiers and others, but the beginning of a '*new century*' that involves the most amazing advances in modern engineering [italics in original]." There were also billboards along the right-of-way and radio spots that told of this century of service. Early on the company sponsored a "Monon Railroad Centennial Essay Contest" for high-school students, with county and state winners. These young people received signed certificates and a dinner that honored them and their families at the French Lick Hotel. And in twenty-one Monon towns and cities the local chambers of commerce selected beauty queens. These "Queens of the Monon" participated in the main-line train ceremonies.

John Barriger relished every moment of what turned out to be the successfully orchestrated Monon centennial gala of July 1947. Here he waves from the engineer's seat of the historic William Mason 4-4-0 steam locomotive that the company borrowed from the Baltimore & Ohio Railroad. (John W. Barriger III Collection, Barriger National Railroad Library at UMSL)

The "Queen of New Albany" also had her own court of six "Belles of the Monon," each dressed in long antebellum period dresses, and together with the twenty other queens joined in the various festivities, including the grand finale. Barriger took great pride that on February 22, 1947,

the Indiana Society of Chicago made the Monon the theme of its annual dinner, and a month later the Lafayette Chamber of Commerce, in
collaboration with Purdue University, similarly honored the railroad.[42]

The extensive and most remembered centennial celebration occurred in New Albany, being the hometown of James Brooks, founder
of the New Albany & Salem Rail Road. From July 27 through July 30,
1947, a variety of events took place: Homecomers' Day, Exhibitors' Day,
Youth Day, and the all-important Transportation Day. Coinciding with
these activities the Monon dispatched the Centennial Train Show, a
steam-powered special that started in Hammond, stopped in a score
of Indiana communities and terminated in New Albany for the finale
on Transportation Day. As with several other centennial celebrating
railroads, the Monon borrowed from the Baltimore & Ohio its historic
William Mason, a classic 4-4-0 American-type locomotive, and two
vintage cars. Aboard the Centennial Train were Barriger, the four male
singing "Mononeers," and songstress Marie Lawler. Everyone, including Barriger, was dressed in historic costumes. John McGee, a professional music entertainer who served as program director, wrote eight
centennial songs, the most popular being "Up and Down the Monon."
Its memorable lines came from the chorus:

> Up and down the Monon
> Everything is fine,
> 'Cause that rootin' tootin' Monon
> She's a Hoosier line.
> All aboard!
> All aboard!
> It's my Indiana home that I'm
> a headin' toward, Oh!
> Up and down the Monon
> Everything is fine,
> 'Cause that rootin' tootin' Monon
> She's a Hoosier line.

Soon 10,000 albums of these 78-rpm phonograph records became
available for purchase, and Barriger expected that these tunes would
"become popular permanent additions to Indiana's song bag." When
the Centennial Train steamed into New Albany, there was a parade,
which featured a Monon float and an assortment of dignitaries, including

Indiana governor Ralph Gates. Also for Transportation Day thousands of attendees toured the new Hoosier streamliner and saw the Southern Railway's Best Friend of Charleston, an operating replica of that much-heralded locomotive that on Christmas Day 1830 chugged along the first 6 miles of the South Carolina Canal and Rail Road. An estimated 100,000 people "Up and Down the Monon" viewed the centennial events, and Barriger and his board of directors had no qualms about the $150,000 the company spent for this public relations sensation.[43]

While not the center of attraction, Barriger made certain that the Monon had a presence at the Chicago Railroad Fair of 1948–49. This grand gala, spearheaded by the publicity department of the Chicago & North Western Railway (C&NW), was designed to focus attention on this pioneer Midwestern railroad and the post–War World II railroad industry. The year 1948 held significance for the C&NW; the first locomotive to operate in the Windy City belonged to its predecessor, the Galena & Chicago Union Rail Road. On a mile-long strip of land along Lake Michigan, thirty-five railroads joined the C&NW to sponsor this well-orchestrated celebration. Resembling the Monon centennial, the Chicago fair exceeded all expectations. Between July 20 and October 2, 1948, more than 2.5 million visitors paid several million dollars to learn about the way railroads revolutionized Chicago and the nation. This enthusiastic public response led to a repeat performance when, during the summer and early fall of 1949, more than 2.7 million people visited the extravaganza.[44]

How would the Monon be represented? Barriger sent the F-3 diesel unit No. 81, resplendent in the passenger livery of Indiana University colors, and a new Pullman-Standard 40-foot boxcar with the unusual number of "CI&L 1." Barriger thought that boxcar numbers should be simple. "Each unneeded digit eliminated from a car number reduces opportunities for error and saves thousands of lead pencil strokes, typewriter impressions, teletype impulses and spoken numerals." He could have added that the "One Spot" became a curiosity and brought more attention to the Monon as it traveled in freight trains throughout the country. Being wedded to a policy of good public relations, Barriger firmly believed that the Chicago Railroad Fair was well worth Monon's participation. "[It] gave many of its visitors their first clear realization that the railways, through private enterprise, had within a century transformed a continental wilderness into the greatest nation on earth."[45]

THE FUTURE MONON

John Barriger realized that the Monon could never become a super-railroad. The financial resources were not available. There was no practical way to allow streamliners between Chicago and Indianapolis, for example, to operate at speeds of 90 to 100 miles per hour. Yes, dieselization, the Cedar Lake Cutoff, track and roadbed improvements, and an aggressive program of publicity and traffic solicitation produced positive results. As for the latter, the company increased its handing of national freight tonnage from 0.14 percent in 1945 to 0.2 percent in 1950. Passenger betterments were less successful, although the impact of the streamliners bolstered employee morale and may have had that marque value among shippers, politicians, and others. Barriger, moreover, understood that as time passed, railroads faced stiff and growing modal competition. "Like all railroad men who come in direct touch with patrons, I am painfully aware of the growing inroads of motor trucking upon rail traffic," he observed in early 1952. "Industries are steadily enlarging the areas within which they receive and distribute most of their freight by highway." That trend hardly augured well for a small Class I carrier like the Monon.[46]

What should the Monon become? Barriger knew that the carrier was "small potatoes" in the railroad world. In fact, when the talented John Kenefick, a 1943 mechanical engineering graduate of Princeton and US naval officer from 1943 to 1946, applied for a job at the Monon, Barriger turned him down. He told Kenefick, "The Monon is too small. Get with a bigger, stronger railroad to learn the business more quickly." Kenefick did just that, joining the New York Central, and in time he became one of President Alfred Perlman's "boys." Much later Barriger supported Kenefick in his successful quest for a top post at Union Pacific.[47]

Barriger, who knew intimately the national railroad map and the regional one as well, thought that one way to strengthen revenues would be to promote the Michigan City line with its virtual straight and level tangent as a convenient way to circumvent the freight traffic bottleneck of Chicago. This north–south route connected with every Eastern railroad that served the Windy City. Significantly, at San Pierre, 23 miles north of Monon, the New York Central could avoid the Chicago gateway, and at Reynolds, 7 miles south of Monon, there was an interchange with the Pennsylvania that directly linked with the outer belt Toledo, Peoria & Western at Effner, Illinois. Even though he was that consummate salesmen, Barriger was able to grab only a few Chicago bypass cars.[48]

Ultimately the fate of the Monon should involve a merger or sale. As Barriger revealed in the Prince Plan, he preferred side-by-side regional unifications, and his first choice for the Monon would be with the Chicago & Eastern Illinois. This comparable road, except for its major through passenger train service, would provide the consolidated company with access not only to Chicago but also to gateways at Evansville, Indiana, Louisville, and St. Louis. Moreover, neither carrier was plagued with a plethora of branch lines. Barriger knew well the C&EI from his time at Kuhn, Loeb & Company and later as a C&EI reorganization manager and member of its board of directors. Unfortunately for Barriger the C&EI was not interested, notwithstanding a greatly improved Monon property. Yet after his departure, the C&EI in the mid-1950s warmed somewhat to a Monon union, although ultimately the L&N became owner of the Monon and the Evansville–Chicago line of the C&EI. Knowing that the C&EI might not become a merger mate, Barriger made attempts to sell the Monon to the L&N and also to the Southern, but the time was not ripe for such a transaction. The beginnings of the end to a highly "Balkanized" industry were a decade or so in the future.[49]

If the Monon were to find a corporate home, John Barriger would not be involved. At the close of 1952 he left his "Guinea Pig" road to take the vice-presidency of the New York, New Haven & Hartford Railroad, a career move that turned out badly. For Barriger's replacement the Monon board of directors selected the less flamboyant yet capable Warren Brown effective January 1, 1953. This decision assured a continuation of Barriger policies and kept the railroad financially in the black. But as board member Arthur T. Leonard said, "The company suffered a regrettable loss through the resignation, on December 31, 1952, of Mr. John W. Barriger."[50]

Why resign? Even though Barriger relished the challenges of heading a troubled carrier like the Monon, there seemed little more that he could do with the available resources and his overall notions of how a railroad should be run. The obvious exception would be to find a merger partner or buyer. Already Barriger had established a restlessness in his professional career. As Jack Barriger remembers his father saying, "There is no worse featherbedding than a president of a 500-mile railroad. You should move on."[51]

John Barriger learned much as a first-time railroad president. Most of all he saw firsthand the positive impact of dieselization and experienced the benefits of good public relations. Barriger remained convinced that speed, frequency, price, and public service were basic factors in creating and operating a modern railroad company. In 1948 he contributed to *Railway Age* a piece that he called "A Railroad Officer's Creed." The final paragraph summed up his basic thoughts about being an executive, and they were ones that he consistently embraced:

> The title of an official position should not be regarded by the incumbent as the measure of the prestige, honor and respect due him by the organization below him in rank. Instead, he should look upon it as a measure of the capacity and responsibility with which his superiors and associates have entrusted him. Titles tend to become confused with honors in the mind of many of the holders of them. This is wrong; titles should be wholly related to work, duties and responsibilities. Titles of officers of corporations should never be corrupted by subconsciously thinking of them as one does of titles of nobility – held without regard to performance.[52]

FOUR

Transition Years

NEW HAVEN INTERLUDE

On January 1, 1953, John W. Barriger returned to the East. While his family remained in Winnetka, Illinois, this new vice president of the New York, New Haven & Hartford Railroad (New Haven) commuted between his home and office in New Haven, Connecticut. Ready to leave the Monon and always seeking challenges, he accepted an offer from Frederic C. "Buck" or "Bucky" Dumaine, Jr., New Haven board chairman and president, to manage this 1,800-mile road at a handsome salary of $50,000 annually ($478,000 in current dollars).[1]

The New Haven, which once dominated freight and passenger traffic in southern New England, traced its history back to the mid-1840s with formation of the New York & New Haven Railroad (NY&NH) that opened in 1848 between the two cities of its corporate name. Initially, this road provided only passenger service, but in 1851 it began handling carload freight. Then in 1872 the NY&NH united with the Hartford & New Haven, an even older road, to create the New York, New Haven & Hartford Railroad. Expansions followed. By 1895 the New Haven main line extended between New York City and Springfield, Massachusetts, and the company operated a maze of secondary and branch lines, most of which were leased. By the eve of World War I, financier J. Pierpont Morgan Sr. and his New Haven lieutenant, Charles S. Mellen, had largely shaped the modern company. The railroad sported nearly 1,200 miles of mostly owned trackage, including its busy Shore Line between New York, New Haven, Providence, and Boston. That popular passenger route, together with its other lines that served this densely populated region, explains why passenger traffic generated a substantially higher proportion of its revenues than for most railroads. The New Haven also had become heavily invested in street and interurban railways in Connecticut, Massachusetts, and Rhode Island. And the railroad owned all of the region's steamship companies. "In short, almost everything that moved in southern New England was a New Haven vassal in one form or another," explained railroad historian Herbert H. Harwood Jr.[2]

After World War I the mighty New Haven faced growing challenges. The high price paid for its traction properties and their rapid decline in the 1920s imposed a severe financial drain. Efforts to combat increasing private automobile usage with its bus subsidiary New England Transportation Company proved lackluster. Increasing the dollar strain was the continued loss of highly rated freight to motor carriers. Only in 1928 and 1929 did the company pay dividends to its common and preferred stockholders. Then the Great Depression struck. The New Haven attempted to cope, including abandonment of its remaining trolley lines, reduction of maintenance on its rolling stock and physical plant, employee layoffs, introduction of an early streamlined passenger train, and a $16 million ($205 million in current dollars) loan from the Railroad Division of the Reconstruction Finance Corporation. Its economic health still deteriorated. On October 23, 1935, the company gave up the battle and petitioned a federal court for bankruptcy protection. This receivership would last eleven years.[3]

In 1947 the prospect for the reorganized New Haven looked mixed. Although its financial house was in good order, the company relied heavily on an extensive and labor-intensive commuter operation, deriving about half of its passenger revenues from this source. Outdated and counterproductive labor agreements hardly helped. Notably, too, the New Haven had only three routes that were longer than 100 miles, and most consisted of less than 70 miles – no long-haul freight revenues for this carrier. Moreover, erosion of freight traffic appeared endless. President Howard Palmer aptly described his railroad as "one extensive terminal, with traffic spreading out all over the rail lines, with few well-defined main lines and a very high proportion of secondary routes and branches."[4]

Bucky Dumaine's father, Frederic C. Dumaine Sr., began the family's association with the New Haven. This rags-to-riches businessman, who headed textile giant Amoskeag Manufacturing Company and was "a dominant force in Boston's financial world since the turn of the century," led the Boston Railroad Holding Company, a large stakeholder in the three principal New England railroads: New Haven, Boston & Maine, and Maine Central. Dumaine also served as a pre-bankruptcy director on the New Haven board. Described as "miserly, dictatorial and inflexible," the eighty-two-year-old Dumaine in August 1948 orchestrated an investor coup that took control of the New Haven. He and his associates, who included Patrick McGinnis, a railroad securities specialist, were unhappy with the conservative dividend policy of the Palmer administration, and they promised greater returns to shareholders. Palmer was soon forced out of the presidency, and Laurence Whittemore, a former Boston & Maine and Maine Central official and Federal Reserve Bank of Boston president, took charge. Policy differences between Dumaine and Whittemore, however, resulted in the latter's brief tenure, and Dumaine assumed the presidency and chairmanship of the board. This maneuvering created a board vacancy, and Dumaine filled it with his eldest son, Bucky. With the death of the senior Dumaine in 1951, Bucky took control over the family-controlled Amoskeag conglomerate, consisting of "everything from one of the nation's biggest textile manufacturers to Fanny Farmer Candy Shops," and he also became the New Haven president.[5]

Frederic Dumaine Jr. resembled his father, although he was more progressive in matters of railroad policy. Born in Concord, Massachusetts, in 1902, Bucky received a top-notch private school education. He attended the small but prestigious Pomfret School in Pomfret, Connecticut, where he excelled both in the classroom and in its athletic programs. Bucky was also popular with his classmates and served as senior class president. He decided, however, to skip college, being anxious to enter the rough-and-tumble world of business.[6]

So what kind of railroad president was Bucky Dumaine? He agreed with his father, whom he greatly admired, that New Haven operations should be streamlined, ending needless expenditures and disposing of unneeded assets. Yet Bucky wanted to improve the railroad, bolster employee morale, and establish good public relations, goals that his late father generally did not share. He was also less concerned about hefty dividend payments. Dumaine considered himself a big idea, and not an operations, person. "He knew the railroad, just not the details of its operations." That explains the offer to John Barriger in late 1952.[7]

Barriger may have had serious reservations about joining the New Haven. He went so far as to travel to Amarillo, Texas, to see his older son, Jack, a recent graduate of the Massachusetts Institute of Technology and the Graduate School of Economics at Yale, who worked as a transportation inspector for the Atchison, Topeka & Santa Fe Railway. His son considered this something of a surprise visit. Jack's response to his father's intentions was straightforward: "You are nuts to leave the Monon for the New Haven." But, of course, the senior Barriger did just that.

Barriger had a vision. He saw the New Haven position as a possible way to bring about a consolidation of railroads in the New England region, most likely unification of the New Haven, Boston & Maine, and Maine Central. Opined Barriger: "New England pays a high price to keep its railroads small in size, and in the scope of their aggregate operations.[8]

When Barriger arrived at his new post, he was predictably optimistic. For one thing, he believed that the New Haven could develop aspects of a super-railroad. Bucky Dumaine had committed resources to modernize the physical plant, and he promised to reinvigorate the railroad's less than stellar freight and passenger operations. Said Bucky, "the business of the railroad is service to the public, and the primary objective can be obtained only through good adequate service." Barriger heartily approved. Making the New Haven a first-class railroad, however, would take time and money. After all, the railroad remained revenue dependent on commuters and intercity passengers, and it continued to be saddled with an immense physical plant. Although twice the size of the Monon, the New Haven was still a small Class I carrier. Barriger, of course, enthusiastically endorsed the Dumaine family desire for a merged New Haven, Boston & Maine, and Maine Central; a more unified New England rail network made sense.[9]

It did not take long before Barriger realized that he never should have accepted the New Haven post. His tenure lasted only five months; May 31, 1953, was his last official day on the job. Later Barriger explained that his decision to resign involved "difference of managerial policy."

Remembered Jack, "Dad left the New Haven because he could not work with owner Bucky Dumaine." Barriger wanted to run the railroad, but Bucky apparently had other ideas, "Bucky made decisions, and sometimes he didn't bother to tell Dad." A case in point: "Dad was downsizing Readville [Massachusetts] Shops when an employee who knew Bucky called him in Florida and Bucky countermanded Dad's order without telling Dad." Furthermore, Dumaine stayed at his Florida home for extended periods and was unavailable for consultations in either the office or other mutually convenient venues. Jack recalled his father telling Bucky: "The two of us can't both run the New Haven." So Barriger left. "Dad was disappointed but not bitter," and the two men remained friends.[10]

It may have been a blessing that Barriger severed his ties to the New Haven. In 1954 Bucky Dumaine was ousted from the executive suite in the wake of a bruising proxy battle with Patrick McGinnis. Since assisting the senior Dumaine in gaining control of the New Haven seven years earlier, McGinnis had been involved with the Norfolk Southern and Central of Georgia railroads, and these associations revealed questionable ethical practices. This wheeler-dealer believed that Bucky's administration was reinvesting too much of the New Haven's earnings back into the property, money he felt should go to stockholders. McGinnis, who barely won the fight that gave him the New Haven presidency, immediately set out to plunder the railroad. Unfortunately for the "McGinnis crowd" the nation's first $1 billion storm, Hurricane Diane, struck southern New England in August 1955 and ravaged the New Haven, a natural disaster that added to its financial woes. McGinnis's growing unpopularity with investors, regulators, employees, and the public forced his resignation in January 1956. Yet he remained a railroader, taking the reins of the Boston & Maine. A decade later a federal court convicted McGinnis on charges relating to a kickback scheme that involved the sale of Boston & Maine passenger cars; he subsequently went to prison.[11]

ROCK ISLAND YEARS

Since joining the Pennsylvania Railroad, John Barriger had never faced unemployment. Before submitting his formal resignation to Bucky

Dumaine, he successfully tapped his network of contacts to find his next position. "There was no one in the industry that he didn't know," remembered one railroader. On June 1, 1953, he joined the Chicago, Rock Island & Pacific Railroad (Rock Island) and would work at its corporate headquarters in La Salle Street Station in downtown Chicago. Unlike other vice presidents at the Rock Island with their specific titles, Barriger was simply "vice president." He described his duties this way: "Staff work on special projects delivered to me by immediate supervisor." What Barriger did during his slightly more than three years at the Rock Island was to work for president John D. Farrington. "Barriger was Farrington's show horse. The person who could give speeches and serve as a liaison with the financial community." There was more. Barriger participated in traffic solicitation. For this "port in a storm" Barriger accepted a substantial pay cut from his New Haven position, receiving $35,000 annually ($327,000 in current dollars).[12]

The Rock Island appointment was well received by company personnel. The only rub likely involved the attitude of Downing Jenks. This rising railroad executive, who held an engineering degree from Yale and previously had served as vice president and general manager of the Chicago & Eastern Illinois, believed that he should replace the aging Farrington as president. When Barriger arrived, Jenks held the position of executive vice president and recently had joined the board of directors. "Dad was not a threat to Jenks," remarked Jack. "That was understood by Farrington and Dad." Yet Jenks may have had his doubts. In 1956 he did become president, and five years later he took charge of a more robust Missouri Pacific Railroad.[13]

Once the Rock Island might have been that "mighty fine line" of musical verse, but by 1953 it claimed a checkered past and an uncertain future. The Rock Island began as the Rock Island & La Salle Rail Road, chartered in the late 1840s. By the early 1850s the company, recast as the Chicago & Rock Island Rail Road, linked the Windy City with the Mississippi River at Rock Island, Illinois. Growth continued. Through affiliate Peoria & Bureau Valley Rail Road, the company reached the Illinois River at Peoria, and through another associated property, Mississippi & Missouri Rail Road, it began its construction march across Iowa. In 1856 the Rock Island opened the first railroad bridge over the

Mississippi River, and this tie-in between Prairie State and Hawkeye State rails augured well for profitability. Later, in 1869, the company, now flying the banner of the Chicago, Rock Island & Pacific Railroad, reached Council Bluffs, Iowa, and a connection with the just completed Union Pacific–Central Pacific transcontinental line. More building followed. As the nineteenth century progressed, the Rock Island gained greater importance. By constructing and leasing trackage, this expanding granger road emerged as a leading Chicago-based carrier. Guided by Ransom Cable, its aggressive president and general manager, the Rock Island by the 1890s controlled a web of rails that stretched from Illinois to Colorado and Texas. The mileage of all lines owned, leased, and operated exceeded 3,500; the company proudly claimed to be the "Great Rock Island Route."[14]

As the twentieth century took hold, a sad chapter in the history of the Rock Island began. Stock plungers Daniel Reid and William and James Moore seized control. This "Reid-Moore Syndicate" bled the company, and in the process they showed little concern about protecting the public interest. Moreover, the syndicate embraced a policy of reckless expansion. By 1910 the system exceeded 8,000 miles, and its debt level soared. Admittedly, the Rock Island had established itself as a major interregional carrier. Its overall importance had increased with a strategic connection in New Mexico Territory with the Southern Pacific Railroad, creating the "Golden State Route" between Chicago, Kansas City, and Los Angeles. With growing financial problems, the Rock Island on the eve of World War I found itself in receivership, and it took three years before its first bankruptcy ended. The company limped through the "Roaring Twenties," but by 1933 a perfect storm had struck: a severe postwar agricultural recession, increasing drought on the Great Plains, expanding highway competition, and the deepening Great Depression.[15]

A nearly empty treasury forced a second bankruptcy, and court control would last from 1933 to 1948. Slowly better times came to the beleaguered Rock Island. In 1936 John D. Farrington joined the company as operating head and immediately embarked on what he called a program of "Planned Progress." This veteran railroader, who had spent most of his career with the Chicago, Burlington & Quincy, sparked a Rock Island renaissance. These included line relocations, rebuilt freight yards, and diesel-powered passenger trains – the popular Rocket streamliners. The improvement that likely helped the company the most was an upgraded Golden State Route, providing the best long-haul for its freight and passenger traffic. These betterments appealed to John Barriger, but as he remarked that "being a penny pincher [Farrington] limited his plans to the minimum necessities of the present rather than expanding them to the opportunities of the future." Still in Barriger's mind, "Mr. John D. Farrington is Mr. Rock Island."[16]

The World War II era meant a Rock Island that operated at or near full capacity. Operating revenues predictably spiked. The company had more money than ever, although legal complications prevented it from exiting bankruptcy until after the war. By the early 1950s the Rock Island appeared to be an up-to-date railroad with its all-dieselized motive power and fleet of Rockets that sped along its principal routes in portions of fourteen states. The company continued to improve its physical plant, including line relocations, grade reductions, and equipment upgrades. Yet there were indications that the Rock Island was about to face serious challenges. Competition from automobiles, barges, and trucks increased, and the railroad remained dependent on agricultural traffic and "had no real industrial base at all." Another concern was its money-draining Chicago commuter operations that in 1954 alone posted a deficit of $1.5 million ($13.4 million in current dollars).[17]

As with his previous railroad jobs, John Barriger worked long hours. At the Rock Island this meant not only time spent in his La Salle Street Station office but also travels along its far-flung system and offline sites as well. Much of his attention focused on strengthening the freight sector, carloadings that this railroad always needed. Barriger and Farrington, though, held divergent notions about traffic solicitation. Barriger liked to say that his boss "believes that traffic, like rain, falls on the just and the unjust alike." At best this was naive thinking. Farrington failed to show much enthusiasm for meetings of traffic associations or encouragement of traffic people. Barriger, on the other hand, was a constant booster of such gatherings and individuals. "Dad loved going to those traffic meetings and meeting with shippers." Since Barriger lacked a title other than vice president, he made this addition to his business card: "Vice President and Senior Traveling Freight Agent." This may have brought smiles to those who noticed this self-initiated title, but it represented his feelings about what his role should be on the Rock Island. Farrington did not object; "Farrington respected Dad."[18]

Barriger did more than support the traffic department and its personnel. With his vast understanding of railroad finance, he represented the Rock Island at various financial meetings. In November 1953 he explained before a gathering of the New York Society of Security Analysts in New York City the progress that his company had made since the start of the Farrington administration. His core argument: "The Rock Island is not only strong from the standpoint of property condition, management and operations, but likewise has one of the most conservative capital structures in relation to its property value, revenues and earning power of any American railway." He closed his extended remarks on a most optimistic note. "This company's earning power has already been well tested and seasoned for whatever the future may bring. Rock Island will register another year of progress in 1954." Barriger was perhaps the consummate "spin doctor."[19]

There were other tasks. One involved exploring a possible acquisition of the Illinois Terminal Railroad (IT). Barriger used his knowledge of the railroad network and his financial skills to report to Farrington and the Rock Island board on how the company might benefit from the proposed sale of this 400-mile property. The IT was unusual; this carrier once had been a mighty electric interurban. In fact, as the Illinois Traction System (McKinley System), it was the largest interurban property in the Midwest, serving such cities as Danville, Decatur, Peoria, Springfield, and St. Louis. Through the early part of its existence, the IT did a strong passenger business, even operating sleeping and parlor cars, and competed effectively with neighboring steam roads. But as the 1920s ended, it had become more dependent on freight revenues. As weaker regional interurbans scaled back their trackage, entered bankruptcy, or abandoned altogether, the IT (known as Illinois Terminal after 1923) continued to prosper. It did so by increasing its carload freight business and expanding terminal facilities in the Alton and East St. Louis area. To expedite a diversified freight business IT constructed belt lines around major cities to avoid excessive street running, frequently the bane of electric roads that handled carload freight.[20]

By the early 1950s the Illinois Terminal had reduced its passenger operations and abandoned sections of trackage. Largely dieselized, its freight maintained substantial earnings, and in 1953 they amounted to more than $10.5 million ($94.3 million in current dollars). By this time IT investors, however, had decided that they wanted to liquidate. "I suspect that the IT stockholders forecast a downward spiral for their small railroad and just wanted to get their money out," recalled a Santa Fe official.[21]

Rock Island management knew of the availability of the Illinois Terminal. But would it be a good acquisition? Barriger would explore; he spent considerable time examining the property and considering its potential. In his initial report, dated October 29, 1953, his thoughts, based on extensive research, were positive. "The geographical pattern of the Rock Island provides only interior and no exterior connections between its principal terminals; Chicago, Peoria, St. Louis, Memphis, et al. Traffic gathering power and operating flexibility would be improved by system control of connections between these extremities." Barriger continued, "One of the few opportunities available to secure such supplementary mileage lies in the possible acquisition of the Illinois Terminal Railroad Company. The latter's direct line from East Peoria to St. Louis would provide a satisfactory route that would make all Rock Island mileage in Illinois, Iowa and Minnesota accessible to the St. Louis gateway over the Illinois Terminal. The latter would also provide Rock Island with direct access to several important industrial districts." Study, though, revealed that the Toledo, Peoria & Western (TP&W) was strongly interested in the property. Significantly, before any line sale occurred, the IT, Barriger learned, planned to sell its monster McKinley Bridge over the Mississippi River to Venice, Illinois. If that occurred, the new owner would likely charge "exorbitant" rental fees for use of this critical structure. From Barriger's perspective the Rock Island purchase of the IT would come at a substantial cost. In addition to bridge charges, it would have to compete against the TP&W or other possible bidders, forcing up the final sale price.[22]

The Rock Island, however, did become financially involved in the Illinois Terminal. Not long before Barriger left the company a consortium

Being a Rock Island vice president allowed John Barriger more opportunities to continue what he so much loved, attending professional meetings and giving public talks. On April 25, 1956, he participated in the second annual Michigan Management Seminar held at the University of Michigan in Ann Arbor, where he joined a panel discussion on automation and train operation. To Barriger's left is George Baughman, vice president of Union Switch and Signal, and to his right is Al Kalmbach, president of Kalmbach Publishing Co. (John W. Barriger III Collection, Barriger National Railroad Library at UMSL)

of nine (later ten) railroads, including the Rock Island, through its Illinois-Missouri Terminal Company, acquired the property, completing the sale on June 15, 1956. Yet this takeover did not provide the advantages that Barriger had envisioned for his employer.[23]

Throughout his tenure at the Rock Island, Barriger remained active on the speaker's circuit. Take his June 1956 presentation to the Association of American Railroads Safety Section in Louisville, Kentucky. At this conference he argued for the industry to raise minimum interchange requirements for freight cars. "There are good many freight cars running on American railways today that are nothing more than railway jaloppies [sic]." Barriger contended that these pieces of rolling stock might be suitable for low speed, short trains, but they "constitute a hazard to high-speed movement of heavy trains, especially where these inadequate vehicles happen to be placed among cars at the head end where stresses and strains are most severe." These "jaloppies" were not appropriate for his vision of super railroads.[24]

SUPER-RAILROADS

Unlike the presidency of the Monon and his stint at the New Haven, his tenure at the Rock Island allowed John Barriger more time at home. This gave him opportunities to work on a project that he had contemplated for years, namely a study on how the national railroad system could be improved, creating "a package of advice for American railroading." As Jack recalled, "Dad was constantly talking about super-railroads long before he joined the Rock Island."[25]

The title of Barriger's sole book publication reveals the thesis: *Super-Railroads for a Dynamic American Economy.* In his mind it was possible to create an efficient, high-speed core rail network through imaginative industry self-help and reduced regulatory involvement. In an age of growing and government-subsidized model competition, a railroad renaissance was badly needed. If a transformed railroad industry became reality, the American economy would prosper more than it did at mid-century. Barriger explained his basic thinking this way: "My theme song has long been 'It is a paradox that America – with its burgeoning economic life – should have superhighways, supermarkets, and super everything else, but there are no super railroads.' Since economical railroad transportation is the foundation on which 'super everything' in present day American economic life is based, the United States urgently needs super railroads."[26]

Barriger crafted this four-chapter work largely in 1954, although during the following year he placed finishing touches on the manuscript, mostly updating and checking statistical data. "Dad worked at home evenings and weekends hunt and pecking on an upright typewriter," recalled his son. "He'd create a rough draft and then have a secretary type a clean copy." Simmons-Boardman, an established New York City firm that specialized in railroad publications, including *Railway Age*, was

SUPER-RAILROADS

For a Dynamic American Economy

... "The consuming public, as well as the railroads, are direct beneficiaries of all measures calculated to promote near-capacity use of railroad plant ... The margin of profit will be increased by physical improvements that improve train and yard operation, and by a reduced ratio of investment per mile compared to revenue per mile— hence spreading the burden of all indirect expenses. In this way, growing density ... enables the railroads to provide the public with an enormous volume of transportation at a very moderate price. No other means of transportation can haul so much, so far, for such little expenditure of man-hours, of fuel, and of capital."

by John Walker Barriger

☆

SIMMONS-BOARDMAN PUBLISHING CORPORATION
NEW YORK

The cover of *Super-Railroads for a Dynamic American Economy*, published by Simmons-Boardman in New York City, lacks sexiness. Yet the promotional copy suggests its contents. (John W. Barriger III Collection, Barriger National Railroad Library at UMSL).

the publisher. The list price for this ninety-one-page book was a modest $2.00 or ten copies for $17.50. It featured a 8 × 10-inch double-column format but lacked illustrations of any kind, although there were five appendixes that included a plethora of industry and transportation statistics.

Later when Barriger served as president of the Missouri-Kansas-Texas (Katy) Railroad, the company reprinted the book. He then handed out copies to the interested.[27]

In a nontheoretical fashion John Barriger nimbly laid out his cause for super-railroads. He began with an explanation of what he called the "Railroad Problem." He believed that a pressing issue involved severe overregulation and the real threat of public ownership. Since subsidized model competition was becoming more intense, railroads required a freer hand in managing their affairs. If the Interstate Commerce Commission and state regulatory bodies provided a level playing field, this would permit carriers to accelerate their own physical betterments, thus providing benefits for customers and all Americans. There were other concerns, including the increasing costs of labor and materials, deferred maintenance, and insufficient earnings to finance modernization.

Barriger took time to explore the "Operating and Economic Characteristics of Railroads," creating an almost textbook-like approach to this complex topic. He stressed the point that much business left the rails because of service inadequacies that could have been minimized or perhaps avoided. He saw expanding plant capacity, provided that it was properly utilized by increasing traffic, as essential to successful railroad operations.

Super-Railroads does not overlook what Barriger considered "Accomplishments of Railroad Management." He contended that technological and managerial progress had occurred, especially during the post–World War II years, but at times it had been uneven. Dieselization, most of all, had been a revolutionary force, the greatest technological advance since the air brake. "The diesel locomotive made maximum-capacity motive power available for the first time to all lines having the capacity to utilize it. The transition from steam to diesel motive power is a remarkable achievement – one of the most brilliant and encouraging chapters in railroad history." Barriger also considered centralized traffic control (CTC) essential for high-speed operations on both single tracks and double-track heavy-density lines, and thought this technology should be expanded. He repeatedly emphasized that "a modern, efficient and economical plant – equivalent in technological standards to the diesel locomotive – must be constructed, wherever resources permit, so that the industry's full potential for efficient, high-speed mass transportation can be fully realized."[28]

If trunk roads enhanced their physical plants with lower grades, less curvature, and heavier rail, and modernized their motive power, rolling stock, communications, and terminal facilities, faster-moving and more dependable freight service would result. Traffic would increase, helped by recapturing shipments that motor carriers had been taking away since the 1920s. Corporate coffers would fill, and carriers would find it easier to finance capital expenditures that would make these super-railroads ever better.

With physical improvements realized, there would be real possibilities for improving passenger operations. While some railroad executives were giving up on the passenger train, Barriger thought that there was a potentially lucrative market for this service. "Seventy miles per hour overall passenger schedules, terminal to terminal, will be required to make train travel more attractive than motor travel." He added, "Such speeds will reduce travel time to the point where the travelers, when weighing other advantages of trains over airlines, will prefer to go by rail, except when the pressure of time is extreme or some other feature of air travel may have compelling attraction on particular trips, e.g., for particularly long distances." The results were clear: passenger sector revenues would increase because trains thus would have a larger share of the intercity movements of people, express, and mail. When it came to passenger train commentary (and elsewhere, too) Barriger placed old wine in a new bottle. In his 1947 "The Monon Is a Guinea Pig" article, he wrote, "Passenger traffic is a gold mine if speed is combined with low unit cost of operation."[29]

Barriger spent the majority of his time, thirty-four pages, dealing with his greatest love, "Requirements for a Modernized Railroad System." Since his college years and even before, he had found matters of technology fascinating. He insisted that investments in the best engineering practices and the smartest replacement technologies were critical for bolstering the industry. For one thing, Barriger cogently argued that the profile and alignment of most railroads in 1954 had not changed much during the previous forty years. "The real problem is that too small a part of total railway property is representative of the best, due primarily to lack of capital." And he made clear what he thought was the "best." Except in mountainous terrain, ideally trains should operate over a ruling grade of no more than 0.5 per cent and maximum curvature of 1 degree. When lines cross rugged territory, 300 miles of tunnels should be bored to reduce mountain barriers down to a maximum grade of just 1 percent.[30]

Additional technologies should be employed or developed, especially in communications. "The need is for equipment to transmit all printed, audible, and visual information used in railway operation, whether transmitted over wires or without them." A strong advocate of centralized traffic control (CTC), he hoped that this proven technology might be refined, seeing the possibility of it "freed from the use of wires, even to actuate switch and signal movements at distant points and to record train locations."[31]

Barriger endorsed other technological betterments, ranging from retarder-equipped hump yards to installation of continuously welded or "ribbon" rail. He seemed especially enthusiastic about main-line electrification. Barriger liked the potential cost savings and efficiencies that heavy traction offered. "The principal operating advantage of electrification lies in its capacity to provide the all-electric locomotive with the full quantities of power required to utilize the maximum capacity of traction motors for producing torque, or tractive effort, while running in the higher speed ranges." He thought that "the busiest 5–10 percent of the mileage of super-railroads (compared with but 1 percent of present railroads) will have the density necessary to support the fiscal burden of constructing and maintaining the power-transmission system." Yet he surely realized that the fundamental weakness is that the *entire* motive-power system, including locomotives, overhead catenary structures and wires, power supply, substations, and specialized shop facilities must all be installed at once. An expensive proposition, indeed. Barriger also believed that steam-turbine-electric locomotives could help to make super railroads a reality. He showed interest in the current work being done by the Norfolk & Western with its prototype Jawn Henry 4-8-0+4-8-0 coal-burning, steam-turbine-electric, one that promised impressive power and fuel economy. Creating super railroads would not come cheaply. He

John Barriger became that perpetual "evangelist" for his concept of super-railroads. On March 6, 1961, he stands by a special exhibit in Boston that indicates what Washington lawmakers must do to realize his goals of making railroads great again. (John W. Barriger III Collection, Barriger National Railroad Library at UMSL)

That same day he poses with Elizabeth and Herbert H. Harwood, executive
representative agent for the New York Central System, with the same sign. (John W.
Barriger IV Collection)

estimated that the "out-the-door" price tag to create the industry that he envisioned would reach $20 billion ($180 trillion in current dollars).[32]

In the closing paragraph of *Super-Railroads* the perennially hopeful Barriger summarized his hopes for the future of American railroading: "Imagination and determination – these are the qualities which, if exercised, will make the second century of railroading one of far greater accomplishment in public service than the first. No other means of transportation can haul so much, so far, for such little expenditure of man-hours, of fuel, and of capital; and, by so doing, confer benefits on so many people."[33]

The contemporary response to the Barriger book was favorable. *Railway Age* said, "Probably no other book, since L. F. Loree's 'Railroad Freight Transportation' appeared in 1922, has come along with so much professionally important information for all railroad men who have a serious interest in their work." It added, "All in all, John Barriger has provided a convenient body of information and inspiration, which, if widely read in the railroad industry, could easily banish all inclinations to defeatism and set the sights for the industry's progress upward and onward." The most glowing review, however, came from David P. Morgan, editor of *Trains*. "Of course, *Super-Railroads* is selling out. It is *the* book on the subject, a railroad library in one volume. It is theory, definition, practice, prescription, and prophecy." He was so bold as to call it "a bible for railroading." Morgan closed his extended commentary with these thoughts: "John Walker Barriger, then, has climbed the mountain and returned with the commandments, some of which we knew, all of which were never before so briefly yet fully and effectively placed in print. The prophet has done his job."[34]

With historical hindsight, it is apparent that Barriger had both good and not-so-good ideas. Moreover, no one, not even a leading railroad expert, has a crystal ball that is capable of predicting the future. Barriger rightly recognized the need for a better physical plant. Shadowing James J. Hill, the "Empire Builder," and others much later, he championed low grades, less curvature, and the like, making for more efficient and cost-effective railroads. Barriger understood the amazing impact of dieselization, although his notions of large-scale electrification had limits, mostly because of high costs and the non-interchangeability of locomotives with nonelectrified trackage. His faith in the future of coal-burning gas turbine engines went nowhere. Barriger did not foresee computers, jumbo hopper cars, or containerization. He also accepted the makeup and breakup of trains in the established fashion rather than the unit-train revolution (what Barriger later called "multiple cars") that began in the early 1960s with coal movements on the Southern and Baltimore & Ohio. Barriger seemed traditional about labor, hardly anticipating two- or possibly one-person freight train crews. Surely he was overly optimistic about the future of passenger trains. After all, the remaining passenger-carrying railroads (with three exceptions) happily shed themselves of their last "varnish" when in May 1971 the quasi-public National Railroad Passenger Corporation (Amtrak) began its modest operations. Admittedly, Amtrak eventually introduced its popular higher-speed, electric-powered Acela trains on the Northeast Corridor, convincing some experts that this might be the harbinger of a new rail-passenger era. But Barriger was right on with his insistence that Washington allow carriers greater freedom from out-of-date regulatory restraints. That would come about with passage of the Staggers Act in 1980 and the later dissolution of the Interstate Commerce Commission and its replacement with the less intrusive Surface Transportation Board. Yet for a person writing in the mid-1950s, Barriger made recommendations that were sensible; there was no lunatic-fringe thinking on his part.

John Barriger took satisfaction with the praise that he received for *Super-Railroads.* There was also that pleasure that he gained from putting into print his various notions about how the industry could be substantially strengthened. He repeatedly promoted his ideas long after the book appeared. As he told a luncheon meeting of the Railroad Community Committees of New England in March 1961, "The development of super-railroads is a subject dear to my heart," and then summarized the basic concepts. Yet Barriger took greater delight in finding an executive position with a company that had elements of the super-railroad that he relished. In August 1956 he left the Rock Island to become president of the Pittsburgh & Lake Erie Railroad, an affiliate of the New York Central System. Barriger would happily stay with the "Little Giant" until he was sixty-five years old, the mandatory retirement age for its executives.[35]

FIVE

Pittsburgh & Lake Erie

THE LITTLE GIANT

By the time John Barriger joined the Pittsburgh & Lake Erie Railroad (P&LE), this Pittsburgh, Pennsylvania–based company had long been the industry's "Little Giant." Since the road's founding by local interests in the mid-1870s and its official opening in 1879, it had developed impressive traffic volume and profitability.[1]

Unlike most trans-Chicago railroads, the P&LE did not take root in a frontier environment. Rather the road appeared in a long-settled and growing area on the western fringes of Appalachia. Initially this single-track, 65-mile line linked the thriving industrial city of Pittsburgh with Youngstown, Ohio, a developing steel center on the Mahoning River inland from Lake Erie. The route from Pittsburgh followed the Monongahela and Ohio Rivers northward to the mouth of the Beaver River where it crossed the free-flowing Ohio. Tracks then paralleled the Beaver and its Mahoning tributary to the Ohio border before reaching Youngstown. The P&LE possessed a mostly level right-of-way; no need for the company to attach a helper locomotive on a heavy freight drag to negotiate steep gradients.[2]

Ownership of the P&LE morphed rapidly from area-owned to Vanderbilt family control, allowing this wealthy New York City clan, headed by William H. Vanderbilt, to gain access to Pittsburgh, a traffic-rich market dominated by the Pennsylvania Railroad (PRR), its arch-rival. By 1889 Vanderbilt interests, through their Lake Shore & Michigan Southern affiliate, had acquired a majority of the P&LE's capital stock.

This financial relationship meant that its well-being was likely assured. As the twentieth century progressed, the New York Central (NYC), legacy of the Vanderbilts, took ownership. By the 1950s it possessed 52.6 percent of the outstanding capital stock. The Pittsburgh property additionally expanded its core route, including lease of the 58-mile Pittsburgh, McKeesport & Youghiogheny Railroad (Pittsburgh to Connellsville, Pennsylvania, and McKeesport to Brownsville, Pennsylvania) and joint interest with the PRR in the 70-mile Monongahela Railway (Brownsville to Fairmont, West Virginia). The P&LE also acquired a 50-percent position in the eight-mile Lake Erie & Eastern Railroad between the Ohio communities of Girard and Struthers in the north Youngstown area that offered both a connecting link to a newly opened direct NYC line to Cleveland and valuable industrial trackage. There were shared interests in several other rail properties. Over time the P&LE main line between Pittsburgh and Youngstown became a multitrack speedway, sporting heavy rail, knife-sharp ballast, and automatic block signals.[3]

While the steel industry became the bread and butter for the P&LE with shipments of coal, coke, limestone, ore, and metal products, the railroad also created a vibrant passenger business. The company dispatched commuter, local, and limited trains from its massive and architecturally striking Pittsburgh Terminal Building, located near the city center. This volume peaked in 1923 with 196 daily movements. During the passenger era the P&LE developed a longtime association with the Erie Railroad to provide first-class service between Cleveland and Pittsburgh though Youngstown. On the eve of World War II the P&LE and Erie joined the Baltimore & Ohio (B&O) to inaugurate the Washingtonian, a deluxe train that sped between Cleveland, Pittsburgh, and Washington, DC. This service was an outgrowth of an agreement signed in 1934 (extended for twenty-five years in 1937) that granted the B&O trackage rights over P&LE rails for its main-line passenger and freight trains between McKeesport and New Castle Junction, Pennsylvania, a distance of 58 miles. This gave the B&O the advantages of a water-level route rather than its own hilly, twisting, and roundabout line through greater Pittsburgh. As late as 1950 the Erie and P&LE introduced the Steel City Limited, designed to attract businessmen who sought a convenient, dependable, and comfortable way to travel between Cleveland and Pittsburgh. For much of the pre–World War II years passenger-train miles equaled or surpassed freight-train miles.[4]

When Barriger entered the executive suite in the Terminal Building in August 1956, the P&LE served a territory that had yet to gain "Rust Belt" status; this economic malaise developed a decade or so later. Total freight tonnage in 1956 stood at an impressive 33,400,909, somewhat down from the recent high of 39,256,609 set in 1951 during the Korean War traffic boom. Although passenger business declined rapidly after the early 1950s, the railroad in 1956 operated a score of passenger trains (excluding those that belonged to the B&O) over its Pittsburgh–Youngstown stem. As the years passed, this sector became less remunerative. By the mid-1950s the railroad's remaining mileage was for "freight service only"; the short-haul passenger market, except for commuters, had declined rapidly since World War II. Nevertheless, the 221-mile "Little Giant" remained the jewel in the crown of the NYC.[5]

PRESIDENT AGAIN

It would be Alfred (Al) E. Perlman, president and chief executive officer of the New York Central Railroad and chairman of the P&LE board, who hired John Barriger for the presidency. Recalls Barriger's son Jack, "Perlman enjoyed saying that he rescued Dad from the Rock Island." These men, both of whom adored railroads, developed a long-standing relationship. Each had graduated from the Massachusetts Institute of Technology (MIT), Barriger in 1921 and Perlman two years later, and that is where they first met. When Barriger headed the Railroad Division of the Reconstruction Finance Corporation (RFC), Perlman, who had gained railroad engineering and operating experience on the Northern Pacific, joined him as a special examiner for a year beginning in May 1935. Before his marriage in the late 1930s to Adele Emrich, Perlman accompanied the Barriger family when it vacationed at the Padlock Ranch in Wyoming, guests of Frederick Prince. While on the RFC payroll it would be Barriger who recommended to Chicago, Burlington & Quincy officials that Perlman take charge of a line reconstruction in Nebraska, Kansas, and Colorado following the devastating floods that had occurred largely along the Republican River in late May and early June

1935. Perlman excelled at this challenge. "When the line was rebuilt, it was raised above the flood plain of the Republican River and was decidedly stronger than the old line had been, and more secure against flood damage than ever before." The Republican River triumph led Perlman to engineering and managerial posts on the Denver & Rio Grande Western (D&RGW), becoming general manager in 1948 and president four years later. Under his leadership the letters D&RGW in the minds of its critics no longer stood for "*Dangerous & Rapidly Getting Worse*." When the flamboyant "populist of Wall Street" Robert R. Young won control of the NYC in 1954 after a bitter proxy battle, he turned to Perlman, whom he correctly recognized as an innovative and successful operating man, and made him president.[6]

Barriger and Perlman were cut largely from the same piece of cloth. Both of these highly intelligent railroaders embraced innovation, although Perlman showed greater imagination when it came to technical improvements. While at the D&RGW, for example, Perlman brought about a workable redesigned railhead and opened the first railroad testing laboratory. Both men as executives sought out bright individuals who excelled in marketing and operations. Barriger and Perlman also expressed enthusiasm for passenger trains, yet Perlman realized earlier than Barriger that the future of intercity service was diminishing if not doomed. Each shunned being the silent type, enjoying talking about the industry they loved. Both, too, had little or no use for lawyers, and they didn't think that the legally trained made good railroad executives. Jervis Langdon Jr., a lawyer and a highly innovative and successful president at the B&O and Rock Island, was not admired by either man.

As might be expected, there were differences between Barriger and Pearlman. The most noticeable was temperament. In his book *The Men who Loved Trains*, journalist Rush Loving Jr. describes Perlman as "a short, feisty man whose brilliance was matched by a devastatingly blunt tongue." That was hardly a description of Barriger. Even with his abrasive personality and occasional outbursts of temper, Perlman appeared to be more inspirational than Barriger. "Working for Perlman would be a special education in itself," observed Loving, "something like getting a doctorate in railroad management." Perlman had a strong love "for the almighty dollar. Dad didn't," reflected son Jack. Both men also tried not

Alfred (Al) Perlman, president of the New York Central System and backer of John Barriger as head of its prosperous Pittsburgh & Lake Erie Railroad affiliate, stands near a Howard Fogg watercolor of the Central's crack Twentieth Century Limited–Super Greyhound of the Rails–when the powerful 4-6-4 Hudson-type steam locomotive ruled. Little argument exists that this was America's most famous train. The *New York Evening World* once editorialized that its name was "so magnificent that it should never be printed save in capital letters, thus 'THE TWENTIETH CENTURY LIMITED.'" For many this train had become a "national institution." (John W. Barriger III Collection, Barriger National Railroad Library at UMSL)

to let their egos overrule their good judgement, although at times that was difficult for Perlman.[7]

John Barriger had no reservations about leaving the Chicago, Rock Island & Pacific (Rock Island) for the Pittsburgh & Lake Erie. "Dad liked working for a rich railroad. He said that this was the first railroad that I worked for that wasn't broke." Moreover, Barriger admired Al Perlman. "Dad was impressed with what he had done on the Rio Grande and what he was doing on the Central." Then there was a considerable salary boost. Initially Barriger received $45,000 annually ($405,000 in current dollars) and when he retired on December 31, 1964, his base salary stood at $50,000 ($392,000 in current dollars) plus bonuses and

In 1957 the internationally acclaimed photographer Louis Fabian Bachrach Jr., known professionally as Fabian, took this formal portrait of the mature railroad executive. (John W. Barriger IV Collection)

stock options that amounted to more than $10,000 in each of his last five years. There was more. Perlman allowed his old friend to have mostly free rein at the P&LE, but that was not the case with his relationships with vice presidents at the NYC. Of course, Perlman was not taking much of a risk; the P&LE had been and continued to be profitable. During the

A few years earlier Elizabeth arranged for her husband to be photographed by the more famous Yousuf Karsh of Ottawa, Ontario. "Dad was not particularly excited or honored but he liked the [Karsh] portrait," recalled son Jack. Presumably, Barriger also approved of Fabian's work. (John W. Barriger IV Collection)

post–World War II period the company usually paid dividends of about $8 annually on each share of common stock, although that dropped to an average of about $6 between 1957 and 1962, reflecting the impact of the serious recession of 1958–59. The P&LE was unquestionably the crown jewel of the NYC. The road became the freight car supplier for the larger system; it could get better credit terms than its parent. This resulted in the P&LE generating favorable car-hire balances and a high portion of its cars traveling offline.[8]

Barriger inherited a railroad that had been superbly managed. His immediate predecessor, John F. Nash, a career NYC system employee and also a lover of railroads, had done an excellent job as P&LE vice president (July 1952–December 1955) and as president. Nash left Pittsburgh for NYC headquarters in New York City to become vice president–operations, and later he served as NYC senior vice president. According to a P&LE colleague, "While eager to accept the challenge of this demanding position, [Nash] was reluctant to leave Pittsburgh where he felt comfortable and the P&LE which was running so well."[9]

It did not take long for John Barriger and his family to start a new life in Pittsburgh. Their house in Winnetka, Illinois, was sold, and a spacious one was bought at 213 Tennyson Avenue near the campus of the University of Pittsburgh. Edith (Didi) Barriger did not relocate, remaining in the Chicago area until her job at the Great Lakes military facility ended, and then she moved to an apartment on Delmar Avenue in St. Louis. Daughter Elizabeth (Betty) did join her parents and found a local grade-school teaching position. The other three children had left home: John W. Barriger IV (Jack) was working for the Santa Fe; Ann had graduated from Wellesley College and had married in 1955; and Stanley (Stan) was a student at MIT. With Pittsburgh being a relatively compact city, unlike Chicago, John Barriger did not face a lengthy commute to his office (and office car No. 99) in the P&LE's Pittsburgh Terminal complex or to the nearby Duquesne Club, site of his frequent business and social events, including his legendary breakfast gatherings.[10]

Barriger did not enter the presidency blindly. After arriving in Pittsburgh he examined the internal operations of the company, more deliberately than he had at the ramshackle Monon. To assist in his efforts Barriger brought in outside consultants, usually ones who had recently retired, and these trusted individuals explored specific aspects of the road. "He got his department heads to accept these men as helpers who would assist them in discovering and adopting the latest and best methods," recalled P&LE general counsel Harold McLean. "The consultants completed their assignments within the first year and Barriger had the

As a railroad executive John Barriger took great pains to make certain that shippers, politicians, railroaders, and others received the attention that he believed they deserved. While he was Pittsburgh & Lake Erie president, two trusted attendants, chef and steward, worked on office car No. 99 to create memorable breakfasts, luncheons, dinners, and receptions. (John W. Barriger III Collection, Barriger National Railroad Library at UMSL)

satisfaction of finding that he already had a good operation and that his department heads were adopting many of the suggestions made by the consultants. What had seemed like an inquisition to be feared turned out to be the helping hand he intended." Barriger demonstrated to one and all that he wanted to make the P&LE the best possible railroad, and he showed, too, his deep love for the business. Moreover, his work ethic demonstrated his commitment to the P&LE, admitting that he put in one hundred hours a week.[11]

When it came to the daily operations of the P&LE, Barriger benefited from the presence of Donald Fleming, an experienced, hands-on railroader. Since joining the New York Central System following his graduation from the University of Michigan in 1929, Fleming had held a variety of operating and supervisory positions, including trainmaster,

John Barriger knew how to entertain. While his breakfast gatherings became
legendary, he also hosted luncheons and dinners. With a larger discretionary
budget at the Pittsburgh & Lake Erie than he had at the Monon, he felt comfortable
entertaining large groups such as the Community Relations Committee of Pittsburgh
Railroads in the palatial P&LE station. And he never hesitated to say a word or two.
(John W. Barriger III Collection, Barriger National Railroad Library at UMSL)

assistant division superintendent, and division superintendent. In February 1954 he came to Pittsburgh as general superintendent of the P&LE,
and in August 1957 Barriger promoted him to general manager. "The
P&LE executives knew their business, and the railroad was not too complicated." And there was this comment attributed to Barriger: "Let the
operating people do their work." These factors permitted him to focus
on other matters.[12]

Paralleling his years at the Monon and Rock Island, Barriger turned
his attention to promoting the P&LE among customers, public officials,

For years John Barriger relied on Howard Fogg, a gifted commercial artist, to produce a variety of railroad and railroad-related scenes that were used for both corporate and personal use. The two men stand in front of works designed to promote the Pittsburgh & Lake Erie. (John W. Barriger III Collection, Barriger National Railroad Library at UMSL)

and the greater service area. "He viewed his primary role as that of
P&LE's chief salesman, not by assuming the functions of his chief traffic officer, Thomas Fitzpatrick, a good salesman himself, but rather as
promoter of the railroad in the eyes of its customers and the public at
large." Barriger admired Fitzpatrick and joked, "Tom did my drinking
and soaked up a great deal of Virginia Gentleman Bourbon during this
tenure on the P&LE." Even more so than during his first presidency,
Barriger spoke time-after-time to a mixed variety of groups. It might be
at a meeting of a chamber of commerce, an industrial organization, or a
traffic association. He might also host such gatherings. Not to be overlooked were those repeated formal and not-so-formal meals. "At the drop
of a hat [Barriger] gives breakfast, luncheon, and dinner parties at the
lordly Duquesne Club in Pittsburgh, at the Chicago Club, or wherever
a quorum of potential shippers can be found to drink the P&LE's Jack
Daniels and perhaps route their merchandise over its well-maintained
rights-of-way," observed raconteur, columnist, and railroad enthusiast
Lucius Beebe. "He himself doesn't tipple at all, but the best of everything
liquid flows in veritable Niagaras at the parties he gives to encourage
shippers and other useful characters to take an interest in his railroad."
And Barriger always enjoyed making his favorite public toast: "Let us
pour a wee libation upon the altar of friendship."[13]

Barriger never missed opportunities to escort shippers and others on
tours of the railroad. He would cover aspects of operations and service,
hoping to convince guests that the P&LE should be their railroad of
choice for freight routings, or at the least that it was a premier property.
"When John Barriger hosted a meeting of railroad people, it always involved an inspection trip," recalled a one-time participant. "When this
trip occurred, he lectured on the history of the P&LE, the steel industry and related subjects. It was absolutely fascinating." Barriger enjoyed
these talks and travel experiences, and he firmly believed in what he was
doing. As he frequently said, "The railroad industry is not very good at
selling its services," and he did what he could to change that situation.[14]

One creative way to remind shippers and others of the P&LE was
to use commissioned watercolor paintings of industrial and business
scenes together with railroad images. This art work came from the brush
of Howard Fogg, a talented commercial artist. A graduate of Dartmouth

College and the Art Institute of Chicago and a lifelong admirer of trains, Fogg became the official artist for the American Locomotive Company (Alco) following World War II. It was at an Alco-sponsored event at the Waldorf Astoria Hotel in New York City in 1946 that Barriger first made contact with this artist. "Dad loved the realism of a Fogg painting," remarked son Jack. Soon Fogg began to paint various images along the Monon, eventually numbering nearly a score. Barriger used them for promotional purposes, including calendars and postcards. When he joined the P&LE Fogg played an even more important role in this unusual advertising strategy. The original watercolors, which cost on average of about $500 each, would be given at some ceremony to the featured company. But before these paintings left Barriger's possession, they would be copied for advertising and promotional purposes, appearing mostly on booklets, calendars, and postcards. Fogg painted about fifty images for the railroad, including nearly a dozen of subjects other than the railroad, ones that depicted the principal industries that feed it traffic. After Barriger retired from the P&LE, this business relationship continued when he served as president of the Missouri-Kansas-Texas Railroad, as did their personal friendship.[15]

The image of a Fogg watercolor on a holiday card became another advertising ploy. Business associates received a Fogg-illustrated card and so did family members and close friends. Dating back to the Monon years, Barriger continually added to and updated his card lists. The widely held joke: "It's easy to get on John Barriger's Christmas card list, but it's hard to get off." While P&LE president, Barriger sent out annually 5,000 or more cards. Recipients often kept these cards with their handwritten messages; some even framed them.[16]

There was another way that Barriger sought to instill goodwill toward his railroad. He created a "Book-of-the Month" program. It was described in this way: "[It] involved sending books on railroads and related subjects to a special list of high traffic potential friends, not every month by any means but only when Barriger could find what he felt was a worthwhile book." Apparently the book project was popular and "some who would like to have had their names on the list never made it." The book giveaway reflected Barriger's own tastes. He was an avid reader, not of fiction but of nonfiction. Railroad and transportation titles were his first love, but he also enjoyed works on military history, particularly the Civil War and World War I. Barriger also consumed a range of newspapers and periodicals, but he largely ignored television, except to watch a special event or personage. While reading at home, he enjoyed listening to classical music, especially works by Johann Strauss.[17]

One memorable undertaking that Barriger instigated meshed well with his perceived duties as president: the commission of an exhaustive study of the economic potential of the P&LE service territory. In 1960 he engaged Arthur Longini, an experienced railroad economist, to prepare what became a skillfully researched publication, *Region of Opportunity: Industrial Potential along the Pittsburgh-Youngstown Axis*. Explained Barriger, "The [study] depicts the industrial resources and opportunities of a 77-county economic area converging upon Pittsburgh, Pennsylvania, and Youngstown, Ohio, the principal cities served by the Pittsburgh and Lake Erie Railroad." The purpose was to woo businesses to the area and ideally to trackside. "Let the P&LE be given the first opportunity if not preference, in the matter of plant site selection." This massive 1,450-page work provided P&LE representatives with what was in reality a valuable sales or marketing manual. Much later Henry Posner III, founder of the Pittsburgh-based Railroad Development Corporation that in the early 1990s attempted to acquire the P&LE, described this Barriger-inspired study as "extremely dry reading but [it] is one of the pioneering industrial development works for railways."[18]

This awareness and sensitivity to promotional and public relations opportunities produced a rather singular event on the New York Central System. Even though Al Perlman admired the intercity passenger train, he realized that at his financially troubled NYC the growing out-of-pocket losses from "varnish" operations meant mandatory service curtailments. Long-distance trains might well be slashed to one daily round trip between New York City and Chicago and also between New York and St. Louis. Perlman thought of having more shorter intrastate trains – Empire State Service – and they would save money by winning regulatory approval to eliminate the big losers. While Barriger endorsed the concept of Empire State Service, he saw value in retaining and maintaining the legendary flagship of the NYC passenger fleet, the once

It's a joyous time at the Duquesne Club in downtown Pittsburgh, and John Barriger reads from a book, likely the newly published *Twentieth Century Limited* by Lucius Beebe. Seated to Barriger's right are Beebe, whom he had long known, and Adele Perlman, wife of Al Perlman. (John W. Barriger III Collection, Barriger National Railroad Library at UMSL)

incomparable extra-fare, all-Pullman Twentieth Century Limited. In April 1958 the NYC had downgraded the Century, and its future was in doubt. It could no longer claim its previous deluxe status, having been downgraded to a standard coach-and-sleeper train. Barriger realized that on June 15, 1962, the nation's most famous name-train would celebrate its sixtieth anniversary, and he believed that it should be upgraded and celebrated. And upgraded it would be, thanks to Barriger convincing Perlman that this was the right thing to do. "There would be better cars, dining service and the like," and so for a brief period the Twentieth Century Limited regained much of its former glory.[19]

Barriger had always seen the marquee value of a first-class passenger train. Although he had been a "Pennsy man" and proud of that road's Broadway Limited that sped between New York City and Chicago, he

A triumph of the Barriger presidency at the Pittsburgh & Lake Erie was the opening
of Gateway Yard, located in East Youngstown, Ohio. This facility was a modern,
electronically operated hump classification facility, although today it no longer exists.
After CSX purchased what remained of the P&LE, it closed Gateway Yard in 1993. (John
W. Barriger III Collection, Barriger National Railroad Library at UMSL)

expressed a fondness for the Twentieth Century Limited. In a 1926 report
for the Pennsylvania Railroad, Barriger revealed his feelings. "Unquestionably *The Twentieth Century Limited* is the finest name that can possible be coined for a train and its natural appeal has been so magnified
and exploited that the train which bears it has a remarkable powerful
hold on the public imagination. Passengers almost feel that their own
personal prestige is enhanced by using that train and that the extra fare is
a social investment as well as a purchase of travel comforts and service."
In his mind, the tradition should continue as long as possible. This con-
viction led Lucius Beebe to write a book-length history of the Twentieth
Century Limited, which he dedicated to Barriger.[20]

Although the largely freight-hauling P&LE already featured elements of a super railroad – easy grades, heavy rail, centralized traffic

control (CTC), and good rolling stock – it was not without need for regular upgrading. Barriger sought betterments, and he usually had the resources to make them. On May 1, 1958, a major achievement took place when the railroad opened a state-of-the-art electronically operated hump classification facility at East Youngstown, Ohio, named Gateway Yard. It was precisely what the P&LE needed. The complex could classify 3,000 freight cars daily, and it took the place of five separate flat-switching facilities. Gateway Yard reduced the time required for cars to pass through the terminal by approximately 40 percent and generated significant savings in operating costs. Four years later the classification yard at McKees Rocks, Pennsylvania, was completely rebuilt, resulting again in better service and enhanced savings.[21]

Other ways to make the P&LE more efficient and profitable were not overlooked. By the early 1960s upgraded communications, including walkie-talkies and CTC, were added, improved, or expanded. By this time, mechanization of maintenance-of-way operations had been greatly advanced. A comprehensive main-line rail replacement program was also ongoing, and 131- or 132-pound steel, continuously welded, served the busiest sections. Upgrading of motive power and rolling stock continued. In the early 1950s the "Age of Steam" had largely passed, and by 1958 all steamers, having been stored for emergency use, had left the property. Approximately 150 mostly first-generation diesel-electric locomotives provided dependable service. Freight cars were repeatedly rebuilt at the McKees Rocks shops or replaced, essential for online customers and also an important source of income from per-diem payments when in interline movements. Significantly, the number of full-time employees dropped: 5,259 in 1956 but only 3,162 in 1962, money-saving reductions that were continual.[22]

Always an advocate of the best possible service, Barriger took delight in a new technology that he believed enhanced customer satisfaction, namely adoption of the New York Central's coordinated road-rail Flexi-Van service. "Highway trailers minus the wheels ride on special flatcars." On April 16, 1958, less than a year after the NYC introduced this imaginative intermodal option, Flexi-Vans appeared on the P&LE main line between Pittsburgh and Youngstown. Noted Barriger, "Flexi-Van gives

Being a man who loved railroads, John Barriger enjoyed inspecting rail properties. As Pittsburgh & Lake Erie president, he spent considerable time in office car No. 99, taking advantage of his ringside viewing seat. (John W. Barriger III Collection, Barriger National Railroad Library at UMSL)

the shopper the advantages of door-to-door pick-up and delivery service plus fast, dependable rail transportation and a minimum of loading and unloading." He happily embraced the gestating intermodal revolution.[23]

Physical improvements were no exception to Barriger's concern about details. As would be expected of a cracker-jack salesman, Barriger wanted to make certain that online businesses benefited from P&LE's capital expenditures. Minutes of a Barriger staff meeting capture this commitment: "Mr. Barriger said all concerned should make certain that steel for our new freight cars is from Pittsburgh-Youngstown district steel

John Barriger, the action railroader, takes a swing at a track spike on the P&LE's rehabilitated Monongahela River bridge with ample onlookers, including his personal chauffeur. That day Barriger could truly say that he'd been workin' on the railroad. (John W. Barriger III Collection, Barriger National Railroad Library at UMSL)

mills. He charged Mssrs. Le Suer and [W. F.] Kascal [chief mechanical officer] to make sure this is the case. If they have any trouble in this regard, they are to notify Mr. Barriger immediately so he can see what he can do."[24]

Barriger kept an eagle eye on the property. It would usually be on weekends that he made his inspections. This might involve riding a scheduled train or a hi-rail vehicle or being driven by automobile to the desired locations. He made known his comments to the appropriate personnel. In the transcript of one staff meeting, the secretary noted that "Mr. Barriger stated that in riding over the railroad recently, he noticed a lot of the usual debris that accumulates around a railroad" and that there needed to be the "usual housekeeping." Barriger was no armchair executive.[25]

John Barriger continued to have a good working relationship with Al Perlman. While there were those executives throughout the NYC system who lived in mortal fear of Perlman or were at least cautious of perhaps offending him, Barriger spoke his mind. Harold McLean recalled a budget meeting, chaired by Perlman, where Barriger defended a proposal to spend $25,000 for fencing the perimeter of the McKees Rocks shops but "was having difficulty showing a rate of return." The P&LE board chairman intervened. "'John, why not put up half the fence this year and the other half next year?' Barriger replied, 'Mr. Perlman, half a fence is about as much use as half a bridge,' which got a laugh from everybody, including Perlman." Commented McLean, "Nobody else would have had the temerity to make such a retort." The following year the fence was installed, and it cost only $13,000.[26]

As president Barriger worried about the revision of the trackage-rights agreement with the Baltimore & Ohio for its use of the P&LE between McKeesport and New Castle, a twenty-five-year arrangement that was due to expire in 1963. "This is a very complex and important immediate issue confronting the P&LE," Barriger told Jack Bader, assistant vice president of the NYC system, "and I have a considerable part to play in the preparation and presentation of our case [before the ICC]." Under the existing document, the B&O compensated the P&LE on a train-mile basis, but over time the B&O had significantly lengthened the size of its trains without increasing its compensation to the P&LE. "In order to obtain an increase," explained Harold McLean, "the P&LE was obliged to give the requisite one-year notice of cancellation and seek an order from the ICC requiring either to discontinue the operation or pay more rent." After considerable maneuverings, negotiations, and hard work Barriger, took satisfaction in an agreement that provided substantially increased payments from the B&O. The new yardstick for compensation would be based on the number of cars rather than the number of trains that ran over this strategic trackage, and minimum usage of the line by the B&O was also established. Perlman and his fellow officers, too, were pleased with how Barriger handled in a confidential and professional manner this tricky and financially important matter. There is no question that Barriger effectively followed their wishes "to keep the pressure upon the B&O, and not to yield."[27]

INDUSTRY MAN

With a well-functioning, money-making railroad, John Barriger could devote more time to speaking locally and nationwide about industry topics. When at his office or in his home study, he wrote a prodigious number of these presentations. Annually they totaled more than when he worked for either the Monon or Rock Island. Unlike some industry spokesmen who lectured extensively, Barriger usually prepared his remarks from scratch and tailored them to his intended audience. In one remarkable example of his dedication to speech writing, he prepared a presentation while attending a World Series baseball game with his son Jack. The range of topics was impressive. While at the P&LE Barriger spoke to the conference of the Southern Research Institute on "The Prospects for Railway Electrification"; National Defense Transportation Association on "Railroad Capacity for National Defense"; National Motor Freight Traffic Association on "An Interpretation of the Railroads' 'Magna Carta' in Transportation"; Syracuse Transportation Conference on "Where Do We Go from Here?"; and the Transportation Management Institute at Stanford University on "Why Consolidation." There were scores more, including less formal presentations to rail enthusiast groups. Barriger even gave a talk on "Civil War Railroads" at the University of Southern California for Jack's wife, Evie, who was teaching there. Not to be overlooked were Barriger's testimonies on varied subjects before regulatory bodies, most of all at the ICC.[28]

A recurring theme in Barriger's speeches involved his decades-long passion for railroad consolidations. In July 1963 he spoke to the Jonathan Breakfast Club in Los Angeles, California, on "The Urge to Merge." By this time, merger activities were accelerating. Such corporate marriages as the Erie with the Delaware, Lackawanna & Western and Chicago & North Western with the Minneapolis & St. Louis had already occurred. Barriger heartily approved. And he looked forward to the real possibility of a unification between the New York Central and Pennsylvania. "It will be found that the railroad with the best route characteristics frequently does not have the heaviest traffic. Consolidation will concentrate tonnage on the route having the best physical characteristics and make them available without capital expenditures. This is particularly applicable in the PRR-NYC consolidation. The PRR has the heavier traffic density but the NYC has better route characteristics. The merger will make the superior grades and curves of New York Central routes available for PRR traffic without capital cost." Asked Barriger, "What could be more in the public interest?"[29]

The P&LE president also participated in a well-attended public debate. This memorable event took place two days after Christmas 1962 in Pittsburgh at a meeting of the American Transportation Research Forum held in conjunction with the annual convention of the American Economic Association. Barriger met head-to-head with Leon Keyserling, a Columbia- and Harvard-educated economist and lawyer who had been a staunch New Dealer and Fair Dealer. As for the latter, he had chaired the Council of Economic Advisers in the Harry Truman administration between 1949 and 1953. Although Keyserling was no firebrand "leftie," he was an outspoken liberal and the intellectual nemesis of the conservative Barriger.

The subject of the Barriger-Keyserling debate: "The Effect of Mergers on Competition." Hardly a surprise to anyone in the audience was that Barriger favored corporate consolidations; Keyserling did not. Barriger made clear their core disagreements. "Dr. Keyserling will assert that the railroads are actually in satisfactory financial condition, although some details of their services and the record low level of their employment disturb him. The railroads' present difficulties, he implies, are readily correctable if these stubborn and on the whole prosperous companies would only run more trains, buy more equipment and spend more money on maintenance." He revealed that liberal-conservative split: "Deficit spending is his panacea for private as well as public problems." Barriger closed with this heartfelt observation: "The simplicity of consolidated operations is far more conducive to efficient service than the imaginary virtues of small size."[30]

The increasing public exposure to John Barriger made him known not only to those individuals whose work had a direct or indirection connection with the industry but also to railroad "wannabees." During his tenure at the P&LE Barriger graciously responded to those young men who either wished to join his railroad or wanted his guidance about a possible railroad career.

The encounter between Edward (Ed) A. Burkhardt and Barriger reveals how the senior railroad executive handled a job applicant. At an early age Burkhardt, son of a New York City physician, fell in love with trains. While in high school he landed seasonal jobs on a Great Northern track gang, and in subsequent summers took employment with the Santa Fe and Rock Island. These work experiences, however, did not prevent a collegiate education. Burkhardt enrolled at Yale University, and in 1960 he received a bachelor of science degree in industrial engineering. As a Yale student he took course work from the popular and widely respected Kent T. Healy, professor of transportation, and Healy knew Barriger. During Burkhardt's senior year, "Professor Healy called around about a job for me," and this led to interview with Barriger. "And I got free [rail] transportation to Pittsburgh," happily recalled Burkhardt. At their morning meeting in the P&LE offices Barriger surprised him with a quiz. "One question involved leaders of American railroads, including who's the president of the Seaboard." Burkhardt believed that he did reasonably well with his responses. "Barriger wanted to learn if I was really interested and knowledgeable about the rail industry." The interview also included a "rather lengthy" tour of Barriger's personal (and always growing) railroad library. When Barriger finished his part of the interview, he turned the process over to other officials. It was during this time that P&LE personnel warned Burkhardt that the all-powerful NYC controlled the railroad; their somewhat negative comments about this corporate relationship dampened Burkhardt's enthusiasm for Barriger's road. Burkhardt did become a railroader, initially with the Wabash and later with the Chicago & North Western, where in time he became vice president, transportation. Rather than remaining a "North Western man," he sought his own railroad, and in 1987 he led a group of investors that purchased the Lake States Transportation Company, a subsidiary of the Soo Line, resulting in the successful 2,000-mile Wisconsin Central Ltd. After his career with Wisconsin Central Burkhardt launched Rail World Inc., a Chicago-based firm that invested in various non-American rail properties.[31]

William (Bill) J. McKnight was another college student who was attracted to John Barriger. In August 1961 this Rochester, New York, resident, a student at the Wharton School of the University of Pennsylvania, wrote Barriger to inquire about opportunities in railroading. To his pleasant surprise he received a long, thoughtful, and personalized reply. The substance of the advice: "The answer to your question relating to the career opportunities for young men who will enter the railroad industry over the next few years depends upon whether or not the railroads will be permitted to survive as private enterprises." Explained Barriger, "Unfortunately, this is a political rather than an economic, technological or commercial question. If the future status of the railroads could be determined by their capabilities in these three latter fields, I would have no hesitancy in giving you an enthusiastically affirmative reply. However, I hesitate to venture any predictions respecting ones so completely interlaced with politics as are the reforms of national transportation policy that will be necessary to permit the railroads to have opportunity for competitive equality."[32]

McKnight took the Barriger advice to heart. After receiving his MBA degree from Wharton in spring 1963 with a concentration in transportation and public utilities, he accepted an offer from the Ford Motor Company in its transportation and traffic office. "Fourteen years later I jumped to GTWRR [Grand Trunk Western Railroad]," noted McKnight, "and finally went railroading." His position at the Grand Trunk Western: director of automotive marketing. Barriger would have been pleased.[33]

In a somewhat different scenario, William (Bill) F. Howes Jr., an avid railfan and a young man who longed to work for a railroad, was well aware of the professional stature of John Barriger. While a graduate student at Purdue University in 1962 working on his master of science degree in chemical engineering, he wrote "New England Railroads: A Plan for Their Survival." This study of contemporary railroad problems in New England had been "prompted by my experience working for the New Haven in 1960 and 1961 as it slid into bankruptcy." Proud of his work, Howes sent off copies to several dozen railroad presidents, and he got either no responses or only polite replies, "but not much encouragement." However, there was one exception – John Barriger. The P&LE president not only thanked him for sending the study, but he had read it and "offered some thought-provoking critiques." Further, recalled Howes, "Several days later I was surprised when I got another letter from

Mr. Barriger stating that he had reread the report and he made some additional comments." Still later Howes received a postcard from Barriger that invited him to have breakfast in his office car. "Exhilarated though I was at that prospect, I panicked! I was petrified and I never did go. And what an experience I missed." Eventually that feeling of being overawed by a famous railroad executive faded away. At a professional meeting of the American Association of Railroad Superintendents Howes, who had become an officer at the Baltimore & Ohio, explained to Barriger why he had declined that breakfast invitation. After that personal exchange "I received a copy of every speech that Mr. Barriger gave, and I got onto his famous Christmas card list."[34]

DEPARTURE

This second railroad presidency of John Barriger could be termed an unqualified success. When he retired from the P&LE on December 31, 1964, he left behind a solid property that effectively served the needs of its customers and provided essential income for its New York Central parent. Barriger, too, was pleased that his replacement would likely replicate the same results. In a seamless transition Curtis D. Buford took the throttle, first as executive vice president between September and December 1964 and then as president beginning January 1, 1965. The son of a former president of the Milwaukee Road and a 1942 graduate of MIT, Buford had risen up through the managerial ranks of the New York Central. But in August 1959 he left the NYC to join the Association of American Railroads as vice president, operations and maintenance, a position that "gave a window to the entire world of railroading." This was exactly the type of railroad executive who appealed to Barriger.[35]

Forced retirement because of age was bittersweet for Barriger. "There had been happy years for dad," related Jack. "Perhaps this was the happiest part of his life. Dad did not want to step down as president, but he had no choice in the matter." Fortunately for Barriger his railroad career continued, offering a variety of new opportunities and challenges, including two more presidencies.[36]

SIX

Missouri-Kansas-Texas

OFF TO THE KATY

During a dual retirement and sixty-fifth birthday party held on December 3, 1964, at the ritzy Duquesne Club in downtown Pittsburgh, John Barriger announced his plans to return to his boyhood hometown of St. Louis, Missouri. Yet he made it clear to everyone assembled that he was not about to retire. "You [guests] have been swindled if you think I am going to retire. It is my intention to start looking for a new job tomorrow morning." As he liked to say, "I've been fired for old age," a reference to the inflexible personnel regulations of the New York Central System (NYC). In the same fashion, Barriger indicated to the press that "the cemetery is the only place where I can be happy in retirement." Barriger was not about to accept retirement gracefully.[1]

An official retirement ceremony usually comes with one or more gifts. When Barriger left the Pittsburgh & Lake Erie (P&LE), this long-standing tradition was embraced. Lucius Beebe presented him with a much-treasured Howard Fogg painting, "Thoroughbred at Work," depicting the all-Pullman Broadway Limited of the Pennsylvania Railroad being pulled by a K4-class steam locomotive (Barriger's favorite) and traveling through the Appalachian Mountains during daylight hours. Then there was a more substantial one. NYC president Alfred (Al) Perlman asked Elizabeth Barriger what her husband would like for his retirement gift. Always quick on the uptake she knew exactly what to request. Recently the family had purchased a large three-story house at 15 Washington Terrace, located on a gated street of forty-eight grand late nineteenth-century homes in the Central West End of St. Louis. Elizabeth suggested that Perlman arrange and pay for the moving. He agreed. This would be no small, inexpensive undertaking, requiring four truck vans to transport the household goods but mostly Barriger's massive library. The weight of the latter meant that the ballroom on the top floor of the St. Louis home had to be strengthened with steel beams.[2]

Where would the "retired" Barriger find employment? When past positions ended, he tapped his extensive industry-wide network of contacts, and again he repeated this tactic. Barriger landed a job, likely temporary, before he left Pittsburgh. His friend Louis (Lou) W. Menk, the young, talented, and hard-driving president of the St. Louis–San Francisco Railroad (Frisco), soon to lead the Chicago, Burlington & Quincy Railroad, hired him as a special consultant. On January 4, 1965, Barriger arrived at corporate headquarters in the Frisco Building in downtown St. Louis. His assignments: marketing and statistical projects.[3]

But Barriger remained at the Frisco for only eleven weeks; he soon found his third railroad presidency and his first board chairmanship. After having accepted an offer from representatives of National Industries, who controlled the Missouri-Kansas-Texas Railroad (Katy), Barriger began on March 11, 1965, his five-year stint with the company.[4] Initially Barriger's salary was fixed at $50,000 ($381,00 in current dollars) annually; later it exceeded $60,000 ($457,000 in current dollars). Also after creation of Katy Industries Inc., he acquired more than 17,000 shares of its common stock. His appointment to head this 3,017-mile, seemingly doomed, St. Louis and Dallas, Texas–based road would be no caretaker position. Unlike the P&LE, the Katy was the antithesis of a "super-railroad"; it resembled, in Barriger's words, a "transportation slum." Yet as seen with his career at the Monon, he liked challenges; this would be the ideal job for an executive later called by some in the industry the "Doctor of Sick Railroads."[5]

KATY'S TORTURED PAST

The Missouri, Kansas & Texas Railway (MK&T), later the Missouri-Kansas-Texas Railroad, claimed a fascinating history. In 1869 the original unit won incorporation as the Union Pacific Railway Company,

Southern Branch to build from Junction City, Kansas, on what became
the main line of the Kansas Pacific Railroad (later acquired by the Union
Pacific), to the border of Indian Territory (today's Oklahoma), a distance
of 180 miles. Yet it took five years before that destination was reached,
and when accomplished, the corporate name was altered to the more
appropriate MK&T. During the next two years construction crews
marched southward across Indian Territory, and on Christmas Day 1872,
the first train chugged across the newly completed bridge over the Red
River into Texas. The terminus became Denison, a nearby community
destined to play an important role in company history. With arrival of
connecting carriers in the region, the MK&T made possible an all-rail
route into the Lone Star State from the north and east.[6]

The Katy was the quintessential frontier railroad: it was built largely
through unsettled country; it was cheaply constructed; it owned inadequate rolling stock; and it was overcapitalized. Although the company
was promised a 3.11-million-acre federal land grant in Indian Territory,
legal and political issues prevented it from receiving this potentially lucrative award. The company got only a 200-foot-wide right-of-way strip
along with land needed for stations, shops, and yards. Moreover, this
financially weak road faced a series of hard times and reorganizations.
Resembling some other Class I carriers, including the Erie and Rock
Island, it went through the bankruptcy wringer on multiple occasions,
1875–76, 1888–91, and 1915–23.[7]

When the Katy emerged from its first receivership, Jay Gould, the
legendary "robber baron" of the Gilded Age, took control. Then in 1880,
the road was leased to his Missouri Pacific Railroad. While within the
Gould orbit, the Katy expanded. This trackage was designed largely to
connect with other components of the growing Gould system. This resulted in a link to Fort Worth and a much longer one that gave access
to San Antonio. That integrated construction also led to rails reaching
the Missouri towns of Moberly and Hannibal. The dissolution of the
Gould relationship in 1888 prompted the MK&T to build its own lines
(or to secure trackage rights) into Kansas City, St. Louis, San Antonio,
and Houston.

After its second period of court protection a revived Katy embarked
on another wave of expansion. The formative years of the twentieth

century produced a building boom throughout the company's service territory, but most of all on the southern Great Plains. The company expanded considerably through control of two long feeder lines, one built by the Texas Central Railroad between Waco and Rotan, Texas, and the other the legacy of the Wichita Falls & Northwestern Railway that linked Henrietta and Wichita Falls, Texas, with Forgan, Oklahoma. Additional construction and purchases also occurred.

During the 1910s and 1920s, what officially became the Missouri, Kansas & Texas Railway and its companion Missouri, Kansas & Texas Railway of Texas developed into a modern railroad. Much of this progress occurred under the direction of Charles Schaff, president or receiver between 1912 and 1926. He oversaw the rebuilding of tracks and construction of a number of attractive depots, along with shops and engine houses of improved designs. And primary lines were equipped with automatic block signals. Rolling stock, including locomotives, also received upgrades. Most of these betterments took place during that third receivership. The casual observer, however, likely did not see a problem created during Schaff's tenure, namely top-heavy capitalization. "Possibly as a consequence of its rehabilitation, instead of being thoroughly reorganized financially, as it was physically, the railroad emerged from receivership in 1923 with a debt of $165,000,000 – extremely heavy for a railroad whose gross revenues were but $55,000,000," related Barriger. "The MK&T capital structure, designed in 1922, probably evidenced the optimism with which the financial world regarded the southwestern railroads at that time. This area was flourishing under the double impetus of a boom in petroleum production superimposed upon the general post–World War I prosperity."[8]

The mid-1920s became a turning point for the Katy. Schaff, the modernizer, retired, and his capable successor, Charles Whitehead, died only a few months after his former boss's departure. The next Katy chief executive, Columbus Haile, was "a rather ordinary man"; the momentum provided by Schaff and Whitehead vanished.[9]

As the executive suite seemed to have a revolving door, there continued to be hope that the Katy could become a stronger road. This involved corporate consolidations, what became an obsession with John Barriger. Leonor Loree, the flamboyant and innovative president of the

Delaware & Hudson and board chairman of the Kansas City Southern (KCS), proposed unification of the KCS, Katy, and St. Louis Southwestern (Cotton Belt). He (and others too) believed that if consummated, this well-connected southwestern system would ultimately be acquired by the Southern Pacific, a fate that later befell the Cotton Belt. Loree forged ahead. The KCS acquired substantial stock holdings in the Katy and Cotton Belt, and the KCS interests in the Cotton Belt were sold to the Katy. In July 1926 Loree became Katy chair. The Interstate Commerce Commission (ICC), however, rejected a KCS-Katy-Cotton Belt merger, branding it as "not in the public interest." Although Loree did not immediately give up, the scheme went nowhere "much to the subsequent detriment of the MKT." In 1928 he left the board.[10]

Optimism for creating a vibrant Katy faded. After Leonor Loree resigned, a succession of managerial changes followed. The next board chair was Michael Cahill, formerly operating vice president at the Seaboard Air Line. In 1930 after serving four years as Katy president, Columbus Haile retired, whereupon Cahill became president as well as chair. The quality of Katy leadership left much to be desired, largely because of its inability to respond effectively to a host of financial woes and its determination to slash expenditures for essential betterments. The Cahill regime ended in 1934, and Matthew Sloan, former president of Brooklyn Edison Company, took charge. Keeping the railroad out of the hands of a federal court became Sloan's principal goal, and it proved to be a daunting challenge. Not only had the Great Depression descended upon "Katyland," but these were the "dirty '30s," the time of infamous Dust Bowl. Yet Katy survived while its main competitors – Cotton Belt, Frisco, Missouri Pacific, and Rock Island – went bankrupt. It would be the Railroad Division of the Reconstruction Finance Corporation (RFC) that saved Katy. Two loans, the first in 1935 and another one three years later, kept the company afloat. But Barriger, who then headed the RFC's Railroad Division, did not support these cash infusions. "Initially [I] recommended to RFC's chairman, the Honorable Jesse Jones, that these loans to MKT not be made," he recalled. "My reason for doing so was a belief that it would be to M-K-T's ultimate best interest to give up the financial struggle to avoid recapitalization through deferring maintenance and development." Continued Barriger, "I believed that the means taken to avoid reorganization would place it under a serious competitive handicap against its stronger neighbors in future years, which proved to be a correct forecast."[11]

As with virtually every American railroad, the period of World War II, 1939–45, produced a flood tide of freight tonnage. The Katy was no exception. Vast quantities of cotton, grain, livestock, lumber, petroleum, and other products moved over its rails. Moreover, the government selected several online sites as locations for ammunition plants and other war-related industries. Management unfortunately continued to skimp on improvements to the physical plant both before and after Pearl Harbor. "The Katy's preference for maximizing debt retirement rather than upgrading maintenance led it to plan its maintenance expenditures so as to minimize capital expenditures," explained Barriger. "Consequently, year after year, the Katy made less progress in respect to maintenance and development than its competitors achieved."[12] The Matthew Sloan presidency brought about a relatively stable management for more than a decade. In 1945, however, Edward Claughton, a large investor in Katy common stock, spearheaded a successful proxy contest against Sloan. With victory came the appointment to the board chair of Raymond Morfa, a businessman associated with the Alleghany Corporation led by Wall Street financier Robert Young. Morfa, though, did not assume the Katy presidency; Donald Fraser, a company veteran, took that post. Under the new regime the railroad limped along, failing to adequately maintain either physical plant or equipment.[13]

A decade after the Claughton takeover another ownership change occurred. Robert Thomas, an official in the Pennroad Corporation (subsequently the Madison Funds), led a syndicate comprised of Pennroad, Bear Stearns & Company, and State Street Investment Company that acquired the Katy holdings from the estate of the late Edward Claughton, giving it ownership of about two-thirds of the outstanding common stock. That year Thomas joined the Katy board and took control of its finance committee. About this time Fraser became seriously ill, and so his replacement was sought. Thomas served as the interim de facto president.[14]

In January 1957 a tough operating leader came to Katy. William (Bill) Neal Deramus III assumed the presidency and emerged as its most

controversial executive. Deramus was the son of veteran railroader William N. Deramus Jr., who in 1945 became president of the Kansas City
Southern (KCS) and its Louisiana & Arkansas affiliate. Unlike his father,
Bill Deramus received an excellent education, graduating from the University of Michigan and the Harvard Law School. Rather than pursuing a
legal career, he went to work for the Wabash in 1939 as an assistant trainmaster and later became assistant to the general manager of the KCS.
In 1948 Deramus joined a Kansas City investor group, which included
his father, that took control of the struggling 1,500-mile Chicago Great
Western Railway (CGW). A syndicate member, Grant Stauffer, became
president, and Deramus at age thirty-three served as his principal assistant. Stauffer soon died, and Deramus took his place.[15]

The nine years Bill Deramus spent at the Chicago Great Western
became a rehearsal for his much shorter stay at Katy. The CGW gained
financial strength, benefiting from physical improvements, dieselization, passenger-train cutbacks, abandonment of low-density lines, and
a restructured freight service. Following his father's lead on the KCS,
Deramus orchestrated administrative centralization; state-of-the art
technology, including two-way radios, teletypes, IBM data-processing
machines; and industrial park development. During his tenure he took
a bitter strike by operating personnel that shut down the railroad for six
weeks, and he also became famous for his abrasive personality, excessive
profanity, and snap decisions. "Young Bill was not diplomatic," recalled
a financial adviser, "and he lacked the charm of his father."[16]

At Katy Bill Deramus sought to upgrade and modernize the property. As he told *Railway Age*, his sole objective was "to get this railroad
back on a sound economic footing as soon as possible." Deramus got off
to a good start. "[He] began to attack the road's maintenance deficiencies
vigorously as evidenced by tie insertions reported for 1957, by diesel locomotives repaired and rebuilt, and by other physical measures, and also
plans for a modern yard at Denison." The Deramus regime also equipped
locomotives, cabooses, and supervisors' automobiles with radio communications and installed teletype machines throughout the system.
Unfortunately for the Deramus administration, a recession soon hit the
country, ending the so-called "Eisenhower prosperity" and causing on

the Katy a sharp drop in freight revenues. Results were predicable: the Katy cut back, curtailing its maintenance programs much more than it had during previous economic downswings. The company also shelved plans for that upgraded yard facility in Denison and similar improvements at Parsons, Kansas, and Waco, Texas.[17]

Reductions in maintaining and improving the railroad were reasonable responses to growing hard times, but Deramus took some draconian steps. Employment was slashed to the bone. On the eve of his arrival, the railroad employed about 8,000 workers, but by 1960 the number had dropped to only 2,817. The Deramus philosophy: "Cut all personnel to the lowest possible number that will still permit daily conduct of business." All "frills" ended, including the discontinuation of the Katy's monthly employee magazine and abolishment of its public relations department. Although these actions received local press coverage, one gained national attention. In March 1957, without notice to Katy employees, Deramus ordered the closing of offices in St. Louis and Parsons. Under the cover of darkness, records and equipment were placed in moving vans and hauled off to Texas. As Deramus explained tersely in a public statement, the relocations to Denison were due to "the immediate need for economy and increased efficiency of operation." Said *Railway Age*, "Like a corporate Arab, the Missouri-Kansas-Texas seems to pack its furniture and records and silently steal away." Those employees who had enough seniority to hold their jobs had only a few days to relocate to either Dallas or Denison. Needless to say, office morale plummeted. One notable public response: the St. Louis Chamber of Commerce expelled the Katy from its membership; its executive committee unanimously made this unprecedented decision.[18]

In 1961 Bill Deramus resigned to succeed his father as Kansas City Southern president. The Katy board selected as his successor Charles Williams, vice president of operations. Since financial conditions had reached "panic" conditions, he intensified the program of curtailment of maintenance and service. As for the latter, the company reduced operations to one daily freight train to and from St. Louis and established a similar schedule in and out of Kansas City. Switching was also drastically curtailed, and train movements were cut to a weekly basis on its

Northwestern District and tri-weekly between Denison and Wichita Falls. Then late in 1964 freight trains on the Parsons to Oklahoma City line ran only triweekly. "Williams hacked and chopped instead of pruned until the Railroad was brought to the very brink of physical, financial and service collapse," explained Barriger. "The basic elements of the business had all but been liquidated and its bankruptcy was expected by the end of 1964." Too much red ink flowed across company books.[19]

BARRIGER TO THE RESCUE

John Barriger realized that the Missouri-Kansas-Texas Railroad was in dire straits. He knew he must act quickly in order to prevent bankruptcy and possible liquidation. "At that time [1965] I found that the Railroad's current carloadings were running more than 10% below the corresponding period of the previous year. Unless this traffic hemorrhage could be quickly staunched, 1965 gross would fall below $45 million thus making liquidation inevitable." He opined further: "I do not believe it is an exaggeration to state that at that time the Katy was on the brink of physical dissolution, following the dismal precedents of the Fort Smith & Western, New York, Ontario & Western, and the Rutland railroads." The Katy would become the Herculean challenge of Barriger's career, but he was up to the task. This sixty-five-year-old accomplished executive possessed the necessary drive, enthusiasm, and knowledge to do the job, and he put in seventy-hour or longer weeks to save the railroad. "What he walked into might have daunted a less seasoned railroader," noted an industry writer. Commented another: "[Katy] required in the spring of 1965 a missionary, realist, salesman, and magician. It requires a certain moxie, a touch, and indefinable quality that you can't put through a computer or print in an annual report. John Barriger has it and Katy demands every iota of it." Said still another: "The greatest railway booster in the world and the most courageous operator would never have taken the risk of rebuilding the Katy."[20]

From a physical standpoint the Katy was in terrible shape. Years of deferred maintenance "had left Katy a railroad in name only." The largely unmaintained track had become "center bound," causing ties to seesaw under the weight of passing trains, snapping many like match sticks. On the principal lines three of every ten ties were bad, and on its secondary and branch lines the situation was worse. Outside experts concluded that over 3 million ties needed to be replaced, or about one-third of all ties on the railroad. Few miles had heavy, modern rail, and on branches most rail was light and ancient. Ballast often was missing or was too thin, and in places vegetation choked the right-of-way. The basic deterioration of track standards forced reductions of operating speeds even on the busiest lines to the point where there were few long stretches where a 25-mph speed was safe for freight trains. Derailments became epidemic, averaging twenty or so a month. Perhaps an exaggeration, but one writer indicated that "the Katy claimed the distinction of being the only line in American railroad history that had derailments of trains standing still."[21]

Rolling stock likewise had deteriorated. More than 20 percent of Katy's nearly 10,000 freight cars were in bad order. To save money the Williams administration four years earlier had closed the car shops in Denison, and the company had almost stopped buying new cars. Equipment supply had reached desperate proportions. The diesel locomotive picture was hardly any better. "Locomotive condition at the outset of 1965 was so bad that the Katy had few completely dependable units," reported Barriger. "Failures on the line were numerous, running from one or two to ten per day, and totaling from 125–150 per month. Many of these were serious."[22]

There were additional concerns. Although bridges were in relatively good shape, including the monster span over the Missouri River at Boonville, Missouri, most needed minor repairs and nearly all required painting. That was also true for the vast majority of depots and other trackside structures. Office equipment and procedures were often outdated. Communications, too, demanded improvements. "The Katy is equipped with its own communication system for dispatching trains and for transmission of oral and printed messages," said Barriger. "These facilities are long overdue for modernization."[23]

How did Barriger respond to the Katy crisis? Generating immediate cash became a pressing priority. Payrolls had to be met, and rehabilitations started. After viewing the railroad, he realized that there was a modest amount of money to be found in the weeds. Obsolete and badly damaged equipment littered the property, and Barriger soon found about $750,000 worth of salable scrap. He also negotiated a $1 million bank loan, which according to one observer was "secured by the sheer weight of Barriger's personality." Fortunately, he learned about the $4.7 million that remained from an ICC-guaranteed loan of $12 million obtained in 1963. This unspent money had been earmarked for the Katy to acquire an ownership share in several smaller roads controlled by the Muskogee Company, principally the Kansas, Oklahoma & Gulf and Midland Valley railroads. That deal, however, had fallen through. "[Barriger] was able to persuade the Commission to allow Katy to spend the money to put its house in order." While Barriger scrambled to fill corporate coffers, he needed to know the state of company accounts, and so he ordered a comprehensive outside audit.[24]

Realizing that substantial increases in freight traffic would be the salvation of the railroad, John Barriger put his sales skills to work. As he had done in the past, particularly on the Monon, he reinvigorated the sales department. "To help reverse the railroad's image from one of failure to one of success," he noted, "several of the principal sales offices were moved into attractive, efficient quarters situated in well known, centrally located buildings. These improvements have been made at New York City, Kansas City, Tulsa, Pittsburgh, Chicago, New Orleans, Austin and Houston." Barriger did more. "As quickly as he could, he traveled up and down the railroad and with what one newspaper praised as 'engaging candor' told shippers and communities exactly how bleak the situation was, and his plans to rehabilitate the property and its freight service. 'Give us freight,' he entreated shippers on line and off." Commented Barriger publicly, "We're like the Christian martyrs in the dungeon, hoping with great faith to be saved. But we don't want to wait for salvation until the hereafter. We want it now. We say to shippers 'don't punish us with a traffic dead penalty for past sins. Forgive us. Allow us to prove our ability to serve you adequately again. At least start returning some of the traffic you gave the Katy before her fall from grace.'" The appeal worked; carloadings and revenues increased. So much progress had been made that in 1966 the Railway Progress Institute presented the Katy with its

Golden Freight Car runner-up award "for its remarkable comeback from financial trouble."[25]

Still the Katy had to deliver. The Barriger axiom: "You must first give service to get business." Track had to be improved, motive power made dependable, and cars available for customers' needs. Under Barriger's command, the company swung into action.

Where to begin with the miserable track? Tapping once more his industry connections, Barriger turned to Ernest Poole, retired chief of Southern Pacific's Bureau of Transportation Research, to assist with a comprehensive study of deferred maintenance. The decision was made to focus initially on upgrading key corridors. This first involved the route between Kansas City (specifically Paola, Kansas, where the Katy left Frisco trackage 40 miles south of Kansas City) and Denison, a distance of 370 miles. Four mechanized tie, ballasting, and surfacing units went to work, and by the end of 1965 trains could run from Kansas City to Denison without those time-delaying slow orders. Maintenance crews next turned to the Houston section of the main line and later the track between Parsons and St. Louis. Branches got modest attention, largely places where train speeds had been forced to barely a crawl and derailments happened all too often.[26]

Motive-power deficiencies could not be ignored. Not long after Barriger took charge, the Katy revved up the Parsons locomotive shop. In the following months, most of its approximately 180 diesel locomotives were given repairs, some of which were major and cost about $25,000 to $30,000 each. About 30 or so units were retired. Then in 1966 the company took possession of a dozen new 3,000-horsepower Electro-Motive Division GP-40 road locomotives. These units were the company's first second-generation diesel power, and they significantly bolstered its fleet. By mid-1967 Barriger happily noted, "This repair program, along with the 12 new locomotives, has led to the important expense reductions now appearing in the cost of locomotive repairs, consequently transportation performance, efficiency, and economy have been improved. Locomotive failures are now averaging only one per week and these are generally of minor consequence, whereas, two years ago most of the failures on the line entailed serious delays and high repairs costs." As part of this attention to motive power, Al Perlman, who made an early inspection trip

The Katy did not go unrecognized by the railroad industry for the Barriger administration betterments. John Barriger gladly accepts the "Award of Merit" for these accomplishments from the Railway Progress Institute. Fellow railroad president and friend Louis (Lou) Menk makes the formal presentation. (John W. Barriger III Collection, Barriger National Railroad Library at UMSL)

with Barriger, suggested ways to improve efficiency and cost savings at the Parsons facility, resulting in converting the servicing and light-repair work into an assembly-line basis.[27]

One reason why Katy declined so badly before the Barriger regime took hold involved its inability to supply equipment to shippers. It did not take long before the idled car-repair shop in Denison hummed with activity. A large number of bad order cars were returned to service at minimal cost, but a sizable number went to the scrap heap. Being hard-strapped for funds, Barriger found it difficult to come up with the 20 percent cash down payment needed for installment-plan equipment trusts. So what the Katy couldn't buy, it leased. Soon nearly 4,000 new freight cars, including cushion-underframe boxcars and covered hoppers, arrived to meet customers' needs. Moreover, they reduced money-draining per diem charges on "foreign" cars. Barriger took pride that by mid-1967 the Katy had not only repaired a large number of coal hopper cars for its three major coal mine operators, but had acquired 100 new ones and more were to be reconditioned or purchased. Commenting about the impact of the car rehabilitation program, he optimistically predicted: "[F]reight cars are its most effective salesmen and as soon as its 12,000 car program is completed, [Katy's] fundamental traffic and revenue difficulties will vanish."[28]

John Barriger found another way to husband funds. When he arrived, the Katy still operated a limited passenger service. The company dispatched two daily trains between Kansas City and Dallas, remnants of its once-popular Texas Special. Few people rode them, with an average of only ten revenue passengers per train mile. These trains, of course, produced substantial money losses, estimated at $4 million annually. In a complicated takeoff case, the ICC initially approved the Katy's abandonment petition, but then rescinded its order. Due to Katy objections and a legal technicality, the ICC finally sided with the railroad. Barriger earmarked these out-of-pocket savings for track and other betterments.[29]

While Katy "varnish" vanished, Barriger did something with an ICC decision that may have caught shippers and the public by surprise. The previous administration had decided to abandon its long Northwestern District, a mostly grain-carrying appendage that extended into the Oklahoma Panhandle. The ICC agreed that because of declining tonnage and deteriorating track, which drained precious resources, the Katy could retire the line. But following an inspection trip in April 1965, Barriger saw that an excellent wheat crop was in the making following several poor harvest years. So he decided to forgo abandonment. Commented railroad historian Don Hofsommer, this came about "particularly in view of a potentially profitable grain-movement year." Barriger's hunch was correct. Carloadings on the Northwestern District soared from 3,516 in 1964 to 7,100 the following year. Added Hofsommer, "Withdrawal of the abandonment application would be a public relations coup; it would demonstrate that the new management embraced a philosophy of service quite different from that which had been offered by previous administrations." Later, though, grain traffic diminished, track conditions became worse, and operating losses mounted. Katy had no alternative but to reactivate its abandonment petition, and the ICC once more blessed this request to retire the trackage. Crews subsequently removed the rail and other salvageable materials.[30]

The consummate cheerleader and publicity hound, Barriger showed off his well-honed skills. Even though he lacked an appropriate centennial to celebrate – he had been blessed with such an event while at the Monon – he took advantage of the sixtieth anniversary of the founding of the Texas oil boom town of Burkburnett, located on the Wichita Falls to Forgan line. Barriger arranged to have the Katy play a leading role in this celebration. Railroad workers painted the Burkburnett depot, spruced up the station grounds, and inspected the track. Then on June 15, 1967, a special train departed from Wichita Falls for the 14-mile trip to Burkburnett. On board were Barriger and a host of invited guests, including the Texas lieutenant governor. Not only did they devour a "sumptuous brunch," but they had ringside seats to watch a mock train robbery where mounted "bandits" shot off blank ammunition. Upon arrival in Burkburnett, members of the Barriger party encountered hundreds of men, women, and children who had descended upon town to see the train and its dignitaries, to hear a speech by Barriger, and to enjoy other festivities, including a parade, rodeo, and barbecue.[31]

Always on the lookout for ways to enhance the image of the Katy and to make it a good corporate citizen, Barriger in September 1966 recognized the crowning of Miss America, Jayne Anne Jayroe, a native

John Barriger takes the podium at the sixtieth anniversary of the founding of the oil boomtown of Burkburnett, Texas. On Thursday, June 15, 1967, the Katy operated a special train between Wichita Falls and Burkburnett and officially participated in the community's day-long events, including a speech by Barriger to a large outdoor gathering. (John W. Barriger III Collection, Barriger National Railroad Library at UMSL)

of Laverne, Oklahoma. Why this interest? Laverne was a station on the Katy's Northwestern District. An excited community decided to honor its most famous daughter by making "the Home Town of Miss America spic and span." Barriger ordered the shabby wooden depot, located at the head of Main Street, repainted and flower boxes placed under its windows. In his words, "to make the M-K-T presentable and reasonably worthy of the distinction of serving the home town of Miss America." This connection with a Miss America led to a new corporate advertising campaign that featured the "Miss Katy" theme, depicting a vivacious, miniskirted young female who embodied this reviving railroad.[32]

It is impossible to determine if the publicity conscious John Barriger enhanced the corporate bottom line with either the Burkburnett Boom Town celebration or the attention paid to the Laverne depot, but his continuous contacts with existing and potential customers did. After all, he could honestly promote a "new Katy," a railroad with better track, motive power, and freight equipment. A print advertisement, "KATYDID!"

from 1967, captured this feeling in a not-so-exaggerated way, saying in part: "Helping companies find profitable plant sites is only part of Katy's speedy service in the great and growing Southwest. New diesels and cars get products and materials to market fast. More than 3000 miles of improved track provide convenient schedules and on-time connections to the whole country." Barriger's artist friend Howard Fogg depicted these improvements in a series of paintings, and they appeared in print advertisements and, of course, on his Christmas cards.[33]

The financials bore out the "KATYDID!" hype. Although it was far from being a money machine, Katy's overall financial health by 1970 was much improved. During his presidency, Barriger cut the deficit to less than $3 million from more than $7 million, although he never eliminated it. Using freight revenues as a barometer of performance, total revenues for 1964 stood at $46.4 million and for 1969 $64.3 million, having grown each year during the Barriger tenure. Although better revenues contributed to enhanced investor interest in Katy, they soared in 1967 when the railroad, backed by Barriger, created Katy Industries, a Delaware-based holding company. "A contact that Dad met through a M. I. T. event suggested mining the Katy's losses by forming Katy Industries," recalled Jack. "Dad agreed to the plan with the understanding that Katy would receive cash for a share of the tax savings that would result." Taking advantage of the railroad's substantial federal tax-loss carryforward credits, the firm provided opportunities for diversification into nontransportation fields that eventually included Elgin Tools, Martha Washington Candies, and others, and all with positive earnings. By 1968 company stock rose a whopping 153 percent, attributed in part to investor confidence in Barriger himself.[34]

The presence of John Barriger unquestionably increased employee morale. Both blue- and white-collar workers no longer worried about their job security as they did during the Williams and Deramus regimes. They likewise appreciated those much-needed betterments and improved operating and administrative policies. Top management personnel, though, did not always applaud the Barriger work style. Don Hofsommer remembered remarks made by William (Bill) Thie, Katy's general counsel. "[He] often recalled the groans in Dallas when Barriger's office car came down from St. Louis. John Barriger did not recognize the distinction between weekdays and weekends; his sessions with managers were like marathons. How happy they were when the markers headed north."[35]

What did John Barriger have in mind for the future Katy? He believed that with its upgraded stems, reduction of branchline trackage, and healthier balance sheets the railroad could become a merger partner with a large, financially robust carrier. As in the past Barriger wanted to reduce the number of railroads, and Katy, he asserted, was ideally suited for helping to achieve that restructuring. Toward the end of his presidency, he thought that either the Burlington Northern (BN) or Union Pacific (UP) might be likely candidates. In a summer 1970 interview with Tom Shedd, editor of *Modern Railroads*, Barriger believed that BN would be the buyer. He bubbled with excitement. But, alas, the recently created BN was too involved in making unification of the three old Hill Lines work to consider a Katy acquisition. "Management was more interested in cementing the BN merger." Still, there was the assumption that talks would resume. Although Barriger had a good relationship with John Kenefick, who headed UP, it seemed problematic that that carrier would absorb Katy. Yet ultimately it did; the ICC approved a merger of the two roads, going into effect on May 19, 1988. UP was pleased, benefiting from a shorter, straighter route to the Gulf of Mexico and acquiring valuable real-estate holdings in the Dallas–Fort Worth area.[36]

Inclusion of the Katy into an expanding Union Pacific system would have delighted Barriger. Unmistakably he and his successor, Reginald (Reg) Whitman, whom he had sought out as his replacement, made the woebegone Katy into a respectable railroad. Whitman showed off his considerable administrative talents, especially at obtaining government loans and grants. A physically improved property and an increasing traffic base created real value. Whitman, though, was critical of Barriger, saying that he saddled the railroad with heavy financial commitments for motive power and equipment. He also did not care for the "Miss Katy" campaign and other advertisements. "I think Whitman was too harsh, ignoring Katy's state when Barriger arrived," observed Don Hofsommer. "Simply stated, I think John Barriger was the right man for Katy at the time – maybe the only man for Katy at the time."[37]

SEVEN

More Retirements

BOSTON & MAINE RAILROAD

John W. Barriger caused his own retirement from the Missouri-Kansas-Texas Railroad. Although he said that the reason why he left the presidency at the end of June 1970 was "over age limit," the real explanation involved his desire to obtain a "better" position, and one that he desperately wanted. If Barriger succeeded with his objective, this could become the crowning achievement of his long, distinguished career.[1]

What did Barriger seek? He had his eyes set on a job in Philadelphia. When Penn Central Transportation Company entered bankruptcy on June 22, 1970, only 871 days after its much ballyhooed corporate birth, the US District Court of the Eastern District of Pennsylvania needed to appoint a full-time chief trustee along with several trustees who could assist on a part-time basis. John P. Fullam Jr., the jurist who oversaw the bankruptcy, made it clear that he was not about to appoint any unqualified people; there would be no political hacks. Soon the judge compiled a list of more than fifty nominees for lead trustee. No one denied that this would be a difficult position. "It was an absolutely terrible job," remarked railroad executive James (Jim) Hagen. Nevertheless, some individuals considered this post to be highly desirable, and Barriger was one. After finishing up at Katy, he spent time in Washington, DC, and elsewhere to promote his cause. Although Judge Fullam had Barriger on his short list, his efforts to win the position failed. Jervis Langdon Jr., the talented Cornell University–educated lawyer and former president of the Baltimore & Ohio and Chicago, Rock Island & Pacific (Rock Island), came out victorious. Barriger was badly disappointed with the Langdon appointment, believing that "lawyers made poor railroad executives because they think defensibly and don't seem to delegate very well." Judge Fullam, however, made the right decision; Langdon performed admirably as head trustee. Recalled Barriger's son Jack, "Dad was becoming frail and would fall asleep in meetings and he would not have been a good choice." Barriger, of course, was badly disappointed in not becoming a force at Penn Central. After all, he probably knew the physical and financial characteristics of the combined New York Central-Pennsylvania-New Haven company and its traffic generating possibilities better than almost anyone.[2]

After Judge Fullam selected Jervis Langdon, Barriger took advantage of his industry-wide reputation to become chief executive officer of the recently bankrupt Boston & Maine Corporation (B&M). This a position, which officially began on January 1, 1971, would be a better fit than chief trustee of Penn Central, being much easier to manage.[3]

Winning the B&M job came rather rapidly. Said company trustees: "[Barriger's] selection came after an extensive survey of potential candidates," a public statement that may or may not have been totally correct. Early in November 1970 Barriger started employment discussions with the trustees "at their invitation." Action followed. "They called me again Christmas Eve to discuss it further, and on December 26 they made me an offer that was so attractive I couldn't pass it by." His annual salary would be $35,000 ($212,000 in current dollars) and $15,000 ($91,000 in current dollars) in deferred compensation "because that was all the B&M could afford."[4]

Resembling the Monon, New Haven, and Katy, the Boston & Maine was another ailing railroad. In the twentieth century, paralleling the New Haven, it had gone from riches to rags, and like the New Haven it possessed a complex history. And not unlike other latter-day New England carriers, the B&M was not so much built but rather assembled. Its earliest component, the Andover & Wilmington Rail Road, dated back to the mid-1830s, and in what became the B&M heartland construction expanded in the decades before the Civil War. The B&M officially opened its own line in 1845 between North Wilmington, Massachusetts, and Boston and later took over such carriers as the Boston & Lowell,

Eastern, and Fitchburg. By the early twentieth century the B&M had attained its zenith, with major routes radiating out of Boston to Portland, Maine, through New Hampshire to the Canadian border, and west into New York State. In eastern Massachusetts and southern New Hampshire its corporate map resembled a plate of wet spaghetti. For a short period before World War I the company fell into the hands of the New Haven, and in 1916 it slipped into receivership. Following its reorganization in 1919, the B&M functioned well through the following decades, especially during the era of World War II. By 1950 most experts considered it to be a modern, efficient railroad. The traveling public relied on its "Minute Man Passenger Service," and employees took special pride in its expedited freights, especially the Bullet, "a passenger-fast train from Portland to New York." Then came greater highway competition and erosion of regional manufacturing, particularly textile production.[5]

In 1955 a tipping point occurred in the recent history of the B&M when the Patrick McGinnis group, "wreckers of the New Haven," assumed control of management. In January 1956 McGinnis took charge, and for six more years he remained in that position, being followed by a lieutenant, D. A. Benson, who stayed until 1966. Hardly exemplifying the best qualities of railroad professionals, McGinnis and Benson later served short terms in a federal penitentiary for their corrupt business dealings. Following Benson's departure, the presidency was held by the lackluster R. J. Mulhern, who had been the B&M executive vice president and general counsel. He remained in office until shortly after the company went bankrupt.[6]

A red-letter day for the B&M came on March 12, 1970. That was when "the chickens came home to roost," namely its second bankruptcy. Four insurance firms – Connecticut Mutual Life Insurance Company, Equitable Life Assurance Society, Metropolitan Life Insurance Company, and Northwestern Mutual Life Insurance Company – blew the whistle after the company missed an interest payment on $14 million of outstanding first mortgage bonds. It did not take long before a federal bankruptcy judge named three trustees: Dr. Paul Cherington, Harvard Business School professor and former undersecretary of transportation in the Richard Nixon administration; Charles Bartlett, lawyer and official in the US Department of Commerce in the Lyndon Johnson administration and later president of the American Bar Association; and Robert Meserve, lawyer and one-time president of the Boston Bar Association.[7]

Although the "McGinnis dynasty" failed to merge the B&M with the principal New England carriers – an outcome that might have saved the company from bankruptcy, it also failed to make the B&M a viable operation. These railroaders refused to funnel available funds to support critical betterments. "Maintenance budgets were placed on Draconian policies of austerity." Therefore the physical condition of the property declined, motive power became less dependable, and equipment shortages proved costly. By the mid-1960s the company fortunately had extricated itself from its financially draining intercity passenger service; such fine trains as the Pine Tree Limited and the Flying Yankee had become merely pleasant memories. The B&M also received a subsidy from the Massachusetts Bay Transportation Authority (MBTA) to support its extensive Boston area commuter operations. The freight sector, the principal source of revenues, found itself in a downward spiral. Because of continuing deterioration of the physical plant and inadequate equipment, customers found its schedules unreliable, and as Barriger later indicated, "Its connecting lines were indifferent to fulfilling their responsibilities toward interline services." Former B&M traffic went either to other railroads or more likely to motor transport. As would be expected, worker morale sagged, and some left for other jobs or retired.[8]

By the early 1960s the precarious financial condition of the B&M and other railroads that served the Northeast was widely recognized. As a result of the Norfolk & Western (N&W)-Nickel Plate-Wabash merger proceedings that began in 1961, the N&W agreed that if the ICC sanctioned this union, the combined carrier would negotiate "in good faith" for inclusion of several weaker roads. Following the successful expansion of the N&W in 1964, its leadership fretted about the likelihood of a giant New York Central-Pennsylvania merger. The response: a proposed merger of the N&W with the Chesapeake & Ohio. If this were to come about, what would be the fate of other faltering railroads in the East and Northeast? The result was formation of Dereco, a "protective" holding company that would bring together five distressed carriers – Boston &

Maine, Central Railroad of New Jersey, Delaware & Hudson, Erie Lackawanna, and Reading. After considerable maneuvering, B&M management rejected the Dereco arrangement because it "viewed itself as the
core for an expanded system in New England." Nevertheless, Dereco
suggested that the B&M was anything but healthy.[9]

When John Barriger arrived at Boston & Maine headquarters at 150
Causeway Street in Boston, he joined a company that was much ma-
ligned as the "Busted & Maimed." His new position did not result in the
sale of the family's beloved house at 15 Washington Terrace in St. Louis;
rather, John and Elizabeth spent most of their time in an apartment on
Tremont Street in Boston. Their daughter Betty remained at their St.
Louis home, receiving assistance from a retired African American Katy
business car porter and chauffeur, Fred Tyler, who after 1965 became a
full-time Barriger family employee.[10]

Immediately Barriger went to work. His game plan was not that different from how he had approached the Monon and the Katy. He quickly
assessed his management team and made several key appointments. For
his chief operating officer, he selected H. E. Ring, a former Penn Central
general manager; John Patten, who previously served as vice president
of sales and service for Penn Central, became his chief traffic officer; his
head of labor relations and personnel, L. B. Lee, also came from Penn
Central; and he promoted the capable Peter Carr from the B&M accounting department to comptroller. Later Barriger found a new chief
engineer. He also brought in outside consultants. Two were P. F. Kraber,
retired comptroller of the Pittsburgh & Lake Erie (P&LE), and Herman
Strahl, retired auditor of revenue, who likewise hailed from the P&LE.
He used them to put into effect methods for improving accounting procedures, focusing on measuring costs, expediting monthly statements,
and the like. Barriger made good choices, except for the conniving Ring.
"Ring wanted John's job and tried to get him out of the picture. His personality was the opposite of John's."[11]

Early on Barriger sought to get input from representatives of other
bankrupt or financially hard-pressed Eastern carriers. He organized a
meeting of railroaders that was held in the Ritz-Carlton Hotel in Boston. A major theme: "How can we improve service?" These men also

discussed the closely related matter of how their gross incomes could be increased.[12]

Being a hands-on railroader, Barriger frequently inspected the property, examining its physical condition and spending time at the North Billerica and Boston car and locomotive facilities. As he would tell the ICC, "I have covered much of this railroad by high-rail car, freight train and special train trips."[13]

Deferred maintenance had to be addressed. At the time that he took charge, the property verged on becoming a transportation slum. "The railroad was in terrible shape," recalled Alan G. (Dusty) Dustin, who would serve as B&M president from 1974 to 1984. "There were lots of speed restrictions. There were also all sorts of wrecked cars along the rights-of-way." Although Barriger lacked unlimited funds for improving track structure, noticeable progress occurred. Take tie replacements. In 1966, for example, the B&M installed a mere 20,032 ties, but in 1971 the total reached 82,406, and for 1972 it exceeded 130,000. Similarly, expenditures for locomotive and car repairs increased. "The North Billerica shops hummed with activities." By 1972 the bad order ratio of freight equipment had dropped from about 10 percent to less than 5 percent.[14]

The Barriger regime bolstered marketing, reduced excessively high freight car rental debits, and increased service dependability. Efforts also began toward the abandonment of money-draining branchlines. Barriger, too, expanded the efficiency of the B&M bureaucracy. One involved consolidation of the two operating divisions into a single division. He also did not ignore applying the latest technologies. The railroad had pioneered the use of computers, having installed first-generation equipment in 1956. Upgrades followed in the 1960s, and in June 1971, a third-generation computer began to whiz away, the sophisticated UNIVAC 9300 tape-disc system that a few years earlier had become available. These critical betterments enhanced the bottom line.[15]

Barriger did not ignore organized labor. Even though he had blasted featherbedding practices for decades, he always tried to establish good working relationships with the various brotherhoods. This meant personal meetings with union officials, local chairmen, and rank-and-file members. Dating back to his tenure as Monon president, Barriger would invite brotherhood representatives to join him in his business car, often for breakfast meetings, and occasionally as dinner guests in his home. "Dad was not hostile toward unions," remarked son Jack. "He was always honest with them." Barriger developed a close relationship with Charles Luna, who between 1963 and 1969 headed the powerful Brotherhood of Railroad Trainmen, based in Cleveland, Ohio, and one of the "Big Four" railroad brotherhoods. Then in 1969 Luna became the first president of the consolidated United Transportation Union. As Barriger told the *New York Times*, "I'm kind of one of Luna's pets," and made it clear that he considered Luna to be a "true railroad labor statesman." In one example of their friendship, Luna invited Barriger to participate in a celebratory event that honored the eighty-eighth anniversary of the founding of the Brotherhood of Railroad Trainmen in Oneonta, New York, and Barriger gladly accepted this September 1971 invitation. As with past executive positions, Barriger discussed with B&M workers his plans to upgrade (and in this case to save) the railroad, and he asked for their ideas about what was needed to improve efficiency and profitability.[16]

With the progress taking place at the B&M, efforts by the first-mortgage bondholders to seek liquidation in order to pay off the claims secured by this debt went nowhere. What seemed likely toward the end of 1972 was that it would reorganize independently under the bankruptcy laws since "the railroad is not going to run out of cash," thanks to the impressive start made by the Barriger team at rerailing the company. Nevertheless, he faced a host of obstacles. "Barriger was really paddling against the wind," remarked a B&M employee. He believed that his boss "lacked the political connections in Boston to really allow the railroad to succeed." Yet Barriger remained hopeful that the B&M might join a stronger interregional railroad, or at the least couple itself to other New England carriers, and ultimately that occurred. But there was the nagging problem of his health. "It became apparent that John was well past his prime," observed Alan Dustin. "He'd fall asleep during staff meetings and wake up 10 or 15 minutes later and continue as if nothing had happened. Age was against him." And Barriger's poor hearing was becoming a concern.[17]

After Barriger left the B&M at the end of 1972, a reorganized company continued to make a range of improvements, and in the early 1980s it expanded somewhat by adding trackage in Connecticut and Massachusetts acquired from Conrail, the quasi-public corporation that emerged out of the wreckage of Penn Central. Then in 1983 the B&M fell into the hands of Guilford Transportation Industries, a holding company launched by Timothy Mellon of the wealthy Mellon banking family. Two years earlier Guilford had acquired the Maine Central, and in 1984 it would take control of the Delaware & Hudson from N&W subsidiary Dereco. Unfortunately for shippers, Guilford rapidly gained the reputation as the "bad boy in the East" because of its poor service and other shortcomings.[18]

John Barriger seemed content with his role at the Boston & Maine, relishing the work of reviving a faltering railroad. Yet another retirement would take place, not so much because of age or lack of interest but due rather to the power of B&M trustee Paul Cherington. This James J. Hill Professor of Transportation at the Harvard Business School, who for years had maintained a packed schedule of academic and nonacademic activities, decided that he wanted Barriger's job as chief executive officer. So he "arranged" Barriger's retirement, and also arranged "a big salary step up for himself." Barriger, though, did not want to leave the B&M; still, he remained on speaking terms with the devious Cherington, who because of poor health "didn't provide much leadership for the railroad." Then on August 11, 1974, the B&M head died at age fifty-six from a chronic heart condition, having been hospitalized periodically for nearly a year. A few days later Barriger attended the Cherington funeral in Boston. "I remember that Dad got all dressed up," recalled son Jack, "and went to the funeral to show his former B&M officers and other railroaders that the 74 year old ex-CEO was still healthy and vigorous."[19]

For Barriger the year 1973 started out on a somber note. In his diary for New Year's Day 1973 he wrote these introspective thoughts: "Midnight finds me at the end of my two years' run over the Boston and Maine and jobless for the first time since I entered PRR service at Altoona shops in June, 1917. A sad feeling, but I hope that it can soon be cured." With the B&M position ended, there was predictably another retirement party. This one took plan on the evening of February 12, 1973, at the Copley Plaza Hotel in Boston. There was a good turnout, including "friends from near and far." Barriger indicated that he and Elizabeth would not immediately return to St. Louis. "This delay has not been due to not wanting to go there," he confessed, "but to the fear that a return to take up residence in Missouri just now might be regarded as signaling retirement, – something I wish to avoid like the plague. I have always found hours and days at work were so much more interesting than those not working." He closed with these remarks: "I don't know when or where my next retirement dinner will be held, but I hope I shall have some more and that several of you, at least, will come to it." Quipped one who knew Barriger, "You don't worry about missing one of JWB's retirement parties. You knew there'd be another." And he would be correct.[20]

FEDERAL RAILROAD ADMINISTRATION

John Barriger stayed active professionally following his departure from the Boston & Maine. There were industry meetings, social engagements, and work on his home library. Relying once more on his network of contracts, he found support for a position with the Federal Railroad Administration (FRA). In April 1973, Mark Jones, a one-time Barriger associate at the P&LE, wrote Claude S. Brinegar, secretary of transportation, about his friend's availability and skills. "Until recently, Mr. Barriger was the Chief Executive Officer of the Boston & Maine Railroad. Now he is available for something else. I have known him well for a long time. I believe that he is the best informed and most objective overall specialist on the railroad situation in the country." Letters and other contacts made on behalf of Barriger to Brinegar and others in Washington helped pave the way for his official appointment in July 1973 as special assistant to FRA administrator John W. Ingram. It would be Washington-based transportation consultant Robert (Bob) Banks, president of R. L. Banks and Associates, who played a pivotal role in getting Barriger the FRA job. Recalled Ingram, "Bob Banks and I had lunch and introduced me again to John Barriger. Evidently what John wanted to have happen was to come and work for the Federal Railroad Administration, get back in the railroad business, where he could enjoy the kind of people that he liked to be with." Ingram, however, indicated that there was one hiring problem – his age. Fortunately Barriger's future new boss went to bat for him, perhaps doing so "as an act of kindness." Ingram contacted Jeb Magruder, White House aide to President Richard Nixon, and received a waver. "I got a phone call back from him [Magruder]," remembered Ingram. "Well, go ahead and hire him, the next time he's 65 make sure he retires!"[21]

For Barriger this third postretirement job meant a return to government service. Like his employment with the Railroad Division of the Reconstruction Finance Corporation and with Washington wartime assignments, he joined a recently launched government agency. When the US Congress created the US Department of Transportation (DOT), which began operations on April 1, 1967, this cabinet-level office oversaw more than thirty independent or semi-independent programs previously dispersed throughout the federal bureaucracy. Part of DOT included the new Federal Railroad Administration. An administrator, who was a political appointee, headed this agency and reported directly to the transportation secretary. As for responsibilities, the FRA assumed some policy and research activities previously conducted by the US Department of Commerce, and it also became responsible for railroad safety regulatory functions that had been carried out by the ICC. Prior to Barriger's appointment, the FRA had helped to fashion the legislation that established the National Railroad Passenger Corporation (Amtrak), an achievement that Barriger endorsed. When he arrived at the FRA, its Washington staff of one hundred or so had been involved in crafting the Regional Rail Reorganization (3R) Act of 1973 and soon focused on what became the Railroad Revitalization and Regulatory Reform (4R) Act of 1976, both measures designed to manage the collapse of Penn Central, reverse the downward spiral of the railroad sector, and prevent nationalization.[22]

Barriger was happy to play a role in the industry that he dearly loved by joining an influential federal agency. As he told family members, "I have an interesting and challenging job in the Department of Transportation and am working with congenial and capable people and these factors mean a great deal to me." The pay was respectable; Barriger drew an annual salary of $32,000 ($173,000 in current dollars). In order to prevent any charge of a conflict of interest, he disposed of his $200,000 of New York Central Railroad 6 percent collateral trust bonds, having acquired them during his tenure with the P&LE. Rather than cash them in, John and Elizabeth decided to divide them equally between their four children. "Although your mother and I could make good use of the income produced by these bonds," he told them, "we know that you can too, and this knowledge gives us much pleasure."[23]

Living with Elizabeth in an apartment on Virginia Avenue near the Watergate complex in Washington, Barriger worked closely with the young FRA administrator John Ingram. This business graduate of Syracuse University and masters in transportation economics holder from Columbia University began his managerial career with the New York Central in 1955, serving as an assistant to Al Perlman. There he helped to implement a computerized car-location punch-card system and assisted with rate cases before the ICC. In 1966 Ingram left the NYC to begin a five-year stint with the Southern Railway as director of cost and price analysis. Between 1966 and 1971 Ingram worked for the Illinois Central Railroad (IC) as an assistant vice president, marketing, and later he won promotion to the vice president, marketing, position. At the IC Ingram showed an innovative bent, developing a unique "rent-a-train" program that allowed a shipper to rent a full train for a year and then use it as needed. Soon IC rent-a-trains moved Midwestern grain to Gulf of Mexico ports and hauled sludge from Chicago's Sanitary District to a central Illinois plant where it was converted into crop fertilizer. In 1971 President Nixon appointed the professionally ambitious Ingram to head the FRA.[24]

Barriger worked well with Ingram, a surprise to some. Others at the FRA, in government, and throughout the railroad industry often found Ingram to be "abrasive, acerbic, and arrogant" and an overall "difficult guy." Perhaps their closeness came about because both men were strongly committed to marketing and innovation. Each also considered nationalization of the railroad network to be the wrong, even disastrous, alternative to the growing financial crisis that faced multiple carriers. There is reason to believe that Ingram also wished to take advantage of Barriger's stature to advance his own career. "Ingram considered Barriger his watch fob," remarked a FRA associate. "In no way was he ever abrasive toward him." Or maybe there was that element of personal kindness.[25]

At the FRA Barriger functioned as a consultant, preparing various studies for Ingram and his associates. One of these might have been predictable: "The Evils of Railroad Nationalization." The key argument was his long-held belief that "private profit is always less than public waste." Barriger also offered his coworkers background information about aspects of the railroad industry, including history, economics, and politics. He usually attended staff meetings and made his comments, "some of them were quite time-consuming." And Barriger had frequent contacts with his boss. "With his encyclopedic memory, Ingram would ask Barriger about when and why something had happened. He nearly always received an immediate and correct answer." Unlike previous jobs, Barriger did not put in exceptionally long hours. "He had slowed down considerably."[26]

David DeBoer, a talented young railroader at the FRA who had previously been employed by the New York Central, had assignments that focused on how to encourage innovation. He was exactly the type of individual who interested Barriger. DeBoer recalled how Barriger served the agency and his own work:

> We focused on intermodal market studies and intermodal equipment innovation and a cooperative intermodal labor management demonstration project. Part of this project centered on Chicago. I was pouring over Chicago maps when Barriger walked in and asked about "the problem of the day" [part of Barriger's daily routine to keep in touch with FRA personnel]. I said I was trying to see if we could make a physical connection to St. Louis from a currently unused area in Chicago. He looked at the map and gave a tutorial on the route – including elevations and tower locations. At one tower location he explained a route "and there are alternative routes if the interlocking still works, I think it may have been taken out of service." I thanked him and made a series of notes and arranged with a friend from CATS (Chicago Area Transportation Study) to meet me for an on the ground look – especially the interlocking tower.
>
> We drove to the site and found the tower on a level above us up an embankment. We hiked up and entered the tower greeted heartily by the operator. The interlocking machine was British and from the 1930s. I reviewed the notes and asked about the routing. Just as Barriger had described, including the out of service route. "I'm sure we could have it up and running if we oiled the turnout and put in a few ties," said the tower operator.[27]

As in the past Barriger admired young, bright, and energetic rail-roaders. John Ingram was no exception. Barriger promoted Ingram's candidacy for the presidency of the collapsing Rock Island. He believed that since the departure of Downing Jenks in 1961 to head the Missouri Pacific the company had suffered from inadequate leadership. Barriger did not mince words about Jenks's four successors, Ellis Johnson, Jervis Langdon Jr., William (Bill) Dixon, and Theodore (Ted) Desch. In an April 1974 memorandum he called these men the "four horsemen of the apocalypse, blindly taking that once fine railroad to the brink of disaster over which it will plunge this year unless either or both the Union Pacific and USRA [US Railway Administration]-FRA come to its rescue." Bar-riger thought that Ingram could become the road's savior, and he did what he could to make that happen. In the words of Ingram: "While I was at the FRA John Barriger decided I should work for the Rock Island. And he went and talked to a bunch of people on the Rock Island and a bunch of people on the Union Pacific who were involved in merging with the Rock Island at the time, at least that was theory [and] got approvals here and there and everyplace. What do you know somebody asked me if I would like to come and work for us. The Rock Island not being my idea of a dream railroad. But anyway, I finally said yes." This explanation for why Ingram became the Rock Island chief executive on November 1, 1974, may or may not have been completely accurate, but the *New York Times* and other sources indicated that Barriger had been the instigator. Surely Barriger appreciated the fact that Ingram knew the ropes when it came to obtaining federal assistance loans, and the Rock Island desper-ately needed a huge cash infusion. He also thought that with aggressive marketing and extensive betterments the railroad might be spared a trip to the corporate graveyard. As Rock Island head, Ingram won a small federal loan, but it was not enough needed to save it from bankruptcy. On March 17, 1975, the company filed for court protection, and within five years it underwent liquidation and not the traditional reorganization.[28]

ROCK ISLAND AGAIN

After Ingram ascended to the Rock Island presidency, his successor at the FRA, Ace Hall, asked Jack Barriger to see him the next time that he came to Washington. This he did. The FRA head told Jack that he valued his father's work, but he thought he should retire and asked for his help to make this happen. "At that time Dad's hearing was poor and he often fell asleep in meetings. It was obvious that his health was failing, though his mind was still great on details related to the past." Barriger agreed to leave the FRA, and once more there was a retirement party to honor his service. Still, there was one unfinished project; Barriger had committed to writing his autobiography, and he would do so until near the end of his life.[29]

Always being obsessed about having a railroad-industry job, Barriger about this time asked James (Jim) McClelland, who had been with the FRA but then worked for the USRA, about employment with his organization. "I had a poignant conversation with John Barriger in front of my office at L'Enfant Plaza. He pleaded with me to find him a job with the USRA." Added McClellan, "I couldn't believe that a lowly person like me was having this conversation with John Barriger."[30]

Yet Barriger did not exit the world of railroading. There would be another job, albeit his last. John Ingram hired him on a part-time basis to gain traffic for the Rock Island. Said Ingram, "The idea that we wanted him to do was to keep us up to date on what he thought his ideas of the Rock Island should be and go around and meet some big shippers and see if they couldn't put a little more freight on the railroad." Recalled Jack about his father's final railroad job: "I was surprised and shocked when I found out about a week later [after he left the FRA] that Dad and Mother were in Chicago and that Dad was going to work for John Ingram." He added, "I was fairly well established in Chicago as Assistant to President John S. Reed [of the Santa Fe] in charge of Reed's staff. I was not pleased to have Dad show up, contact all of his railroad friends and start having breakfasts and luncheons at the Chicago Club or Union League Club to which I was invited but was often too busy to attend." Barriger's younger son, Stanley, who at this time worked in Brazil studying that nation's railroad needs for the World Bank, seemed pleased with his father's new position, saying, "Jesus Christ had only one resurrection but you are getting to be like a cat with nine lives."[31]

In May 1976, at an undisclosed salary, John Barriger once more dedicated himself to functioning as a salesman. His Rock Island business card, which he handed out to one and all, bore his special title of "Senior Traveling Freight Agent." Soon Barriger crisscrossed the railroad to drum up badly needed business for his employer. He was happy, reflecting, "They could charge me money to let me work as a railroader, and I'd still do it." Again he reiterated his philosophy of retirement: "Retirement is a cruel state of life."[32]

END OF THE LINE

John Barriger expected to stay with the Rock Island, or if that was not possible, to find one or more consulting jobs, dying with his boots on. He also had other ambitions. Barriger planned to complete his autobiography and to continue work on a book-length history of the railroad industry, tentatively titled "The Rise and Fall of American Railroads." This project would rely heavily on research materials located in his magnificent home library. He did not foresee dying on December 9, 1976, at age seventy-seven.

Throughout his professional career, Barriger bragged about his good health. He rarely missed a day from work. Yet he had had a hernia operation while working at the P&LE, and one that the medical profession considered to have been "successful." It was during the course of that procedure he likely received what was probably a contaminated blood transfusion. By the early 1970s there were indications that he lacked perfect health, for example, frequently falling asleep in meetings. Nevertheless when Barriger had his annual physical examination in May 1976, the results were good. "Your physical examination on May 25, 1976 continues to be excellent," noted a physician at the Saint Louis Medical Clinic. "We know that you have the irregular heart action and you probably have some rheumatic valvular defect. The essential tremor of your right hand is no better and no worse than it was. Your hearing seems somewhat reduced for high frequency." The physician suggested that Barriger begin iron medication. "The cause of your anemia may be a moderate loss of blood without your knowing it, and this can occur in the stomach or even from the diverticula of the bowel."[33]

By late fall 1976 health began a critical issue. Returning from a business trip, a somewhat feeble and frail Barriger became confused in the

While not an absolute abstainer from alcoholic beverages, John Barriger more regularly enjoyed coffee and other nonintoxicating drinks. He preferred an ice cream soda to all else. (John W. Barriger III Collection, Barriger National Railroad Library at UMSL)

St. Louis Lambert Field Airport. A security officer found him wandering about, and Elizabeth was contacted. She had him taken to an area hospital, and later she arranged for a hospital bed at their St. Louis home along with medical assistance. "Dad had a liver problem," noted Jack, and in a short time he would die from cirrhosis of the liver. This was ironic since he seldom drank alcohol. "His favorite drink was a chocolate ice cream soda, and he thought Bauer's in Denver made the best." That earlier blood transfusion likely had been the culprit.[34]

On December 11, 1976, two days after his passing, a funeral took place at 1:00 p.m. in Second Presbyterian Church at Westminster Place in St. Louis. This had been John Barriger's longtime church home. The night before there was a home visitation. Elizabeth arranged for an open bar and a buffet in the dining room. Barriger's body lay in an open casket in front of the living room fireplace. Remembered Jack, "Dad was there all night and we family members took turns staying with him." At both the visitation and funeral there were several hundred in attendance. As might be expected, an array of business friends came, including John Kenefick from the Union Pacific, John Ingram from the Rock Island, and a delegation from the Terminal Railroad Association of St. Louis. Following the morning funeral service there was a buffet luncheon at the home; burial took place in the Barriger family plot at Bellefontaine Cemetery in St. Louis. A dozen years later his beloved "Sweetie Pie" would be buried next to him. And the deaths of his daughters Ann and Betty and son Stanley followed. Yet his son Jack lives on, and there would be grandson John W. (Jay) Barriger V and great-grandson John W. (John) Barriger VI, who would carry on this once widely known name in the American railroad industry.[35]

Epilogue

FOLLOWING HIS DEATH, JOHN WALKER BARRIGER III RE-mained remembered and even cherished by those who knew him, having established himself as a revered elder railroad statesman. Although early in his career he gained industry recognition, Barriger failed to join the acknowledged pantheon of the most famous American railroaders. Such talented contemporaries as Bill Brosnan, Ralph Budd, Jervis Langdon, and Al Perlman achieved greater prominence, most likely because they headed major railroads. The peripatetic Barriger, on the other hand, never led a large Class I carrier; the closest he achieved was the Pittsburgh & Lake Erie (P&LE), that heavily trafficked subsidiary of the New York Central. After all, Barriger won acclaim as that "doctor of sick railroads," whether at the Monon, Katy, or Boston & Maine.

There is every reason to believe that Barriger was satisfied with how his railroading career had progressed. To his way of thinking it was *not* important to become a "big shot." If Barriger were to have sought a major presidency, it would have been at the time when he headed the P&LE. But he was happy with that position, and he had no desire to leave for a supposedly better job. Furthermore, Barriger was not interested in earning an exorbitant salary. What he wanted was a railroad industry where there would be massive corporate consolidations and one that faced less burdensome state and federal regulation.[1]

The question arises as to whether Barriger possessed the skills and personality to become a major Class I president. Some who knew him professionally had their reservations. James (Jim) W. McClellan, a top industry planner, strategist, and marketer, thought that Barriger, while bright, energetic, and extremely knowledgeable about the industry, "was too much of a hands-on guy," and believed that he would have difficulty managing a large corporate bureaucracy. "The Monon and Katy were not the NYC or UP!" Similarly, Richard (Dick) Hasselman, a veteran New York Central and Penn Central executive, considered Barriger to be "basically a salesman and not a skilled executive like Al Perlman." Admittedly, any venture into counterfactual historical speculation is just that – speculation.[2]

Nevertheless, no fellow railroad executive had such a rich diversity of financial and government experiences as did John Barriger. He could claim an unequaled professional background. Furthermore, no one was more indefatigable in promoting enthusiasm for the railroad enterprise or for a single company. Barriger's years on the speaking circuit and his scores of articles in newspapers, magazines, and trade publications attest to this personal commitment. No wonder colleagues called him "the greatest protagonist of the rail mode" and "the greatest railway booster in the world."[3]

Then there was Barriger's restless nature. He was a railroad boomer. Commented his son Jack, "Dad's greatest weakness was that he jumped from job to job. Dad was impatient." Yet a case can be made for the merits of a boomer career. In 1956 James Lyne, editor of *Railway Age*, reflected on this pattern and with Barriger specifically in mind. "Booming is such an effective education device that, where it's difficult or impossible to achieve by natural means, maybe it ought to be simulated artificially. Perhaps railroads could profitably 'exchange' superintendents or other officers, temporarily, as colleges do with professors."[4]

Still John Barriger, this man in motion, retained a great consistency in his worldviews. It involved more than his thoughts about creating a more progressive, customer-oriented, and profitable railroad industry. Perhaps to his detriment he never wavered from his strong commitment to conservative values. Barriger was a staunch Republican or pro-business voter, harboring an abiding dislike for New Deal–type "tax and spend" liberals and especially "Reds" during the Joseph McCarthy–inspired anticommunist hysteria of the early 1950s. Jack recalled a memorable event when he was a graduate student at Yale. He commented to his father about the fate of nine Communists who were then being tried in a federal court in New York City. The parental response was not positive. Barriger clearly overreacted when he said, "I've wasted my money on your education and you've ruined your life," his harsh retort to Jack's discussion of the case. When it came to race relations, Barriger was no different from most of his fellow railroad executives; he hardly backed the developing civil rights movement of the 1950s and 1960s. "I can't image having a black man at our dinner table," he once commented. Although Barriger showed respect to people of color, they were in his mind members of a subservient class: blacks could prepare the meals, clean the house, and maintain the yard. And on the railroad they could attend to needs of their superiors on the business car or elsewhere.[5]

Although historians and other writers have spent more time chronicling the achievements of other twentieth-century railroad leaders, no contemporary of John Barriger has achieved this form of lasting immortality – a renowned research library. The core consists of his books, photographs, personal papers, and related items. And with the additional collections of businesses, organizations, and individuals associated with the industry, it has evolved into a treasure trove of financial, engineering, historical, operating, and regulatory data. This is the John W. Barriger III National Railroad Library, a unit of the St. Louis Mercantile Library, located in the Thomas Jefferson Library on the suburban campus of the University of Missouri–St. Louis (UMSL).

The creation of the Barriger library is a remarkable story. With a passion for collecting published and unpublished railroad materials, John Barriger began to assemble during his teenage years what became one of the largest – if not the largest – private railroad research collections in the country. In vacuum-cleaner fashion he sucked up thousands of items and took possession of some important holdings, including the libraries of Walker D. Hines, an Atchison, Topeka & Santa Fe official and second director of the US Railroad Administration, and Leonor F. Loree, longtime president of the Delaware & Hudson and founder of the North American chapter of the Newcomen Society. While working for financial firms,

John Barriger amassed a remarkable collection of railroad-related materials, including complete runs of *Official Guide of the Railways*, *Railway Age*, and other industry publications. It's May 28, 1963, and he is conducting research in his library, housed close to his office in the Pittsburgh & Lake Erie complex near downtown Pittsburgh. (John W. Barriger III Collection, Barriger National Railroad Library at UMSL)

government agencies, or individual railroads, Barriger took advantage of opportunities to expand his holdings. As that avid collector, he did not miss chances to haunt used-book stores. Son Jack recalled this incident: "About 1960 [my father] visited me while I was a Santa Fe Trainmaster at Los Angeles and we stopped at a second hand bookstore in Beverly Hills. There he found a copy of his book 'Super Railroads for a Dynamic American Economy' with a $5 price tag on it. He went up to the owner of the store, identified himself as the author and told him that the book was worth more than $5." The response: "Without even looking up the owner said, 'I will sell it to you for $10 if it will make you feel better.'"[6]

Over the decades the expanding Barriger library has had various venues. At first it was housed at home, but eventually that became impractical. When Barriger left the federal government in 1944 and moved to Illinois, the collection was placed in the Chicago offices of Fairbanks-Morse on Michigan Avenue. He did keep at home his nonrailroad history collection, mostly books that pertained to the Civil War and World

Owning a camera since childhood, John Barriger constantly photographed railroad subjects. His love of photography resulted in thousands of historically valuable and at times unique images. (John W. Barriger III Collection, Barriger National Railroad Library at UMSL)

War I. After Barriger joined the Monon, the library remained in the Windy City but was relocated to company headquarters on Dearborn Street. When he assumed the P&LE presidency, the materials followed him to Pittsburgh. Rather than transportation in moving vans, two New

York Central baggage cars facilitated this transfer. The collection found space in a warehouse adjacent to Barriger's office in the P&LE station. Following his retirement from the P&LE and move to St. Louis, the next site for his books became the steel-reinforced ballroom on the top floor of the Barriger house on Washington Terrace. And the basement held forty or more metal filing cabinets of papers and photographs.[7]

With Barriger's death in 1976, what would be the fate of the railroad books, papers, and photographs? According to his will, the nonrailroad historical collection went to his daughter Ann, and the railroad books and related materials went to sons Jack and Stanley. According to Jack, "[Dad] thought that Stanley and I would somehow divide the railroad books and materials and that all of us would keep collecting as enthusiastically as he had." That was not realistic. "We had neither Dad's intense interest in collecting nor the space in our homes to accommodate our share of his library." Since the sons agreed that the collection should be in the public domain, they sought an appropriate repository. This noble goal became a daunting challenge. The initial contact was made with the library director at the Massachusetts Institute of Technology (MIT), a logical choice because of family connections with that Cambridge institution. Although interested, MIT wished to have only about half of the books, and it had limited interest in the papers and photographs. The Barriger sons, though, wanted the materials kept intact. Word spread throughout the academic research community that the Barriger collection was available, and several museums and libraries made offers, but nothing tangible transpired. Then in 1981 it appeared that the Smithsonian Institution in conjunction with the Transportation Research Forum (TRF) planned to establish a transportation library in a wing of the federally owned Union Station in Washington, DC. Perhaps the TRF and the Barriger collections could be consolidated under the stewardship of the Smithsonian. Jack and Stanley granted the TRF a one-year option, agreeing not to give their father's holdings to any other organization. This was an attractive plan, but unfortunately the Union Station library proposition fizzled. Finally, a breakthrough occurred. Members of the private and long-established St. Louis Mercantile Library made contact and proposed establishing the John W. Barriger III National Railroad

It is impossible to reveal in a single photograph the extent of the John W. Barriger III National Railroad Library. This image shows a portion of the book holdings. (John W. Barriger III Collection, Barriger National Railroad Library at UMSL)

Library in a special space in this downtown St. Louis facility located at Broadway and Locust streets. There would be incentives, including one-half million dollars earmarked for remodeling, a full-time curator, and a separate board of trustees. On December 28, 1982, a delighted Barriger family signed a formal agreement with the library, and during the following May the massive collection, estimated to weigh 26 tons, was moved into a neighboring warehouse for processing.[8]

Although this was expected to be a permanent site, the John W. Barriger III National Railroad Library did not remain in downtown St. Louis. The Mercantile Library building had physical and locational limitations, and the board of directors wished to have public usage rather than continuity of place, believing that an association with an institution of higher education would be highly desirable. There were also pressing safety concerns. "Safety of the Library from fire, storm, earthquakes and pilfering became an issue," recalled Jack. "Books had disappeared as had maps and photographs cut out and stolen." So in 1998 the Mercantile Library moved to the Thomas Jefferson Library on the UMSL campus. This proved ideal. "The Library had shelf space for the more valuable books in a vault that was bomb, fire and earthquake poof. Also, the Chancellor agreed to use some available funds from the assets transferred to UMSL to endow a 'John W. Barriger III Professor of Transportation' and to create a Degree awarding Center for Transportation Studies." Since the relocation, many more railroad collections and items have been added, resulting in a remarkably comprehensive research facility. These materials, whether they originated in the core collection or from other acquisitions, large or small, attest to the importance of the Barriger legacy.[9]

In what might be considered a related legacy, some of John Barriger's most cherished goals have come to fruition. The result has been the improving, even the saving, of his beloved free-enterprise industry. Two stand out. Dating back to his work on crafting the Prince Plan in 1933, Barriger believed that it made no sense to have hundreds of Class I railroad companies, a situation that led to inefficiencies, waste, and a weakened industry. Consolidation or "system rationalization," as he sometimes called it, became his objective. As demonstrated in the Prince Plan, Barriger wanted side-by-side regional and interregional competitors rather than end-to-end transcontinental ones, and ultimately that was what happened with US-based carriers.[10]

During Barriger's later career, railroad mergers became more popular, and in the 1960s these consolidations started in earnest. At first the movement involved smaller and mid-sized roads, for example, the Erie and Delaware, Lackawanna & Western (1960) and the Norfolk & Western, Nickel Plate, and Wabash (1964). Next the era of mega-mergers began when the Interstate Commerce Commission (ICC) approved the corporate marriage of the New York Central and Pennsylvania, which became effective on February 1, 1968. This watershed event was followed two years later with formation of Burlington Northern, being the unification of the famed Hill Lines: Chicago, Burlington & Quincy, Great Northern, Northern Pacific, and Spokane, Portland & Seattle. In the 1980s and 1990s the list of the largest "fallen flag" carriers increased, whether the 1982 union of Norfolk Western and Southern or the 1997 merger of Union Pacific and Southern Pacific. By the second decade of the twenty-first century, the nation's railroad network was dominated by two competing roads in the East, CSX and Norfolk Southern, and two in the West, Union Pacific and Burlington Northern Santa Fe. Two Canadian carriers, Canadian National and Canadian Pacific, also had established a major presence in the United States. The result: customers had access to "seamless" rail service to many destinations. "Railroads are network operations, and the bigger the network, the more effective you are," commented Robert (Rob) Krebs, a skilled late-twentieth-century Southern Pacific and Santa Fe railroad executive. Barriger would have agreed. These mega carriers also frequently offered "run-through" interline trains, especially for intermodal shipments. Yet these railroads greatly reduced competition, and in recent years some customers have complained vociferously about "excessive rates" and poor service and have agitated for reregulation.[11]

The way that "merger madness" was evolving pleased Barriger. He liked the union of the New York Central, Pennsylvania, and New Haven that created Penn Central (PC), and he believed that it had "the potential of being the GM of railroad transportation." Commenting in June 1970 following the PC bankruptcy, Barriger said, "Penn Central is not a failure of consolidation, but a managerial failure. Instead of getting married, they [PC] started a war. It was management incompatibility. You can't have civil war in the executive suite." He also felt that the former New York Central officials, including Al Perlman, were "unduly influenced by the Pennsy gang of Stuart Saunders." This attack on PC management unfortunately precipitated a break with his long-time friend Al Perlman, who did not take kindly to such thinking about alleged managerial deficiencies. Yet various industry observers agreed with the Barriger assessment of why Penn Central went bankrupt. As a Reading official, for one, reflected, "Incredibly inept advance planning, particularly in the area of employee protection guarantees, coupled with vicious infighting between the 'green team' [NYC] and 'red team' [PRR] managements has assured the failure of this merger before the first train runs."[12]

The corporate rationalization that Barriger longed for also coincided with less regulatory meddling, but this occurred after his death. Passage of the Staggers Act in 1980 was precisely what that doctor of sick railroads had prescribed for decades. This monumental piece of federal legislation – a railroad Magna Carta – essentially permitted the industry to sink or swim financially. As controls set by the ICC dwindled, and partial rate deregulation took hold, there followed a profound and positive impact on all railroads, whether mega, regional, or short-line carriers. Barriger probably never thought that the father of federal regulatory bodies, the ICC, would ever disappear, but it did. On January 1, 1996, the Surface Transportation Board, a unit of the US Department of Transportation, came into being. This Washington agency assumed some of the regulatory functions that had once been administered by the ICC, but it was not a reincarnation of its defunct predecessor.

In a similar fashion, Barriger had long worried about government ownership. He thought that this was a real possibility. After all, Washington took action with formation of the National Railroad Passenger Corporation (Amtrak) in 1971 and the Consolidated Railroad Corporation (Conrail) five years later, but these were actually quasi-public corporations. While a financially struggling Amtrak retained that status, Conrail did not. In 1987 the federal government sold its stake at a handsome profit. Later giants CSX and Norfolk Southern acquired what had become the investor-owned Conrail by splitting its assets. Any fears that Barriger would have had about a nationalized freight rail system vanished, at least for the foreseeable future.

In various ways, the railroad enterprise that Barriger had envisioned in the Prince Plan and *Super-Railroads for a Dynamic American Economy* has been realized. By the second decade of the twenty-first century the industry has achieved greater efficiencies, the best routes or "corridors" utilizations, enhanced physical plants, and state-of-the-art equipment, including powerful and energy-efficient locomotives. Had John Barriger been a railroad prophet? Perhaps so. Indisputably he became an industry legend in his own time.

Notes

PREFACE

1. Interview with David J. DeBoer, June 27, 2016; Tom Shedd, "Why They Made Him Man of the Year," *Modern Railroads* 24 (January 1969): 57.

2. Rush Loving Jr., *The Well-Dressed Hobo: The Many Wondrous Adventures of a Man Who Loves Trains* (Bloomington: Indiana University Press, 2016), 130.

1. EARLY LIFE AND CAREER

1. John W. Barriger III, "An Autobiography of John Walker Barriger, III," November 1975, hereafter cited as Barriger Autobiography, John W. Barriger III papers, John W. Barriger III National Railroad Library, St. Louis, MO, hereafter cited as Barriger papers; "Thirty-Eighth Annual Report of the Association of Graduates of the United States Military Academy at West Point, New York, June 13, 1907," 74, hereafter cited as "West Point Thirty-Eighth Annual Report." The background of the Barriger family is murky. "Barriger does not sound Dutch," commented Dutch historian Augustus J. Veenendaal. "However, the name Berger is not uncommon in the Netherlands. It does occur in Delft, for instance, and in other towns. Another remote possibility could have been a family from Barge, which is a small village in the Dutch province of Drenthe. Berger or Bergere is also common in French, for cowherd or shepherd/shepherdess." Veenendaal thought that there might be German roots. "Many Germans from the neighboring areas of Germany came to the rich country of the Dutch Republic during the 17th and 18th centuries. Many stayed but some moved on to America and South Africa. Barriger sounds more German than Dutch to my ears." Augustus J. Veenendaal to author, January 6, 2016.

2. "West Point Thirty-Eighth Annual Report," 74–76; Barriger Autobiography; William Henry Powell and Edward Shippen, eds., *Officers of the Army and the Navy (Regular) Who Served in the Civil War* (Philadelphia: L. R. Hamersly, 1892), 27; *New York Times*, September 18, 1894, January 1, 1907. The title of John W. Barriger Sr.'s government-published study, "Major and Commissary of Subsistence, and Bvt. Brigadier-General," which he compiled, is the three-chapter *Legislative History of the Subsistence Department of the United States Army from June 16, 1775 to August 15, 1876* (Washington, DC: Government Printing Office, 1877). John W. (Jack) Barriger IV made these comments about his great grandfather: "Family stories from Dad and Didi [JWB III's mother] tell that Lt. JWB's company was heavily involved in the First

Bull Run. JWB's commanding officer was killed and JWB was given a battlefield promotion and put in charge of his Company." John W. Barriger IV to author, January 12, 2017, hereafter cited as JWB IV to author (with date).

3. "West Point Thirty-Eighth Annual Report," 75.

4. Barriger Autobiography; "Copy from a draft for an obituary sent to the American Society of Engineers by Edith Beck Barriger, Sunday, July 24, 1949," in Barriger papers, hereafter cited as 1949 draft obituary; Ralph E. Morrow, *Washington University in St. Louis* (St. Louis: Missouri Historical Society Press, 1996), 167, 192–93.

5. Barriger Autobiography; 1949 draft obituary.

6. Barriger Autobiography; 1949 draft obituary; *The Biographical Directory of the Railway Officials of America* (Chicago: Railway Age Company, 1906), 207.

7. Barriger Autobiography.

8. Barriger Autobiography.

9. Barriger Autobiography; 1949 draft obituary; *Poor's Manual of the Railroads of the United States* (New York: H. V. and H. W. Poor, 1902), 1514.

10. Barriger Autobiography; 1949 draft obituary.

11. *St. Louis Republic*, December 20, 1902; *St. Louis Globe-Democrat*, December 20, 1902; *St. Louis Post-Dispatch*, December 20, 1902.

12. *St. Louis Globe-Democrat*, December 20, 1902; *St. Louis Post-Dispatch*, December 22, 1902; *One Hundred Years of Medicine and Surgery in Missouri* (St. Louis, MO: St. Louis Star, 1900), 312.

13. Barriger Autobiography; *St. Louis Post-Dispatch*, February 1, 1903, February 17, 1903.

14. Barriger Autobiography; JWB IV to author, October 13, 2015. Tom Morton had blood ties to a distinguished American family, the Taliaferros of Virginia. One prominent Taliaferro was James Taliaferro, who served in the US Senate from Florida between 1899 and 1911.

15. Barriger Autobiography. Edith Barriger had her husband buried at Bellefontaine Cemetery in St. Louis. On the large granite tombstone she included this inscription: "Associate Member American Society of Civil Engineers." Her grandson recalled, "None of us [Barriger family] thought that was an important thing to put on a tombstone." JWB IV to author, January 12, 2016.

16. Barriger Autobiography; *Washington Post*, March 29, 1922; *Fifty-Third Annual Report of the Woman's Union Missionary Society of America* (New York, 1914).

17. Barriger Autobiography.

18. Barriger Autobiography.

19. John W. Barriger diaries, 1913, 1914, Barriger papers.

20. Barriger Autobiography.

21. Barriger Autobiography; Barriger diary, 1913, Barriger papers, hereafter cited as Barriger diary with date; Barriger diary, June 3, 1915.

22. Barriger Autobiography.

23. Barriger Autobiography.

24. Barriger Autobiography; Barriger diary entries, February 13, 1915, February 20, 1915; Reuben A. Lewis Jr., "Barriger Will Guide the Monon's Destinies," *Finance* 50 (May 10, 1946): 47.

25. Barriger diaries, 1916, 1917, Barriger papers.

26. Barriger Autobiography; Albert J. Churella, *The Pennsylvania Railroad: Building an Empire, 1846–1917* (Philadelphia: University of Pennsylvania Press, 2013), 681–83.

27. Barriger Autobiography; *The Biographical Dictionary of the Railway Officials of America* (New York: Simmons-Boardman Publishing Company, 8th ed., 1922), 263–64; John W. Barriger III, autobiographical sketch, April 12, 1932, Barriger

papers, hereafter cited as Autobiographical sketch, 1932.

28. Lewis, "Barriger Will Guide the Monon's Destinies," 47.

29. Barriger Autobiography; Robert C. Cottrell, *Roger Nash Baldwin and the American Civil Liberties Union* (New York: Columbia University Press, 2000), 22–45; James Neal Primm, *Lion of the Valley: St. Louis, Missouri, 1764–1980*, 3rd ed. (St. Louis: Missouri Historical Society Press, 1998), 400.

30. Margot McMillen, *The Golden Lane: How Missouri Women Gained the Vote and Changed History* (Charleston, SC: History Press, 2011), 51, 92–93; Virginia Jeans Laas, ed., *Bridging Two Eras: The Autobiography of Emily Newell Blair, 1877–1951* (Columbia: University of Missouri Press, 1999), xiv, 162, 170–71; JWB IV to author, October 13, 2015, January 1, 2017; *St. Louis Post-Dispatch*, November 2, 1917.

31. *St. Louis Post-Dispatch*, December 2, 1918, January 19, 1920.

32. Barriger Autobiography.

33. Interview with John W. Barriger IV, October 3, 2015, hereafter cited as JWB IV interview (with date); JWB IV to author, October 13, 2015.

34. Autobiographical sketch, 1932.

35. Massachusetts Institute of Technology official transcript for John Walker Barriger, III, issued January 11, 2016; Barriger diary, 1921; John W. Barriger III to John W. Ingram, July 14, 1973, Barriger papers; JWB IV to author, December 10, 2015.

36. Autobiographical sketch, 1932.

37. Barriger diary, 1921.

38. Autobiographical sketch, 1932; George H. Burgess and Miles C. Kennedy, *Centennial History of the Pennsylvania Railroad Company, 1846–1946* (Philadelphia: Pennsylvania Railroad Company, 1949), 539–40.

39. Autobiographical sketch, 1932; Barriger diary, June 6, 1922; Harold H. McLean, *Pittsburgh and Lake Erie R.R.*

(San Marino, CA: Golden West Books, 1980), 129.

40. Autobiographical sketch, 1932; Colin J. Davis, *Power at Odds: The 1922 National Railroad Shopmen's Strike* (Urbana: University of Illinois Press, 1997).

41. Letter to the Supt. Fgt. Trans. Requesting Certain Changes in the Transportation Course, February 5, 1924, Barriger papers.

42. Autobiographical sketch, 1932.

43. "Tape recording of interview of Robert E. Bedingfield of the *New York Times* with John W. Barriger, President, Missouri-Kansas-Texas Railroad, at the M-K-T offices in St. Louis, Missouri, on March 18, 1969," Barriger papers, hereafter cited as Bedingfield interview.

44. Autobiographical sketch, 1932; Bedingfield interview.

45. Michael R. Federspiel, *Little Traverse Bay: Past and Present* (Detroit, MI: Wayne State University Press, 2014), 244–55; Lewis, "Barriger Will Guide the Monon's Destinies," 47; JWB IV interview, August 6, 2015; *St. Louis Globe-Democrat*, July 17, 1934. Jack Barriger elaborated on how Thatcher left war-torn Mexico. "Grandfather Thatcher knew that [Francisco "Pancho"] Villa had worked for him and that he had been treated fairly. While Villa started slaughtering gringos and other foreigners, Grandfather sent his wife and children to St. Louis but he was quite ill at the time and stayed behind. When he recovered sufficiently, he sent word to Villa that he wanted to be escorted from Parral to La Junta to take the train back to US. Villa sent a senior officer to escort Grandfather and gave him a knife that was well known to the peasantry as further identification to get through the blockades." JWB IV to author, January 12, 2017.

46. JWB IV interview, August 6, 2015; Bedingfield interview; *St. Louis Post-Dispatch*, January 6, 1924.

47. JWB IV interview, August 6, 2015.

48. Bedingfield interview; John W. Barriger III to Edith Barriger, September 19, 1926, Barriger papers; John W. Barriger IV to author, February 11, 2016; *St. Louis Globe-Democrat*, October 3, 1926; *St. Louis Censor*, May 5, 1927.

49. JWB IV interview, August 5, 2015; John W. Barriger to Elizabeth Barriger, October 29, 1926, Barriger papers; Postal Telegraph Company telegram from John Barriger to Elizabeth Barriger, January 25, 1933, Barriger papers.

50. "Supplementary Statement of J. W. Barriger," n.d., Barriger papers.

51. Bedingfield interview.

52. Bedingfield interview.

53. "Railroad," undated article galley proofs, Barriger papers.

54. Churella, *The Pennsylvania Railroad*, 714; Bedingfield interview; "Nomination of John W. Barriger III for National Transportation Award, National Defense Transportation Association," 1964, Barriger papers.

55. Bedingfield interview.

56. Autobiographical sketch, 1932; "Summary of Interview of J. W. Barriger's Trip to Montreal, Canada, February 1, 2, 3, 1929," Barriger papers.

57. Bedingfield interview.

58. Bedingfield interview.

59. Bedingfield interview.

60. Bedingfield interview; "Supplementary Statement of J. W. Barriger"; editorial appearing in the *Washington Court House [Ohio] Herald* of July 18, 1931," Barriger papers.

61. John W. Barriger III, *The Pennsylvania Railroad* (New York: Calvin Bullock, 1930), 88.

62. "Biographical Sketch," ca. 1933, Barriger papers.

2. GOVERNMENT MAN

1. "Nomination of John W. Barriger, III, for National Transportation Award, National Defense Transportation Association," 1964, hereafter cited as "Nomination of John W. Barriger," John W. Barriger III papers, John W. Barriger III National Railroad Library, St. Louis, MO, hereafter cited as Barriger papers; page proofs, *Railroad Magazine*, n.d., Barriger papers, hereafter cited as *Railroad Magazine* page proofs; "Supplementary Statement of J. W. Barriger," n.d., Barriger papers, hereafter cited as "Supplementary Statement."

2. H. Roger Grant, "Grouping America's Railroads: The Transportation Act of 1920," *Classic Trains* 12 (Winter 2011): 30.

3. Richard Stone, *The Interstate Commerce Commission and the Railroad Industry: A History of Regulatory Policy* (New York: Praeger, 1991), 2.

4. Albro Martin, *Enterprise Denied: Origins of the Decline of American Railroads, 1897–1917* (New York: Columbia University Press, 1971), 350.

5. "Regional Railroad Consolidation," *Railway Age* 94 (April 1, 1933): 465.

6. Ari and Olive Hoogenboom, *A History of the ICC: From Panacea to Palliative* (New York: W. W. Norton, 1976), 92.

7. Richard Saunders Jr., *Merging Lines: American Railroads, 1900–1970* (DeKalb: Northern Illinois University Press, 2001), 45; Julius Grodinsky, *Railroad Consolidation: Its Economic and Controlling Principles* (New York: D. Appleton, 1930), 2–3; *New York Times*, February 24, 1920.

8. Colin J. Davis, *Power at Odds: The 1922 National Railroad Shopmen's Strike* (Urbana: University of Illinois Press, 1997), 57–62; Robert H. Zieger, *Republicans and Labor, 1919–1929* (Lexington: University of Kentucky Press, 1969), 118–21, 192.

9. Clair Wilcox, *Public Policies toward Business*, 4th ed. (Homewood, IL: Richard D. Irwin, 1971), 376–77.

10. William Z. Ripley, ed., *Railway Problems: An Early History of Competition and Regulation* (Boston: Ginn, 1913);

William Z. Ripley, ed., *Trusts, Pools and Corporations* (Boston: Ginn, 1916).

11. William Norris Leonard, *Railroad Consolidation under the Transportation Act of 1920* (New York: Columbia University Press, 1946), 81.

12. Leonard, *Railroad Consolidation under the Transportation Act of 1920*, 307–08.

13. Leonard, *Railroad Consolidation under the Transportation Act of 1920*, 119–27.

14. Leonard, *Railroad Consolidation under the Transportation Act of 1920*, 311–36.

15. John Will Chapman, *Railroad Mergers* (New York: Simmons-Boardman Company, 1934), 39; Saunders, *Merging Lines*, 66–67.

16. Chapman, *Railroad Mergers*, 41–42; *Railway Age* 91 (November 28, 1931): 820–21.

17. "Address of Governor Roosevelt, Mormon Temple, Salt Lake City, Utah, September 17, 1932, 7:15 p.m.," 7, Franklin D. Roosevelt Papers, Franklin D. Roosevelt Presidential Library, Hyde Park, NY, hereafter cited as Roosevelt Salt Lake City Speech.

18. Hoogenboom, *A History of the ICC*, 123.

19. William D. Middleton, George M. Smerk and Roberta L. Diehl, eds., *Encyclopedia of North American Railroads* (Bloomington: Indiana University Press, 2007), 929–30; Chapman, *Railroad Mergers*, 113–22.

20. Roosevelt Salt Lake City Speech, 11–12. Franklin Roosevelt relied heavily on his advisors to assist him in preparing his speeches. It is unclear who helped with the Salt Lake City speech, but A. A. Berle Jr. and Raymond Moley were likely involved.

21. Raymond Moley, *After Seven Years* (New York: Harper & Brothers Publishers, 1939), 45; "Supplementary Statement"; "Tape recording of interview of Robert E. Bedingfield of the *New York Times* with John W. Barriger, President, Missouri-Kansas-Texas Railroad, at the M-K-T offices in St. Louis, Missouri, on March 18, 1969," Barriger papers, hereafter cited as Bedingfield interview.

22. *New York Times*, February 3, 1953; Paul Wesley Ivey, *The Pere Marquette Railroad Company* (Lansing: Michigan Historical Commission, 1919), 292–303. The likely motivation for Frederick Prince to acquire Marble House was that neighbors of his Prides Crossing estate in Beverly, Massachusetts, had largely ostracized him from their community after he allegedly whipped a stable boy. Prince also had homes in Aiken, South Carolina, and in France. Interview with John W. Barriger IV, September 29, 2016, hereafter cited as JWB IV interview (with date).

23. *New York Times*, September 23, 1933; "Eastman Studying Merits of Consolidation Plan," *Railway Age* 95 (September 30, 1933): 471–72; Bedingfield interview; JWB IV interview, August 5, 2015.

24. "Consolidations of Railways," January 7, 1931, Barriger papers.

25. John W. Barriger IV to author, August 27, 2016, hereafter cited as JWB IV to author (with date); *Traffic World* (May 2, 1964), copy in Barriger papers; *Regulation of Railroads* (Washington, DC: U.S. Government Printing Office, 1934), 23.

26. "Prince Rail Consolidation Plan," *Railway Age* 94 (March 25, 1933): 446.

27. "The Prince Plan: A Plan for Coordinating the Operations of Railroads in the United States, March 15, 1933, Revised September 30, 1933," Barriger papers, hereafter cited as "The Prince Plan"; "The Prince Plan (So-called) of Railroad Consolidation, Revised to Sept. 30, 1933, by Mr. Barriger," *Poor's Manual of Steam Railroads* (New York: Poor's Manual Company, 1935), 39–48, hereafter cited as *Poor's* 1935 report.

28. "System #5," n.d., Barriger papers.

29. "Railroad Plan Nears Completion," *Railway Age* 94 (April 18, 1933): 509–10.

30. "The Prince Plan."

31. *Poor's* 1935 report; "Prince Rail Consolidation Plan," 446.

32. *Railroad Magazine* page proofs.

33. Earl Latham, *The Politics of Railroad Consolidation, 1933–1936* (Cambridge, MA: Harvard University Press, 1959), 38; Dudley Hovey, "'Checking Up' the Prince Plan," *Barron's*, December 18, 1933.

34. "Regional Railway Consolidation," 465, 467.

35. *Pittsburgh Press*, January 2, 1934; Latham, *The Politics of Railroad Consolidation*, 38, 291; *Traffic World*, May 2, 1964.

36. *New York Times*, April 2, 1933, January 22, 1934; Claude Moore Fuess, *Joseph B. Eastman: Servant of the People* (New York: Columbia University Press, 1952), 235; "To the Federal Coordinator of Transportation, Statement on Behalf of Baltimore Association of Commerce in Opposition to Proposed 'Prince' Plan of Railroad Consolidation," November 29, 1933, in Barriger papers; *Regulation of Railroads*, 25; *New York Times*, October 12, 1933; "Cornwell, B.&O. Counsel, Criticizes the Prince Plan," *Railway Age* 95 (October 21, 1933): 571–72; "Cornwell Address Scorns Prince Plan," *Railway Age* 95 (December 16, 1933): 861–62; Shelby Cullom Davis, "The Financial Aspects of Railroad Consolidation," *Journal of the American Statistical Association* 34 (June 1939): 273; Kent T. Healy, *The Economics of Transportation in America* (New York: Ronald Press, 1940), 408.

37. Bedingfield interview.

38. Latham, *The Politics of Railroad Consolidation*, 66; Emory R. Johnson, *Government Regulation of Transportation* (New York, 1938), 330–31; *Wall Street Journal*, May 6, 1933; James B. Burns, *Railroad Mergers and the Language of Unification* (Westport, CT: Quorum Books, 1998), 17; Middleton, Smerk, and Diehl, *Encyclopedia of North American Railroads*, 149; Richard C. Overton, *Burlington Route: A History of the Burlington Lines* (New York:

Knopf, 1965), 427–29; William James Cunningham, *The Present Railroad Crisis* (Philadelphia: University of Pennsylvania Press, 1939), 54–55; Julius H. Parmelee, *The Modern Railway* (New York: Longmans, Green, 1940), 217. The 1933 measure repealed the recapture clause of the Transportation Act of 1920, which had proved ineffective and had provoked considerable litigation.

39. "Nomination of John W. Barriger"; Jesse H. Jones, *Fifty Billion Dollars: My Thirteen Years with the RFC, 1932–1945* (New York: Macmillan, 1951), 145.

40. JWB IV interview, August 6, 2015; JWB IV to author, March 2, 2016.

41. JWB IV to author, August 7, 2015; Bedingfield interview; JWB IV to author, March 3, 2016.

42. John Sherman Porter, ed., *Moody's Manual of Investments: Railroad Securities* (New York: Moody's Investors Service, 1945), a13–a24.

43. "Statement of John W. Barrier, III before Subcommittee of Senate Committee on Interstate Commerce, Thursday, May 28, 1936, 10:30 A.M., Washington, D.C.," Barriger papers.

44. John F. Stover, *History of the Baltimore & Ohio Railroad* (West Lafayette, IN: Purdue University Press, 1987), 293; H. Roger Grant, "Missouri Southern: History of a Shortline," *Railway & Locomotive Historical Society Bulletin* 123 (October 1970): 49; "Nomination of John W. Barriger."

45. *Jacksonville (Florida) Times-Union*, November 3, 1934; H. W. Purvis to John W. Barriger III, November 16, 1934, Barriger papers; undated newspaper clipping, ca. 1938, Barriger papers.

46. See H. Roger Grant, *Rails through the Wiregrass: A History of the Georgia & Florida Railroad* (DeKalb: Northern Illinois University Press, 2006).

47. Grant, *Rails through the Wiregrass*, 138.

48. "Memorandum in re Conference on Georgia and Florida Railroad, June 4, 1935," Barriger papers; "Memorandum to the Board of Directors from Hilton M. Moore, examiner, Railroad Division, June 6, 1935," Barriger papers.

49. Frank P. Donovan Jr., *Mileposts On the Prairie: The Story of the Minneapolis & St. Louis Railway* (New York: Simmons-Boardman Publishing, 1950), 199–202; *New York Times*, May 27, 1936.

50. Don L. Hofsommer, *The Tootin' Louie: A History of the Minneapolis & St. Louis Railway* (Minneapolis: University of Minnesota Press, 2005), 181.

51. Hofsommer, *The Tootin' Louie*, 189, 193; Donovan, *Mileposts on the Prairie*, 207.

52. Hofsommer, *The Tootin' Louie*, 198, 209–11.

53. *St. Louis Daily Globe-Democrat*, January 22, 1934; JWB IV interview, August 6, 2015, October 3, 2015.

54. JWB IV to author, October 13, 2015; JWB IV interview, August 6, 2015. Recalled her grandson, "The US Naval Observatory was five or six blocks from 3611 Fulton St., and Didi walked there. She loved the job, her very first, working for the Navy." JWB IV to author, August 27, 2016.

55. John Sherman Porter, ed., *Moody's Manual of Investments: Railroad Securities* (New York: Moody's Investors Service, 1935), 161; John Sherman Porter, ed., *Moody's Manual of Investments: Railroad Securities* (New York: Moody's Investors Service, 1947), 458; *New York Times*, January 11, 1940.

56. J. W. Barriger to H. R. Sampson, n.d., Barriger papers; George H. Drury, comp., *The Historical Guide to North American Railroads* (Milwaukee, WI: Kalmbach Books, 1985), 65–66.

57. Helen C. Boland to Mrs. [Elizabeth] Barriger, August 7, 1941, Barriger papers; Reconstruction Finance Corporation, Washington, *Resolutions*, n.d., Barriger papers.

58. "Supplementary Statement."

59. "Supplementary Statement"; *New York Times*, December 3, 1941.

60. *New York Times*, October 14, 1941; unidentified clipping, October 10, 1941, Barriger papers.

61. "Supplementary Statement"; John W. Barriger III diary, 1942, Barriger papers, hereafter cited as Barriger diary with date.

62. "Address delivered by Mr. John W. Barriger, Federal Manager of the Properties of the Toledo, Peoria & Western Railroad, at the meeting of the National Industrial Traffic League, held at the Netherland Plaza Hotel, Cincinnati, Ohio, on April 14th, 1942," Barriger papers, hereafter cited as Cincinnati speech, April 14, 1942; *Who's Who in Railroading* (New York: Simmons-Boardman Publishing, 1946), 62.

63. Barriger diary, 1942; untitled biographical sketch, ca. 1956, Barriger papers.

64. Barriger diary, 1942.

65. JWB IV interview, August 6, 2015; *New York Times*, August 7, 1956.

66. Barriger diary, 1942.

67. Barriger diary, 1942; Cincinnati speech, April 14, 1942.

68. Drury, *The Historical Guide to North American Railroads*, 325; *New York Times*, May 28, 1926, June 12, 1926, March 11, 1942, March 23, 1942, March 11, 1947; *Petaluma (California) Post*, October 8, 2012; "Background of T.P.& W Strike," *Railway Age* 122 (March 22, 1947):596.

69. Barriger diary, 1942.

70. Barriger diary, 1942.

71. John Sherman Porter, ed., *Moody's Manual of Investments* (New York: Moody's Investors Service, 1946), 269–70.

72. Barriger diary, 1942.

73. *Chicago Daily Tribune*, March 12, 1947; *New York Times*, March 11, 1947; "Background of T.P.& W. Strike," 596. John W. Barriger IV offered these

comments about the assassination of George McNear: "When I was at MIT attending classes with Denman K. McNear, later of Southern Pacific fame, when his Uncle was killed. Denny's father, also Denman K. McNear, owned the Petaluma and Santa Rosa Railroad. Denny McNear and his father were both certain that George was murdered by Union arrangement with Chicago mobsters." JWB IV to author, August 27, 2016.

3. MONON

1. "Security Investigation Data for Sensitive Position," July 6, 1973, hereafter cited as "Security Investigation Data," John W. Barriger III papers, John W. Barriger III National Railroad Library, St. Louis, MO, hereafter cited as Barriger papers; "Nomination of John W. Barriger, III, for National Transportation Award, National Defense Transportation Association," 1964, Barriger papers; John W. Barriger IV to author, March 6, 2016, January 12, 2017, hereafter cited as JWB IV to author (with date).

2. Mary D. Schopp, *50 Golden Years: An Historical Account of the Central Manufacturing District's First 50 Years* (Chicago: n.p., 1955), 9; "Central Manufacturing District," in James R. Grossman, Ann Durkin Keating, and Janice L. Reiff, eds., *The Encyclopedia of Chicago* (Chicago: University of Chicago Press, 2004), 124.

3. JWB IV to author, December 20, 2015; January 12, 2017.

4. J. Parker Lamb, *Evolution of the American Diesel Locomotive* (Bloomington: Indiana University Press, 2007), 84–85; Albert J. Churella, *From Steam to Diesel: Managerial Customs and Organizational Capabilities in the Twentieth-Century American Locomotive Industry* (Princeton, NJ: Princeton University Press, 1998), 90–91; Jerry A. Pinkepank, "Born at Beloit: The Cinderella of Dieseldom,

Fairbanks-Morse," *Trains* 25 (November 1964): 38–39, 47.

5. Lamb, *Evolution of the American Diesel Locomotive*, 85; Pinkepank, "Born at Beloit," 45.

6. John W. Barriger diary, 1944, Barriger papers, hereafter cited as Barriger diary with date; Churella, *From Steam to Diesel*, 123; "Supplementary Statement of J. W. Barriger," n.d., Barriger papers, hereafter cited as "Supplementary Statement."

7. Barriger diary, 1944.

8. Interview with John W. Barriger IV, August 6, 2015, hereafter cited as JWB IV interview (with date).

9. Lamb, *Evolution of the American Diesel Locomotive*, 86, 88, 107; Hugh S. Norton, "The Locomotive Industry in the United States, 1920–1960," *Bulletin of the Railway & Locomotive Historical Society* 113 (October 1965): 75; Churella, *From Steam to Diesel*, 89–90, 124; John W. Barriger IV to Edward A. Burkhardt, July 28, 2015, in possession of author; JWB IV interview, April 9, 2016; C. H. Wendel, *Fairbanks Morse: 100 Years of Engine Technology* (Lancaster, PA: Stemgas Publishing, 1993), 132.

10. George W. Hilton, *Monon Route* (La Jolla, CA: Howell-North Books, 1978), 163; *Report of the Chicago, Indianapolis and Louisville Railway for the Year Ended December 31, 1946* (Chicago: Chicago, Indianapolis and Louisville Railway Company, 1947), 3; *Railway Age* 120 (May 4, 1946): 921; *Railway Age* 120 (May 11, 1946): 961; "Address," November 13, 1948, Barriger papers; *Indianapolis Times*, September 16, 1946; "Aspirin for a Hoosier Headache," *Business Week*, reprint of March 29, 1947, Barriger papers; *Indianapolis News*, May 19, 1947.

11. Linn H. Westcott, "The Monon System and Its Traffic," *Trains*, July 1947, 21–32.

12. George H. Drury, comp., *The Historical Guide to North American Railroads*

(Milwaukee, WI: Kalmbach Books, 1985), 78–79; *Poor's Manual of the Railroads of the United States* (New York: Poor's Railroad Manual Company, 1906), 348; Maury Klein, *History of the Louisville & Nashville Railroad* (New York: Macmillan, 1972), 310. "Memorandum to Mr. A. E. Perlman," from John W. Barriger III, May 8, 1964, Barriger papers.

13. John Sherman Porter, ed., *Moody's Manual of Investments: Railroad Securities* (New York: Moody's Investors Service, 1935), 135, 140; Drury, *The Historical Guide to North American Railroads*, 79–80; Reuben A. Lewis Jr., "Barriger Will Guide the Monon's Destinies," *Finance* 50 (May 10, 1946): 42.

14. "Aspirin for a Hoosier Headache"; *Indianapolis Star*, January 7, 1947; *Seattle Post Intelligencer*, March 30, 1948; "Making an 'Unnecessary Railroad' an Asset to Shippers and Its Territory," *Railway Age* 132 (February 4, 1952): 73.

15. "Aspirin for a Hoosier Headache"; Gary W. Dolzall and Stephen F. Dolzall, *Monon: The Hoosier Line*, 2nd rev. ed. (Bloomington: Indiana University Press, 2002), 64; John W. Barriger, "The Monon Is a Guinea Pig," *Trains* 7 (July 1947): 16; "Making an 'Unnecessary Railroad' an Asset to Shippers and Its Territory," 73.

16. John W. Barriger, "A Railroad Futurama," December 15, 1943, Barriger papers; Barriger, "The Monon Is a Guinea Pig," 15; Charles Penrose Jr. and John W. Barriger IV, *The John W. Barriger III National Railroad Library* (New York: Newcomen Society, 1999), 8. In 1956 Simmons-Boardman Publishing Corporation initially published Barriger's *Super-Railroads For a Dynamic American Economy*, and later the Missouri-Kansas-Texas Railroad Company reissued the book.

17. Hilton, *Monon Route*, 195; Westcott, "The Monon System and Its Traffic," 20; *Who's Who in Railroading in North America*, 11th ed. (New York:

Simmons-Boardman Publishing, 1946), 85, 117.

18. Westcott, "The Monon System and Its Traffic," 20.

19. Dolzall and Dolzall, *Monon*, 66–67, 70, 71.

20. Penrose and Barriger, *The John W. Barriger III National Railroad Library*, 9.

21. Hilton, *Monon Route*, 187; "What Is the Monon?," n.d., Barriger papers; JWB IV to author, January 12, 2017.

22. Hilton, *Monon Route*, 195, 210; "Making an 'Unnecessary Railroad' an Asset to Shippers and Its Territory," 76; Dolzall and Dolzall, *Monon*, 88–89; Barriger, "The Monon Is a Guinea Pig," 19; *Annual Report of Monon, Chicago, Indianapolis and Louisville Railway for the Year Ended December 31, 1949* (Chicago: Monon, Chicago, Indianapolis and Louisville Railway Company, 1950), 8.

23. Hilton, *Monon Route*, 203, 206–9; Dolzall and Dolzall, *Monon*, 72; *Report of Chicago, Indianapolis and Louisville Railway Company for the Year Ended December 31, 1948* (Chicago: Chicago, Indianapolis and Louisville Railway Company, 1949), 7.

24. Barriger, "Monon Is a Guinea Pig," 16.

25. Hilton, *Monon Route*, 195, 197.

26. Barriger, "Monon Is a Guinea Pig," 16; Dolzall and Dolzall, *Monon*, 86.

27. *Indianapolis Times*, September 26, 1946; Chicago, Indianapolis & Louisville Railway public timetable, August 17, 1947.

28. Chicago, Indianapolis & Louisville Railway public timetable, March 4, 1945.

29. Dolzall and Dolzall, *Monon*, 76–77.

30. Hilton, *Monon Route*, 191; Chicago, Indianapolis & Louisville Railway public timetable, August 17, 1947; Craig Sanders, *Limiteds, Locals, and Expresses in Indiana, 1838–1971* (Bloomington: Indiana University Press, 2003), 23.

31. Hilton, *Monon Route*, 187, 190; Kincaid A. Herr, *The Louisville & Nashville*

Railroad, 1850–1963 (Lexington: University Press of Kentucky, 2000), 283.

32. Hilton, *Monon Route*, 190; Arthur D. Dubin, *More Classic Trains* (Glendale, CA: Interurban Press, 1995), 175.

33. Hilton, *Monon Route*, 191; Dolzall and Dolzall, *Monon*, 84, 90–91; *Annual Report*, 1948, 5; *Annual Report*, 1949, 6; "Fifty Years of Thoroughbreds, 1900–1950," *Railway Age* 129 (October 28, 1950): 120.

34. Sanders, *Limited, Locals, and Expresses in Indiana*, 25.

35. Interview with Herbert H. Harwood Jr., September 17, 2015; David DeBoer, "JWB III," manuscript in possession of author. Barriger's son Jack was not certain about the bottle breakage. "I have heard that story about Dad breaking liquor bottles. I am sure he would have complained about less than the best liquor, but I think it is unlikely that he broke any bottles." Yet he recalled a somewhat similar happening. "I do remember being on the business car riding south when the following occurred. Passing the kitchen, we all saw the standing rib roast being readied for Sunday lunch. Probably it had come from the Union Stockyards Commissary. When it was served, it was brown on both sides and looked greasy, unlike what we were used to. Dad called for the cook and asked how it had been prepared. The cook said he sliced pieces and cooked them in his frying pan in true southern style. Dad asked the cook to bring him the pan and then took it to the back of the car and threw it over the right of way fence, telling the cook he never wanted to see a frying pan on the business car again." John W. Barriger IV to author, August 27, 2016.

36. JWB IV interview, August 6, 2015; JWB IV to author, August 15, 2015, April 18, 2016.

37. "Security Investigation Data"; JWB IV to author, October 13, 2015; March 6, 2016.

38. "Making an 'Unnecessary Railroad' an Asset to Shippers and Its Territory," 74–75.

39. *Indianapolis Times*, September 26, 1946; Linn H. Westcott, "Today's Monon," *Trains*, March 1951, 22; *Railway Age* 128 (June 6, 1950): 39.

40. JWB IV interview, August 6, 2015; John W. Barriger, *A Hoosier Centenarian: "The Monon"* (Princeton, NJ: Newcomen Society, 1947), 9–21.

41. H. Roger Grant, "Celebrating a Century," *Classic Trains* 2 (Fall 2001): 68–69.

42. "A Century of Service," galley page proof, 1947, Barriger papers; *Bedford (IN) Daily Times-Mail*, February 26, 1947; John W. Barriger IV to author, August 27, 2016; *Report of Chicago, Indianapolis and Louisville Railway Company for the Year Ended December 31, 1946* (Chicago: Chicago, Indianapolis and Louisville Railway Company, 1947), 8. In 1997 Mary Etta Ronk Chase, who was "Miss Ladoga," recalled this about these young beauties: "Over the years that followed we always called ourselves Belles of the Monon. There was some confusion as to whether we were Belles of the Monon or Queens. In actuality the six girls from New Albany were the only Belles and we were the Queens, each of us representing our home towns." And she added, "Each queen wore a sash 'Miss Whatever City' we represented." "July, 1947 Monon's Centennial Celebration," *Hoosier Line* 16 (1998):5.

43. Dolzall and Dolzall, *Monon*, 92–93; *Billboard*, May 10, 1947; *Annual Report* 1946, 8.

    If there was a disappointment with the centennial celebration, it was with a commissioned Monon history by the established railroad historian Edward Hungerford. Barriger did not care for the work, and so he decided against publication.

44. H. Roger Grant, *The North Western: A History of the Chicago & North Western*

Railway System (DeKalb: Northern Illinois University Press, 1996), 177–78.

45. Hilton, *Monon Route*, 217; Dolzall and Dolzall, *Monon*, 86–88; "Memorandum for the Information of the Public: Box Car Numbers," June 15, 1947, Barriger papers; J. W. Barriger, "Freedom From Fear," [speech], November 1948, Barriger papers.

46. Hilton, *Monon Route*, 195; John W. Barriger, "Vitamins for the Iron Horse," *Proceedings: The Journal of the Pacific Railway Club* 36 (April 1952): 15.

47. JWB IV interview, October 3, 2015; JWB IV to author, January 12, 2017; Maury Klein, *Union Pacific: The Reconfiguration: America's Greatest Railroad from 1969 to the Present* (New York: Oxford University Press, 2011), 55–56.

48. Hilton, *Monon Route*, 195; *Annual Report of Monon, Chicago, Indianapolis and Louisville Railway Company for the Year Ended December 31, 1950* (Chicago: Monon, Chicago, Indianapolis and Louisville Railway Company, 1951), inside front cover.

49. Dolzall and Dolzall, *Monon*, 105; JWB IV interview, August 5, 2015.

50. Hilton, *Monon Route*, 251; *Annual Report of Monon, Chicago, Indianapolis and Louisville Railway Company for the Year Ended December 31, 1952* (Chicago: Monon, Chicago, Indianapolis and Louisville Railway Company, 1951), 6.

51. JWB IV interview, October 2, 2015.

52. John W. Barriger, "A Railroad Officer's Creed," *Railway Age* 125 (October 23, 1948): 763.

4. TRANSITION YEARS

1. "Supplementary Statement of J. W. Barriger," n.d., Barriger papers, John W. Barriger III National Railroad Library, St. Louis, MO, hereafter cited as "Supplementary Statement."

2. John L. Weller, *The New Haven Railroad: Its Rise and Fall* (New York: Hastings House, 1969), 35–38; *Poor's Manual for 1895* (New York: H. V. & H. W. Poor, 1895), 596,

599; *Poor's Manual of Railroads* (New York: Poor's Manual Company, 1916), 845–46; "Frederic C. Dumaine, President of the New Haven," *Railway Age* 128 (January 28, 1950): 39; Herbert H. Harwood Jr., *The New York, Westchester & Boston Railway: J. P. Morgan's Magnificent Mistake* (Bloomington: Indiana University Press, 2008), 17.

3. Harwood, *The New York, Westchester & Boston Railway*, 106; *Moody's Transportation Manual* (New York: Moody's Investors Service, 1968), 669.

4. Geoff Doughty, "The New Haven Railroad: Darwin's Industrial Stepchild from Industry Giant to Industry Problems," paper presented at the annual meeting of the Lexington Group Inc., Newark, NJ, October 30, 2015.

5. Weller, *The New Haven Railroad*, 140, 142, 206; *Boston Globe*, April 18, 1997; *New York Times*, August 16, 1948; *Time*, June 4, 1951, 98; Doughty, "The New Haven Railroad."

6. George H. Merriam, "Frederic C. Dumaine, Jr.," in Keith L. Bryant Jr., ed., *Railroads in the Age of Regulation, 1900–1980* (New York: Facts-on-File, 1988), 124–25.

7. Doughty, "The New Haven Railroad"; Tamara K. Hareven and Randolph Langenbach, *Amoskeag: Life and Work in an American Factory-City* (New York: Pantheon Books, 1978), 90.

8. Interviews with John W. Barriger IV, April 9, 2016, January 29, 2017, hereafter cited as JWB IV interview (with date); John W. Barriger IV to author, August 27, 2016, hereafter cited as JWB IV to author (with date); *Annual Report to the Stockholders of the New York, New Haven and Hartford Railroad Company for the Year Ended, December 31, 1953* (New Haven, CT: New York, New Haven and Hartford Railroad Company, 1954), 5. Jack Barriger was knowledgeable about the New Haven. "I knew the New Haven fairly well, having traveled the entire system and interviewed

many officers in 1949–50 while writing my Yale Graduate School of Economics thesis on 'A System of Prior Classification for Arranged Service Freight Trains on the New Haven.'" He believed that his father could find a job better than the struggling New Haven. Nevertheless, he came to understand that his father's burning desire was to orchestrate rail consolidation in the New England region.

9. Memo to PBMcG [Patrick B. Mc-Ginnis] from JWB [John W. Barriger], June 25, 1955, Barriger papers.

10. "Supplementary Statement"; JWB IV interview, October 10, 2015; JWB IV to author, April 4, 2016, August 27, 2016.

11. Doughty, "The New Haven Railroad"; William D. Middleton, George M. Smerk and Roberta L. Diehl, eds., Encyclopedia of North American Railroads (Bloomington: Indiana University Press, 2007), 689–90.

12. "Supplementary Statement"; Interview with Edward A. Burkhardt, October 10, 2015.

13. H. Craig Miner, The Rebirth of the Missouri Pacific, 1956–1983 (College Station: Texas A&M University Press, 1984), 46; JWB IV interview, April 9, 2016.

14. H. Roger Grant, "Chicago, Rock Island & Pacific Railway," in Bryant, Railroads in the Age of Regulation, 1900–1980, 79.

15. Grant, "Chicago, Rock Island & Pacific Railway," 80.

16. Who's Who in Railroading in North America, 11th ed. (New York: Simmons-Boardman Publishing Corporation, 1946), 216; Dan Bulter, "John D. Farrington," in Bryant, Railroads in the Age of Regulation, 140–41; Don L. Hofsommer, Steel Trains of Hawkeyeland: Iowa's Railroad Experience (Bloomington: Indiana University Press, 2005), 152.

17. New York Times, August 13, 1955; H. Roger Grant, Visionary Railroader:

Jervis Langdon Jr. and the Transportation Revolution (Bloomington: Indiana University Press, 2008), 123–24.

18. JWB IV interview, April 9, 2016.

19. John W. Barriger, "Rock Island: Address for New York Society of Security Analysts," November 13, 1953, Barriger papers.

20. See Paul H. Stringham, Illinois Terminal: The Electric Years (Glendale, CA: Interurban Press), 1989.

21. John Shedd Reed to author, September 5, 2003.

22. John W. Barriger, "Illinois Terminal Railroad Company," October 29, 1953, Barriger papers; John W. Barriger to Mr. J. D. Farrington, May 14, 1954, Barriger papers; John W. Barriger to Mr. J. D. Farrington, July 12, 1954, Barriger papers; John W. Barriger to Mr. Farrington, "Supplementary memorandum in re. Illinois Terminal," July 27, 1954, Barriger papers.

23. John Sherman Porter, ed., Moody's Transportation Manual (New York: Moody's Investors Service, 1956), 38.

24. "Too Many 'Jaloppies,' Barriger Says," Railway Age 141 (July 2, 1956): 8.

25. JWB IV interview, August 6, 2015; David P. Morgan, "Mr. Barriger Writes a Bible for Railroading," Trains 17 (December 1956): 53; JWB IV interview, August, 6, 2015. During World War II John Barriger outlined the basic components for his vision of a better and stronger national railroad network in an article, "Super-Railroads," which appeared in Trains 4 (December 1943): 4–11. Two years earlier he had told members of the Chicago chapter of the Railway & Locomotive Historical Society that America needed "super-railroads" to confront "'super-liners,' both aerial and marine, 'super-highways,' and 'super-pipe lines.'"

26. John W. Barriger, "Where Do We Go from Here?," speech to Rotary Club of Houston, August 13, 1970, Barriger papers.

27. JWB IV interview, August 6, 2015; John Walker Barriger, *Super-Railroads for a Dynamic American Economy* (New York: Simmons-Boardman Publishing Corporation, 1956); "'Big Opportunity:' Super Railroads Says John W. Barriger," *Railway Age* 140 (June 4, 1956): 41.

28. *Super-Railroads for a Dynamic American Economy*, 24, 33.

29. *Super-Railroads for a Dynamic American Economy*, 34.

30. *Super-Railroads for a Dynamic American Economy*, 39, 47; John W. Barriger III, "The Monon Is a Guinea Pig," *Trains* 7 (July 1947), 18.

31. *Super-Railroads for a Dynamic American Economy*, 49–50.

32. *Super-Railroads for a Dynamic American Economy*, 51, 57, 64–65.

33. *Super-Railroads for a Dynamic American Economy*, 73.

34. Morgan, "Mr. Barriger Writes a Bible for Railroading," 53, 57. Although hardly a Barriger study, the only comparable book on the business of railroading appeared in 1922. D. Appleton and Company of New York published *Railroad Freight Transportation* by L. F. Loree, who served as president of the Delaware & Hudson Railroad and chaired the board of directors of the Kansas City Southern Railway. In the introduction Loree explained his overall intent: "It is the purpose of this book to assemble in reasoned order all of the phases of loading, distribution of cars, movement of engines and trains, handling of men, the features of permanent way and shop plant, the organization through which they are controlled, and accounting made of their activities–as they are related to transportation."

35. "'Big Opportunity:' Super Railroads Says John W. Barriger," 41, 43; John W. Barriger, "The First Steps toward Super Railroads," Railroad Community Committees of New England, Boston, Massachusetts, March 6, 1961, Barriger papers;

1956 Annual Report, The Pittsburgh and Lake Erie Railroad Company (Pittsburgh: Pittsburgh and Lake Erie Railroad Company, 1957), 5.

5. PITTSBURGH & LAKE ERIE

1. John W. Barriger, "The Pittsburgh and Lake Erie Railroad: An Address before the New York Society of Security Analysts," December 19, 1958, John W. Barriger III papers, John W. Barriger III National Railroad Library, St. Louis, MO, hereafter cited as Barriger papers.

2. Harrington Emerson, *Col. J. M. Schoonmaker and the Pittsburgh & Lake Erie Railroad* (New York: Engineering Magazine Company, 1912), 25; Donald Duke, "The Little Giant: The Pittsburgh & Lake Erie Railroad," *Bulletin of the Railway & Locomotive Historical Society* 112 (April 1965): 8–11.

3. Michael Bezilla, "Pittsburgh & Lake Erie Railroad," in *Railroads in the Age of Regulation, 1900–1980*, ed. Keith L. Bryant, Jr. (New York: Facts on File, 1988), 349; Harold H. McLean, *Pittsburgh & Lake Erie R.R.* (San Marino, CA: Golden West Books, 1980), 49–55, 138; Alfred E. Perlman, *Pittsburgh and the P&LE* (Princeton, NJ: Newcomen Society, 1963), 15–16; John Sherman Porter, ed., *Moody's Steam Railroads* (New York: Moody's Investment Service, 1933), 451–59; Barriger, "The Pittsburgh and Lake Erie Railroad."

4. Duke, "The Little Giant," 20–21; *Steel King* brochure, ca. 1950, in author's collection; Peter T. Maiken, *Night Trains: The Pullman System in the Golden Years of American Rail* (Chicago: Lakme Press, 1989), 53; McLean, *Pittsburgh & Lake Erie R.R.*, 149; Janet Greenstein Potter, *Great American Railroad Stations* (New York: John Wiley & Sons, 1996), 205–6.

5. John Sherman Porter, ed., *Moody's Transportation Manual* (New York: Moody's Investors Service, 1956), 1259; *The Official Guide of the Railways* (New York:

National Railway Publication Company, September 1954), 246–47.

6. Interview with John W. Barriger IV, October 2, 2015, January 29, 2017, hereafter cited as JWB IV interview (with date); Russell F. Moore, ed., *Who's Who in Railroading in North America* (New York: Simmons-Boardman Publishing, 1959), 498; JWB IV interview, August 6, 2015; Richard C. Overton, *Burlington Route: A History of the Burlington Lines* (New York: Knopf, 1965), 388.

7. Rush Loving Jr., *The Men Who Loved Trains: The Story of Men Who Battled Greed to Save an Ailing Industry* (Bloomington: Indiana University Press, 2006), 18; Rush Loving Jr., *The Well-Dressed Hobo: The Many Wondrous Adventures of a Man Who Loves Trains* (Bloomington: Indiana University Press, 2016), 66–67.

8. JWB IV interview, August 8, 2015; "Supplementary Statement of J. W. Barriger," n.d., Barriger papers.

9. Russell F. Moore, ed., *Who's Who in Railroading in North America* (New York: Simmons-Boardman Publishing, 1964), 384; McLean, *Pittsburgh and Lake Erie R.R.*, 113.

10. John W. Barriger IV to author, October 13, 2015, March 6, 2016.

11. McLean, *Pittsburgh and Lake Erie R.R.*, 131; *New York Times*, April 6, 1969.

12. Russell F. Moore, ed., *Who's Who in Railroading in North America* (New York: Simmons-Boardman Publishing Corporation, 1959), 204; Interview with Herbert Harwood Jr., September 17, 2015, hereafter cited as Harwood interview; Interview with Richard Hasselman, November 4, 2015, hereafter cited as Hasselman interview.

13. McLean, *Pittsburgh and Lake Erie R.R.*, 131; John W. Barriger to author, August 27, 2016, hereafter cited as JWB IV to author (with date); Lucius Beebe, "Along the Boulevards," *Gourmet*, November

1964, 91; JWB IV interview, September 30, 2016.

14. Harwood interview; Tom Shedd interview of John W. Barriger III, June 24, 1970, audio recording, Barriger Library.

15. Interview with JWB IV, April 9, 2016; McLean, *Pittsburgh and Lake Erie R.R.*, 132–33; Ronald C. Hill and Al Chione, *The Railroad Artistry of Howard Fogg* (San Rafael, CA: Cedco Publishing, 1999).

16. Interview with JWB IV, August 6, 2015, October 2, 2015, October 3, 2015; JWB IV to author, August 27, 2016.

17. McLean, *Pittsburgh and Lake Erie R.R.*, 133; *New York Times*, April 6, 1969.

18. H. Roger Grant, *Railroaders without Borders: A History of the Railroad Development Corporation* (Bloomington: Indiana University Press, 2015), 24: McLean, *Pittsburgh and Lake Erie R.R.*, 133.

19. Hasselman interview; Interview with William (Bill) Howes, October 29, 2015, hereafter cited as Howes interview; Arthur D. Dubin, *Some Classic Trains* (Milwaukee, WI: Kalmbach Publishing Company, 1964), 60, 72.

20. Lucius Beebe, *20th Century: The Greatest Train in the World* (Berkeley, CA: Howell-North, 1962),144. The Beebe dedication, written in his usually flowery prose:

To John Barriger
President of The Pittsburgh & Lake Erie Railroad
Whose Devotion to the History, Folklore and
Iconography of Railroading Identify
Him as an Unique Executive Who Is Also
a Scholar and Patron of the Arts Who
Recognizes No Distinction Between Work
and Pleasure, This Book Is Dedicated.

21. *The Pittsburgh and Lake Erie Railroad: 1957 Annual Report* (Pittsburgh: Pittsburgh and Lake Erie Railroad, 1958), 3; *Pittsburgh and Lake Erie Railroad Company: Annual Report for 1958* (Pittsburgh: Pittsburgh and Lake Erie Railroad, 1959), 1.

22. McLean, *Pittsburgh and Lake Erie R.R.*, 191.

23. P&LE *Annual Report for 1958*, 1, 23.

24. P&LE staff meeting minutes, January 27, 1964, Barriger papers.

25. P&LE staff meeting minutes, February 17, 1964, Barriger papers.

26. McLean, *Pittsburgh and Lake Erie R.R.*, 131.

27. John W. Barriger to I. Jack Bader, March 15, 1963, Barriger papers; McLean, *Pittsburgh and Lake Erie R.R.*, 138–39; *The Pittsburgh and Lake Erie Railroad Company: 1964 Annual Report* (Pittsburgh: Pittsburgh and Lake Erie Railroad, 1965), 4; P&LE Minutes, June 17, 1963, Barriger papers.

28. JWB IV interview, August 6, 2015; JWB IV to author, January 20, 2017.

29. John W. Barriger, "The Urge to Merge," speech to Jonathan Breakfast Club, Los Angeles, California, July 2, 1963, Barriger papers.

30. "Remarks of John W. Barriger in a debate with Dr. Leon Keyserling on the question of 'Railroad Mergers' at a meeting of the American Transportation Research Form," Pittsburgh, Pennsylvania, December 27, 1962, Barriger papers.

31. Interview with Edward A. Burkhardt, October 29, 2015; Grant, *Railroaders without Borders*, 172–174.

32. William McKnight to author, November 6, 2015; John W. Barriger to William McKnight, September 6, 1961, in possession of author.

33. McKnight to author; Don L. Hofsommer, *Grand Trunk Corporation: Canadian National Railways in the United States, 1971–1992* (East Lansing: Michigan State University Press, 1995), 43.

34. Interview with William F. Howes Jr., October 29, 2015; William F. Howes to author, November 30, 2015; William F. Howes, "Presidents Address," *Proceedings of the Ninety-Fifth Annual Meeting and the 19th Winter Meeting American Association of Railroad Superintendents*, January 15, 1991.

35. *Railroading in North America* (New York: Simmons-Boardman Publishing Corporation, 1968), 70.

36. Interview with JWB IV, October 2, 2015.

6. MISSOURI-KANSAS-TEXAS

1. John W. Barriger IV to author, December 20, 2015, hereafter cited as JWB IV to author (with date); JWB IV to author, August 27, 2016.

2. JWB IV to author, December 20, 2015; Interview with John W. Barriger IV, October 3, 2015, hereafter cited as JWB IV interview (with date). Having looked at the all-Pullman "Thoroughbred at Work," which had been commissioned by Barriger's P&LE staff, Lucius Beebe, the next speaker, offered this comment: "The title should be 'Running Fast and Running Late' which caused great merriment among those assembled who knew that the Broadway Limited crossed the Alleghenies both ways in total darkness." JWB IV to author, January 20, 2017.

3. John W. Barriger IV to author, December 20, 2015; Robert L. Frey, "Louis W. Menk," in *Railroads in the Age of Regulation, 1900–1980*, ed. Keith L. Bryant Jr., (New York: Facts On File Publications, 1988), 292–93; William B. Alderman, "How Katy Did," *Texas Parade*, August 1967.

4. The popular Katy nickname sprang from the railroad's stock exchange initials, "KT," and dates from the 1870s.

5. *St. Louis Post-Dispatch*, May 13, 1976; Nancy Ford, "Can Barriger Revive the Katy?" *Modern Railroads* 20 (October 1965): 71, 78.

6. John W. Barriger, "A New Dress for Katy," speech before New York Society of Security Analysts, July 14, 1967, John W. Barriger III papers, John W. Barriger III

National Railroad Library, St. Louis, MO, hereafter cited as Barriger papers.

7. V. V. Masterson, *The Katy Railroad and the Last Frontier* (Norman: University of Oklahoma Press, 1952), 206, 211, 240–41, 282, 284; Sylvan R. Wood, "History of the Katy," *Bulletin of the Railway & Locomotive Historical Society* 63 (January 1944): 9.

8. Barriger, "A New Dress for Katy."

9. Barriger, "A New Dress for Katy."

10. Barriger, "A New Dress for Katy"; Ford, "Can Barriger Revive the Katy?" 74.

11. Barriger, "A New Dress for Katy."

12. Barriger, "A New Dress for Katy."

13. Barriger, "A New Dress for Katy."

14. Barriger, "A New Dress for Katy"; *New York Times*, January 21, 1957.

15. H. Roger Grant, "William N. Deramus III," in Bryant, *Railroads in the Age of Regulation*, 116–17.

16. H. Roger Grant, *The Corn Belt Route: A History of the Chicago Great Western Railroad Company* (DeKalb: Northern Illinois University Press, 1984), 115–53.

17. "Katy Looks for 'Sound Footing,'" *Railway Age* 142 (April 29, 1957): 9; Barriger, "A New Dress for Katy."

18. Grant, "William N. Deramus III," 117; "Katy Looks for 'Sound Footing,'" 9; *Railway Age* 142 (March 25): 14–15; *Railway Age* 142 (April 1, 1957): 15, 17; *New York Times*, March 28, 1957; *St. Louis Globe-Democrat*, March 28, 1957, March 31, 1957.

19. *Annual Report 1965: Missouri-Kansas-Texas Railroad Company* (Dallas: Missouri-Kansas-Texas Railway, 1966), 7–8; Barriger, "A New Dress for Katy."

20. Barriger, "A New Dress for Katy"; Ford, "Can Barriger Revive the Katy?" 69; David P. Morgan, "Can Mr. B. Save Miss Katy?" *Trains* 26 (August 1966): 24–26; 25; Tom Shedd, "Why They Made Him Man of the Year," *Modern Railroads* 24 (January 1969): 57.

21. Morgan, "Can Mr. B. Save Miss Katy?" 25; Barriger, "A New Dress for Katy"; Alderman, "How Katy Did."

22. Barriger, "A New Dress for Katy."

23. Barriger, "A New Dress for Katy."

24. Morgan, "Can Mr. B. Save Miss Katy?" 25; Ford, "Can Barriger Revive the Katy?" 69.

25. MKT *Annual Report 1965*, 10; *Missouri-Kansas-Texas Railroad Company Annual Report 1966* (Dallas: Missouri-Kansas-Texas Railroad, 1967), 5, 7; Ford, "Can Barriger Revive the Katy?" 72.

26. Barriger, "A New Dress for Katy"; Ford, "Can Barriger Revive the Katy?" 71; MKT *Annual Report 1965*, 5.

27. Barriger, "A New Dress for Katy."

28. Morgan, "Can Mr. B. Save Miss Katy?" 26; Barriger, "A New Dress for Katy."

29. Ford, "Can Barriger Revive the Katy?" 73.

30. Donovan L. Hofsommer, *Katy Northwest: The Story of a Branch Line Railroad* (Boulder, CO: Pruett Publishing, 1976), 165.

31. Hofsommer, *Katy Northwest*, 166–170.

32. Hofsommer, *Katy Northwest*, 170; *Missouri-Kansas-Texas Railroad Company Annual Report 1967* (Dallas: Missouri-Kansas-Texas Railroad, 1968), 8.

33. "KATYDID!" advertisement, ca. 1967, Barriger papers.

34. Roy H. Krause, ed., *Moody's Transportation Manual* (New York: Moody's Investors Service Inc., 1970), 365; *Newsweek* 70 (December 25, 1967): 59; "We're Re-Building a Railroad," *Railway Age* 168 (January 5/12, 1970): 34; JWB IV to author, August 27, 2016; MKT *Annual Report 1967*, 21, 24.

35. Don L. Hofsommer to author, September 13, 2016.

36. *St. Louis Globe-Democrat*, March 16, 1970; Audio tape recording of John W. Barriger III interview with Tom Shedd, editor *Modern Railroads*, June 24, 1970, Barriger papers; Interview with Don L. Hofsommer, October 28, 2015; Maury

Klein, *Union Pacific: The Reconfiguration: America's Greatest Railroad from 1969 to the Present* (New York: Oxford University Press, 2011), 191–95; Hofsommer to author, September 13, 2016.

37. JWB IV to author, January 20, 2017; Interview with James (Jim) W. McClellan, July 12, 2016.

7. MORE RETIREMENTS

1. John W. Barriger IV to author, August 27, 2016, hereafter cited as JWB IV to author (with date).

2. H. Roger Grant, *Visionary Railroader: Jervis Langdon Jr. and the Transportation Revolution* (Bloomington: Indiana University Press, 2008), 172; JWB IV to author, August 27, 2016.

3. JWB IV to author, June 6, 2016.

4. "John W. Barriger Named to Head B&M," *Railway Age* 170 (January 11, 1971): 19; *St. Louis Post-Dispatch*, undated clipping, ca. 1971, John W. Barriger III National Railroad Library, St. Louis, MO, hereafter cited as Barriger papers; *New York Times*, January 1, 1971; JWB IV to author, June 3, 2016.

5. *Moody's Manual of Investments: Railroad Securities* (New York: Moody's Investors Service, 1935), 558; R. M. Neal, *High Green and the Bark Peelers: The Story of Engineman Henry A. Beaulieu and His Boston and Maine Railroad* (New York: Duell, Sloan and Pearce, 1950), 37.

6. Statement of John W. Barriger, Chief Executive Officer, Boston and Maine Railroad, at a hearing before the Interstate Commerce Commission in reference to Problems of B&M Railroad, Tuesday, June 22, 1971, Washington, D. C., Barriger papers, hereafter cited as John W. Barriger ICC statement.

7. *St. Louis Post-Dispatch* clipping; *Moody's Transportation Manual* (New York: Moody's Investors Service, 1970), 400.

8. William D. Middleton, George M. Smerk, and Roberta L. Diehl, eds., *Encyclopedia of North American Railroads* (Bloomington: Indiana University Press, 2007), 177; Statement of John W. Barriger, June 22, 1971.

9. H. Roger Grant, *Erie Lackawanna: Death of an American Railroad, 1938–1992* (Stanford, CA: Stanford University Press, 1994), 150–151, 158–159.

10. John W. Barriger IV to author, June 3, 2016, June 20, 2016. After 1965 Fred Tyler became an important member of the Barriger household. Following John's death, Elizabeth relied heavily on Tyler's help, with him serving as her manservant and driver. Remembered her son Jack, "Fred took care of mother in a classic driving Miss Daisy style," JWB IV interview, October 3, 2015.

11. John W. Barriger ICC statement; Interview with Alan G. "Dusty" Dustin, October 18, 2016, hereafter cited as Dustin interview (with date).

12. Dustin interview, October 18, 2016.

13. John W. Barriger ICC statement.

14. Dustin interview, October 18, 2016, November 22, 2016; Roy H. Krause, ed., *Moody's Transportation Manual* (New York: Moody's Investors Service, 1973), 113.

15. John W. Barriger ICC statement; Dustin interview, November 22, 2016; John W. Barriger to Robert W. Meserve, February 11, 1972, Barriger papers.

16. JWB IV interview, October 2, 2015; Audio tape recording of John W. Barriger III interview with Tom Shedd, editor *Modern Railroads*, June 24, 1970, Barriger papers; James Howarth to author, October 18, 2016.

17. Interview with Alden Dryer, September 29, 2016; Dustin interview, October 18, 2016.

18. *New York Times*, October 8, 1971; Middleton, Smerk, and Diehl, *Encyclopedia of North American Railroads*, 177;

Geoffrey H. Doughty, "Anatomy of a Take-over," paper presented at the annual meeting of the Lexington Group Inc., Duluth, MN, September 28, 2016.

19. *New York Times*, August 13, 1974; JWB IV to author, June 20, 2016, June 23, 2016, August 27, 2016.

20. John W. Barriger III diary, January 1, 1973, Barriger papers; "Remarks of John W. Barriger at a Dinner Given to Him by a Group of Friends Following the End of His Two Year Run (1971–1972) over the Boston and Maine," February 12, 1973, Barriger papers.

21. Mark M. Jones to Claude S. Brinegar, April 2, 1973, Barriger papers; Department of Transportation, Federal Railroad Administration, Washington, D.C., News, August 13, 1973, Barriger papers; George H. Drury, comp., *The Historical Guide to North American Railroads* (Milwaukee, WI: Kalmbach Books, 1985), 80; JWB IV to author, June 28, 2016; "An interview with John Ingram," February 7, 2004, Railroad Executive Oral History Program, John W. Barriger III National Railroad Library; McClellan interview.

22. Interview with David J. DeBoer, June 27, 2016, hereafter cited as DeBoer interview.

23. John W. Barriger to [children] Ann, Jack, Stanley, Betty, November 16, 1973, Barriger papers; *St. Louis Post-Dispatch*, August 6, 1973.

24. *Who's Who in Railroading and Rail Transit* (New York: Simmon-Boardman Publishing, 1971), 192; Gregory L. Schneider, *Rock Island Requiem: The Collapse of a Mighty Fine Line* (Lawrence: University Press of Kansas, 2013), 140; John F. Stover, *History of the Illinois Central Railroad* (New York: Macmillan Publishing, 1975), 492–93.

25. Schneider, *Rock Island Requiem*, 139; DeBoer interview.

26. "An Interview with John Ingram"; DeBoer interview.

27. David J. DeBoer, "JWB III," manuscript in possession of author.

28. "An Interview with John Ingram"; *New York Times*, April 27, 1974.

29. JWB IV to author, June 28, 2016; John W. Barriger to Evie and Jack, et al., November 27, 1975, Barriger papers.

30. McClellan interview.

31. *St. Louis Post-Dispatch*, May 13, 1976; "An Interview with John Ingram"; JWB IV to author, June 28, 2016; Stanley Barriger to "Dear Prof. John," May 24, 1976, Barriger papers.

32. Bill Marvel, *The Rock Island Line* (Bloomington: Indiana University Press, 2013), 149; *New York Times*, December 11, 1976; *St. Louis Post-Dispatch*, May 13, 1976.

33. Saint Louis Medical Clinic Inc., to John W. Barriger, June 3, 1976, Barriger papers.

34. JWB IV interview, October 2, 2015; JWB IV to author, August 15, 2015.

35. *St. Louis Globe-Democrat*, December 10, 1976; JWB IV to author, August 15, 2015.

EPILOGUE

1. Interview with John W. Barriger IV, January 29, 2017, hereafter cited as JWB IV interview (with date).

2. Interview with James (Jim) McClellan, July 12, 2016; Interview with Richard (Dick) Hasselman, November 4, 2015.

3. "Katy's John Barriger–Railroad Man of the Year," *Modern Railroads* 24 (January 1969): 61.

4. James G. Lyne, "After Hours," *Railway Age* 141 (August 20, 1956): 30.

5. JWB IV interview, October 3, 2015, October 6, 2015, January 29, 2017.

6. Charles Penrose Jr. and John W. Barriger IV, *The John W. Barriger III National Railroad Library* (New York: Newcomen Society, 1999), 17–18.

7. Penrose and Barriger, *The John W. Barriger III National Railroad Library*, 16–18.

8. Penrose and Barriger, *The John W. Barriger III National Railroad Library*, 18–20; *St. Louis Globe-Democrat*, January 10, 1983. When Elizabeth Barriger died in 1988, her funeral notice asked that in lieu of flowers contributions be made to the Elizabeth T. Barriger Book Fund at the John W. Barriger III National Railroad Library. See *St. Louis Globe-Democrat*, June 24, 1988.

9. Penrose and Barriger, *The John W. Barriger III National Railroad Library*, 23–24; Interview with John Neal Hoover, July 19, 2016; John W. Barriger IV to author, August 29, 2016.

10. JWB IV interview, October 2, 2015.

11. Gus Welty, ed., *Era of the Giants: The New Railroad Merger Movement* (Omaha, NE: Simmons-Boardman Publishing, 1982); Robert Krebs, *Riding the Rails: Inside the Business of America's Railroads*, (Bloomington: Indiana University Press, 2018).

12. Audio tape recording of John W. Barriger III interview with Tom Shedd, editor *Modern Railroads*, June 24, 1970, Barriger papers, John W. Barriger III National Railroad Library, St. Louis, MO; JWB IV interview; Roy Neal, Jr., *The American Railroad: Life after Death (Memories and Milestones)* (London: Minerva Press, 2000), 240.

Index

Index pages in *italics* indicate illustrations

H. ROGER GRANT is Kathryn and Calhoun Lemon Professor of History at Clemson University. He is author of more than thirty books, including *Electric Interurbans and the American People*; *Railroaders without Borders: A History of the Railroad Development Corporation*; *The Louisville, Cincinnati & Charleston Rail Road: Dreams of Linking North and South*; and *Railroads and the American People*.